WESTERN FURNITURE
1350 TO THE PRESENT DAY

IN THE VICTORIA AND ALBERT MUSEUM
LONDON

*Detail of interior of cabinet (p.80), British, c.1700,
showing the crest of Lawson*

WESTERN FURNITURE
1350 TO THE PRESENT DAY

IN THE VICTORIA AND ALBERT MUSEUM
LONDON

Edited by Christopher Wilk

CROSS RIVER PRESS

A Division of Abbeville Publishing Group

NEW YORK • LONDON • PARIS

First published in the United States of America in 1996 by
Cross River Press, a division of Abbeville Publishing Group,
488 Madison Avenue, New York, N.Y. 10022

First published in Great Britain in 1996 by
Philip Wilson Publishers Limited, 143–149 Great Portland Street,
London WIN 5FB

First edition 10 9 8 7 6 5 4 3 2 1

ISBN 0-7892-0252-2

Designed and typeset by Christopher Matthews and Malcolm Preskett
Edited by Moira Johnston
Printed and bound in Italy by Società Editoriale Libraria per azioni, Trieste

Contents

Preface

THE ONE HUNDRED examples of furniture described in this book were selected not only as highlights of the Victoria & Albert Museum's collection, some of its very finest pieces, but also illustrate many of the topics which make the history of furniture so varied and interesting. Some of these pieces demonstrate the greatest craftsmanship in specific techniques such as gilding, carving or marquetry. Others have become classic examples of the most famous styles of decoration, Rococo, Neo-Classical or Gothic Revival. Though many of the earlier pieces in particular remain anonymous, this selection does present many of the most important designers and makers of furniture, including Thomas Chippendale, David Roentgen, A.W.N. Pugin, and the firms of Thonet and John Henry Belter. In some cases it has been possible to identify the design sources for form or ornament, on seventeenth-century cabinets, for example. Viewed from so many tangents it becomes clear that the creation of a piece of furniture was not, in most cases, a matter of the lone inspiration of one 'craftsman', but a complex collaboration of, for example, professional designers, the cabinet-makers who functioned as the business heads of large firms, and the actual journeymen, apprentices or factory workers, who made the pieces. Crucial in this process for furniture of this stature was the role of the patron, client or purchaser and the demands of the marketplace. It would not have been possible to treat every conceivable theme in each entry. For this reason the entries are not controlled by a rigid format and the overriding ambition has been to explain the particular significance of each piece, as we understand it, and its place in the history of Western furniture.

Both the selection of one hundred examples of furniture and the writing of individual texts have been exercises in concision. Many of the pieces have been the subject of specialized studies in journals or books (as is clear from the notes). Collectively, the selection represents one possible version of a history of furniture as illustrated by the major collection of its kind in the world. There are, to be sure, areas left uncovered, by reason of the Victoria & Albert Museum's concentration on the history of design and its emphasis on high-style production; objects which lead taste rather than follow it are more likely to be found in our collection. This means that we largely overlook vernacular furniture made for everyday use, although it must be said that many pieces, especially those dating from after the mid-nineteenth century, reveal the gradual eradication of clear lines between high and popular culture, between the elite object and the commercial one. While, in times past, it was invariably true that it was the top end of the market which influenced the lower end, in recent times the tide of taste moves both ways.

It is hoped that the format of the book will allow those with a casual interest in the subject to read selectively about individual objects or historical periods, while those with a more serious interest will take note of new discoveries and make use of the notes to the text to guide them to further reading.

The process of compiling this book has been a rewarding and revealing one; our view of many of the objects in our care has changed as a result of research and investigation. Much new information appears in these pages: for example, the finely upholstered chair long thought to have been used by Charles I at his trial (p.68) is now, instead, firmly associated with the coronation of Charles II; the 'Coleshill table' (p.92), as it has long been known, appears to have been made for Longford Castle rather than Coleshill House; the lavish, Rococo ornamental casket by Pietro Piffetti (p.94), which carried no provenance when it was acquired, is now known to have been in a Rothschild Collection; a cabinet designed by C.R. Ashbee (p.192) has been discovered to have been owned by the designer himself; as was the most famous of all chairs designed by Charles Rennie Mackintosh (p.182); and, perhaps most unexpectedly, one of the most celebrated objects in the V&A's collection, the so-called Marie de Medici cabinet from Mentmore (originally dated 1630–40), has been withdrawn from these pages as it appears to be largely a nineteenth-century object. It is one of several pieces on the original list of contents which has been omitted following detailed study, underlining the continual development in our understanding of the history of furniture which arises from the constant study and re-interpretation of such a rich and diverse collection. c.w.

Acknowledgements

THERE HAS long been a need for a general book on the V&A's furniture collection and it is singularly satisfying for the Department of Furniture and Woodwork to see it finally published and to be able to express our gratitude to those who assisted us in the project.

Among the many colleagues from outside the V&A who have helped with specific matters of research, thanks are owed to: Barbara Brejon, Palais des Beaux-Arts, Lille; Annette Carruthers; Alan Crawford; Mrs Edward Gibbons; Mary Greensted, Cheltenham Museum and Art Galleries; Dr Barry Harwood, the Brooklyn Museum; Helena Hayward; Maria Haywood; Wilfried de Kesel; Dr Peter Kristiansen, Rosenborg Castle, Copenhagen; Jean MacIntyre; Madame Françoise de la Mouyeyre; David Olby; Margaret Richard, Badminton House; Sigrid Sangl, Bayerisches Nationalmuseum; Jon Whiteley, Ashmolean Museum; and Dr Christian Witt-Dörring, Museum für angewandte Kunst, Vienna. For their comments on the introduction I am grateful to Malcolm Baker, John Cornforth, John Hardy, Simon Jervis, Peter Thornton and Lucy Wood.

All members of the Department of Furniture and Woodwork at the V&A have contributed to the realization of this book. Those who have contributed to the text are listed on p.25; their expertise and co-operation have been most appreciated. In addition, Gareth Williams, Nicholas J. Humphrey, Sorrel Hershberg and Kate McCluskey have deftly handled a range of complicated matters related to photography, conservation, research and administration, while Tessa Murdoch assumed certain administrative responsibilities that allowed me to complete the present task. Sarah Medlam was immeasurably helpful on all matters editorial and organizational, and I am grateful for her professionalism, wide-ranging expertise and good humour.

Most of the new photography for this book was undertaken by Pip Barnard of the V&A Photo Studio. His colleagues James Stevenson and Ken Jackson ensured the smooth running of all matters photographic.

As always, we in Furniture and Woodwork are most grateful to our colleagues (current and former) in Furniture Conservation. Nick Umney, head of Furniture & Woodwork Conservation, his predecessor John Kitchin, and Albert Neher, were particularly involved in this project. We are indebted to them, and also to Timothy Hayes, Tim Miller, Ennio Panetta and Christine Powell for enlarging our understanding of the objects in our care and for their devotion to the field.

For help with matters of research, thanks are owed to numerous fellow V&A curators, including Anthony Burton, Richard Edgcumbe, Peta Evelyn, Julia Hutt, Norbert Jopek, Gill Saunders, Michael Snodin, Richard Dunn and Clive Wainwright. Research for the introduction was made easier by the existence of comprehensive lists of V&A exhibitions and publications compiled by Elizabeth James of the National Art Library, and by the assistance of Serena Kelly and the staff of the V&A Registry. For their work in realizing this book, the contributions of Mary Butler, Head of Publications at the V&A, Anne Jackson and Susan Dixon at Philip Wilson, Moira Johnston, copy editor, and Christopher Matthews, designer, are gratefully acknowledged. Finally, I am deeply grateful for the support of my wife, Ann Curtis. C.W.

Furniture collecting at the Victoria and Albert Museum – a summary history

No MUSEUM in the world can match the breadth and quality of the Victoria & Albert Museum's collection of Western furniture. The Museum has been acquiring objects for nearly 150 years and is now the largest decorative arts museum in the world. Unlike art museums where the decorative or applied arts play second fiddle to the fine arts of painting and sculpture, at the V&A furniture, as well as ceramics, glass, metalwork and textiles, are collected, researched and exhibited with unusual rigour and dedication; and, unlike important museums such as the Louvre, which concentrate primarily on collecting and displaying their national furniture, the V&A collects furniture from all Western nations (and, indeed, from some non-Western cultures).

The collection of 14,000 objects from which the pieces discussed in this book are chosen encompasses a very much wider range of materials and object types which include period rooms, architectural woodwork (including Islamic) and plasterwork, clocks, treen (small wooden objects, many turned) and gilt leather wall hangings. The definition of furniture embraced in these pages includes musical instruments, especially keyboard instruments, which were collected as examples of the history of design and decoration and not purely from the point of view of musicology.

This essay places the objects illustrated in this book within the context of furniture collecting at the V&A. Not only must this be considered a first look at the subject but lack of space precludes an extended discussion of the full and varied range of the collections, the history of furniture displays and exhibitions, and the relationship of the V&A's collecting to that of other institutions.[1]

Collecting at the V&A has always been the result of a mixture of external forces, the implementation of institutional policy, and the actions and taste of individual directors and keepers, and their staffs. The relative importance of such factors has varied throughout the V&A's history as has the impact of individuals and outside organizations. For example, the keepership of Ralph Edwards (1937–54) marked the zenith of emphasis on English furniture, while that of Peter Thornton (1966–84) fundamentally altered the way experts and the public viewed the interpretation of historic interiors, especially the arrangement of furniture, and signalled a revived interest in the collecting of European furniture. Collectors such as John Jones (through his bequest of French furniture, 1882) and dealers, including George Donaldson (through his numerous gifts and sales to the Museum, *circa* 1900), influenced the institutional approach to collecting. Books and their authors, notably Lady Dilke's *French Furniture and Decoration in the XVIIIth Century* (1901) or Percy Macquoid and Ralph Edwards's *Dictionary of English Furniture* (1924), offered a synthetic view of their subject and codified a hierarchy of object types and craftsmen-designers that influenced a

1. The general history of the V&A's collections and displays, as well as its relationship to other decorative arts museums, will be covered in the forthcoming exhibition catalogue: M. Baker and B. Richardson (eds), *A Grand Design: the Art of the Victoria & Albert Museum* (Baltimore/New York: Baltimore Museum of Art/Abrams, 1997). A brief history of the Department of Furniture & Woodwork is provided in S. Jervis, 'The Department of Furniture and Woodwork, Victoria and Albert Museum', *Furniture History*, vol. XXVI (1990), pp.121–31.

generation of curators. And the founding of the Furniture History Society (1964) and the publication of its annual journal, *Furniture History*, represented a crucial break-through in the campaign to put furniture history onto a sound academic base, and the beginning of a new era in furniture studies.

International exhibition pieces and the founding of the V&A

The V&A woodwork collections began as a collection of contemporary examples of techniques, chiefly carving and inlay, including oriental examples (these later trans-ferred to the Far Eastern or Indian and Southeast Asian Departments). They were acquired from 1844 onwards for the new Government School of Design located at Somerset House and were intended to serve as exemplars of design and methods of manufacture for students. The School had been established as part of an effort to combat foreign imports, especially French luxury goods which gained favour after 1825, by improving the quality of British products.

In its early years the Museum evolved two distinct, sometimes conflicting, philosophies of collecting.[2] One approach was identified with its first director (his original title within the Civil Service, from 1852–73, was General Superintendent, Department of Practical Art), Henry Cole (1808–82). He saw its purpose as a collec-tion of mainly contemporary 'manufactures' intended to educate practitioners and improve public taste. Design and craftsmanship were the qualities most valued and the Museum presented in a highly didactic manner the attributes of good and bad design. The second approach, promoted with considerable force by the first Curator, J.C. Robinson (1852–67), focused on the aesthetic merit of objects, and avoided the term 'manufactures' in favour of 'decorative art'. Robinson, a connoisseur and antiquary, helped shift the balance towards the collecting of historic objects, although he acknowledged their usefulness to craftsmen.[3]

The Great Exhibition of 1851 provided the impetus for expansion in the scope of the collection – still part of the Government School – to include contemporary furniture, British and foreign; within the exhibition halls of the Crystal Palace, cabinets by A.W.N. Pugin (p.150) and A. Barbetti were acquired. It was in the aftermath of the Great Exhibition that the first incarnation of the V&A, variously named the Museum of Manufactures or the Museum of Ornamental Art, opened at Marlborough House in 1853, having been founded in the previous year. The 1851 purchases initiated a series of select acquisitions of new furniture made directly from leading international exhibitions, mainly in London and Paris, during the third quarter of the nineteenth century (pp.162, 164). Such pieces, usually large, beautifully made cabinets, were pur-chased for the quality of their design, construction and decoration; their function within the Museum would be primarily to inspire designers and craftsmen and, secondarily, to educate public taste.

In 1857 the Ornamental Art Museum, as it was once again re-named, became part of the larger enterprise known as the South Kensington Museum – which until the later nineteenth century included museums devoted to education, architecture, economics and modern British sculpture – and continued to pursue a vigorous acquisitions policy, buying objects from international exhibitions (including the Paris Exposition Universelle of 1855 and the London International Exhibition of 1862), as well as historic pieces of antiquarian interest. The cabinets by Henri-Auguste Fourdinois (p.162) and by Wright and Mansfield (p.164) were acquired from the Paris

2. On all matters to do with the institutional history of the V&A and its predecessors, I am greatly indebted to the writings and lectures of Anthony Burton, including the extended, unpublished version of his essay 'The V&A: Politics and People' in Baker, op. cit., and 'The Image of the Curator', *V&A Album*, vol.4 (1985), pp.372–87.

3. Cole also actively supported the collecting of historical objects; but he saw this as secondary to the Museum's mission of improving design standards. On Cole and Robinson see Burton, 'The V&A', op. cit., mss. pp.6–7.

Exposition Universelle of 1867, where both were awarded highest honours. They were purchased for the extraordinary skill they demonstrated, their usefulness as teaching objects and, in the case of the 'Adams style' Wright and Mansfield cabinet, its daring use of light satinwood at a time when dark woods, especially ebony, were the fashion.

Further purchases were made from the second London Annual International Exhibition of 1872, but the retirement of Henry Cole in 1873 as Director of the South Kensington Museum, and an accompanying diminution in energy on the part of the new administration, meant that these were the last furniture purchases made directly from international exhibitions. In fact, during the final three decades of the nineteenth century specialist curators were not employed, and decisions on acquisitions were referred to an outside committee of Art Referees.

The only large group of furniture subsequently acquired directly from an international exhibition was the remarkable collection (thirty-eight pieces) of mainly French Art Nouveau objects purchased at the Paris Exposition Universelle of 1900 by George Donaldson (1845–1925) as a gift (p.186).[4] This was perhaps the single most controversial acquisition in the V&A's history and formed a distinguished coda to the nineteenth-century policy of acquiring from exhibitions. Donaldson, a Bond Street dealer, was Vice-President of the Jury of Awards for furniture and part of a contingent of British jurors commissioned by the South Kensington Museum authorities to purchase works of modern decorative art. Donaldson was so impressed by what he saw that he told the Museum that the £500 allocated for purchase was insufficient. In an act of remarkable magnanimity he personally offered the funding required 'to secure an adequate representation of the objects illustrating the "New Movement" to the extent of several Thousand Pounds, if necessary'.[5] Furniture by Majorelle, Gallé and Spindler, as well as lesser-known Hungarian, Norwegian and German designers, was thus represented in the collection.

The acquisition and display of the Donaldson collection at the V&A resulted in a storm of criticism. Leading architects and designers denounced the acquisition in the letters page of *The Times*. C.F.A. Voysey (p.180), who typified the scathing view of the Arts and Crafts men, wrote that Art Nouveau was 'distinctly unhealthy and revolting…we have gone back into savagery on being emancipated from tradition'.[6] The Museum authorities, who had enthusiastically accepted the Donaldson gift, felt sufficiently buffeted to issue a warning to art teachers who might use the collection for teaching purposes:

> Much of the modern Continental furniture…exhibits a style which is not consistent with the teaching at Art Schools of the United Kingdom. It is therefore necessary that students inspecting the examples in this collection should be guided, in forming an opinion as to their merits and obvious faults, by instructors who have given attention to such subjects as Historic Ornament, Principles of Ornament, and Architecture.

Although the collection was retained, exhibited (with the modern collections at Bethnal Green), and requested for loan to institutions throughout the United Kingdom and Ireland, there was subsequently a reluctance to engage with leading-edge contemporary design. Following the Donaldson gift, the V&A ceased to acquire furniture directly from major international exhibitions and, indeed, enshrined as part of institutional policy the exclusion of contemporary objects from most of its collections.[7]

4. E. Aslin, 'Sir George Donaldson and "Art Nouveau" at South Kensington', *Journal of the Decorative Arts Society*, vol. 7 (1983), pp.9–14.

5. Letter, George Donaldson to C.P. Clarke [Director], 23 June 1900, V&A Registered Papers, 'New Art Furniture Collection', V&A Registry.

6. '*L'Art Nouveau:* What It is and What is Thought of It, A Symposium – I', *Magazine of Art* (new series), vol.II (1904), pp.211–12.

7. See the present writer's essay on 'Collecting the Contemporary', in Baker, op. cit.

In later years the importance of objects displayed at major exhibitions of the nineteenth century, and the significance of such a special provenance, were recognized as powerful arguments for purchase (pp.152, 154, 160, 174). Such purchases reflected a growing interest in the Victorian period, beginning in the 1950s and gaining strength in the 1960s, and the retrospective acquisition of exhibition pieces has thus become an active area of collecting.

Collecting collections

While the purchase of new objects proceeded apace from the 1850s, the acquisition of entire collections was seen as the most effective way of building and improving the historic collections. In 1855, a large number of objects from the auction of the distinguished collection of Ralph Bernal MP were acquired, although the only furniture was two pier glasses attributed to Thomas Chippendale.[8] The first wholesale acquisition of a private collection by the Museum, however, was the purchase of Italian and French Renaissance objects from the French collector Jules Soulages in 1856. Eighty-eight pieces of furniture, mainly Italian – including what was described as a mirror 'said to have been the property of the celebrated Lucrezia Borgia' (p.32)[9] – were among the 865 objects purchased from Soulages. Soulages was a lawyer by profession and an assiduous, systematic collector who travelled Italy in search of treasures.[10] He was apparently determined to keep the collection together even after its disposal, and the Museum was unable to secure sufficient funds from the Government for its purchase. Seventy-three subscribers, 'noble, gentle, and industrial, and none the less noble because gentle and industrial'[11] – including the Marquess of Hertford, Herbert Minton, Titus Salt and Isambard Kingdom Brunel – purchased the collection and, eventually, the Government paid in instalments. It was soon exhibited in the South Kensington Museum.

While other important collections came to the Museum during the nineteenth century, it was not until 1882 that one including major examples of furniture was acquired. In that year the military tailor John Jones bequeathed his entire collection of mainly eighteenth-century French decorative arts, notable, above all, for its superb furniture (pp.78, 100, 102, 130) and Sèvres porcelain.[12]

Jones was an enigmatic figure whose outfitting of the military, especially during the Crimean war, brought him great wealth, sufficient for him to retire after twenty-five years in business. His house at 95 Piccadilly was stuffed full of his collection which, with the notable exception of his large *armoire* (cupboard) 'probably designed by Bérain, and executed by Boule [sic] for Louis XIV' (p.78), tended towards smaller objects.[13] Jones sometimes bought directly from collectors, sometimes at auction and sometimes from dealers. Like most nineteenth-century collectors of French furniture he had a particular fondness for pieces with royal associations: the monogram of coupled 'L's on the doors of the *armoire* was thus thought to indicate Louis XIV as its original owner; and among numerous pieces that Jones bought, in part, because of their association with Marie Antoinette, was the combined music-stand and writing-table mounted with a Sèvres plaque (p.130) acquired from the family of Lady Eden.

Through Jones's generosity in making this bequest, the nation acquired in one stroke the greatest public collection of French furniture outside France. From the 1820s French furniture had been widely admired and collected by private patrons in Britain. In 1853 an important public exhibition of 'Specimens of Cabinet Work' had

8. One was, in fact, supplied as one of a pair by Thomas Chippendale to the 3rd Duke of Portland (V&A Museum No. 2387-1855); the other is surely not by Chippendale nor even based on a Chippendale design (2388-1855).

9. J.C. Robinson, *Catalogue of the Soulages Collection* (London: Chapman and Hall, 1856), p.178, and also published in J.H. Pollen, *Ancient and Modern Furniture and Woodwork* (London: Chapman and Hall, 1874), p.187.

10. C. Wainwright, 'Models of Inspiration', *Country Life* (9 June 1988), p.267, which draws, in part, on 'The Soulage [sic] Collection', *Art Journal* (1856), p.381; and Robinson, op. cit, pp.iii–viii.

11. *The Times* (4 November 1856), quoted in Wainwright, op. cit., p.267.

12. D. Sutton, 'A Born Virtuoso', *Apollo*, vol. XCV (March 1972), pp.2–7.

13. *Handbook of the Jones Collection* (London: Chapman and Hall, 1883), p.111. *The Cabinet Maker and Art Furnisher* (1 February 1883), p.145, wrote of the *armoire*, 'It will probably be regarded as the most important piece of furniture in the whole collection'.

been held at Gore House, Kensington, under the auspices of the Board of Trade and of the Department of Science and Art.[14] Several of the more notable collectors of French furniture had lent items, offering to the new Museum a tantalizing view of the riches to which it might aspire. Acquisitions of French furniture of the seventeenth and eighteenth centuries remained few during the next two decades, but during the 1870s the senior staff of the Museum developed the friendly relations with John Jones which ultimately led to his great bequest.[15] The Jones was surpassed only when the collection originally formed by his occasional rival, the 4th Marquess of Hertford, opened to the public in 1900 as the Wallace Collection; the two collections together gave the London public riches of French decorative art which exceeded those then publicly accessible in Paris.[16]

From the late nineteenth century onwards no purchases of major collections of furniture occurred, largely for practical reasons. Money was always a problem but, as the V&A's collection grew, the urgent need of the early decades to form a core collection was satisfied, at least until changing taste and collecting patterns opened up new fields of interest. When the V&A turned its attention to hitherto neglected areas – historic British furniture at the turn of the century, for example – there were no opportunities for the purchase of a major collection. Bequests followed a slightly different pattern. In the twentieth century the V&A has benefited from some remarkable generosity, including the substantial benefactions of George Salting (1910, French, Italian and Spanish sixteenth-century furniture and leather objects), Claude Rotch (1962, eighteenth-century English furniture), Brigadier Clark (1969, eighteenth-century English furniture) and Mrs T.R.P. Hole (1986, the Bettine, Lady Abingdon Collection, Lord Stuart de Rothesay's French Empire furniture). Each was a clear document of period taste, as well as bringing interesting and important items into the collection. With a few exceptions (p.112), however, major masterpieces were lacking.

Continental and British furniture to 1800

The common assumption that the V&A has always concentrated on British objects is unfounded; it is particularly inaccurate for the nineteenth century. In 1864, J.C. Robinson, by then an independent Art Referee (see p.11) for the Museum, indicated a clear preference for continental objects when he commented that there was scarcely anything worth buying in England owing to 'the increasing unfrequency [sic] of importation of works of art from the Continent'.[17] In 1912 – by which time major examples of British, mainly English, design were being sought – it was acknowledged that the V&A, 'so far from being intended as a collection illustrating the decorative arts of England, may be said in fact to have originated with the desire of bringing from abroad such models and examples as might influence and improve English design and workmanship'.[18]

As might be expected, the principal furniture acquisitions of the nineteenth century, other than those from exhibitions and major bequests, included many of the continental forms most valued by and available to collectors and connoisseurs. These included Italian *cassoni* (chests) which were prized in the first instance as tangible symbols of the Renaissance, the historic period most favoured by collectors during the first decades of the Museum's life. (It is worth recalling the popularity of the Neo-Renaissance style for furniture [p.68] and for the Museum's own building programme of the mid-nineteenth century.) *Cassoni* were also valued for their association with

14. Board of Trade, Department of Science and Art, *Catalogue of Specimens of Cabinet Work…Exhibited at Gore House, Kensington* (London: HMSO, 1853).

15. Sutton. op. cit., note 12, p.7.

16. The Wallace Collection had been on public view between 1872 and 1875 when it was loaned to the Bethnal Green Museum while Hertford House underwent renovation. See C.C. Black, *Catalogue of the collections of paintings, porcelain, bronzes, decorative furniture and other works of art: lent for exhibition in the Bethnal Green Branch of the South Kensington Museum by Sir Richard Wallace* (London: HMSO, 1874).

17. 'Report of Art Referee for May 1864', dated 28 June 1864, *Robinson Reports*, vol. II, pt II, p.138 [150/102], National Art Library, V&A. (*Robinson Reports* is the title given to the reports of the Museum's expert Art Referees in the nineteenth century and, although named for J.C. Robinson, include papers written by many.)

18. 'The Purposes and Function of the Museum', confidential printed memorandum, proof dated 5 November 1912, 'Circ 1', V&A Archive , formerly Public Record Office.

notable families (p.28), for the quality of their sculptural carving (and gilding), and for their painted decoration (p.26). Painting and carving allowed *cassoni* to be treated almost as fine art objects.[19]

During the second half of the nineteenth century and the early twentieth, cabinets were regarded as the most significant and representative furniture type, both historically and technically.[20] This assessment derived in part from the role of the cabinet, from the sixteenth century onwards, as the pre-eminent vehicle for display, reflecting new forms or decoration. Some were collected for their royal associations (real or reputed), their provenance from a great house or collection, as well as the quality of design and workmanship; the so-called 'Holbein Cabinet' (p.38), believed to have been made for Henry VIII, and formerly owned by William Beckford, provides an example. Others were acquired solely for the beauty of their design and craftsmanship, and some were bought for their technical ingenuity alone.

French seventeenth- and eighteenth-century furniture was the most highly sought-after furniture in the nineteenth century, as it has remained ever since. The association of such pieces with the most splendid of all royal courts and the virtuoso use of luxurious materials gave French furniture a special aura which accounted for the extraordinary prices it fetched during the nineteenth century.[21] The Jones Collection had provided rich holdings in this area at a stroke, but exceptionally fine pieces continued to be added (pp.66, 72, 74, 126, 134). The opening to the public of the Bowes Museum in Barnard Castle (1892), the Wallace Collection in London (1900) and, later, Waddesdon Manor in Buckinghamshire (1959) further increased the nation's wealth in displays of French furniture. Partly as a result of this, French furniture is now rarely a priority for acquisition by the V&A, with a few outstanding exceptions (p.66).

One unusual aspect of the collecting activity during the nineteenth century was the attention paid to musical instruments, especially keyboard instruments, whose cases served as examples of design and decoration. Instruments were collected from the 1850s, although it was an association with the German historian of musical instruments, Carl Engel (1818–82), which began in the mid-1860s, that led to many great acquisitions and the claim that by 1872 the South Kensington Museum's collection was 'the most comprehensive in existence'.[22] Not only did Engel energetically acquire remarkable instruments on behalf of the Museum, he also wrote the catalogue to, and helped organize an important loan exhibition in 1873 which led to further acquisitions. These included the spectacular Rossi jewelled spinet (p.44) and the lacquered and giltwood Taskin harpsichord (p.134), both notable examples of craftsmanship and both signed and dated, as indeed are the majority of antique instruments, unlike their furniture counterparts. Although certain instruments such as the so-called 'Queen Elizabeth Virginals' (p.42) were, like furniture, collected partly for their historical associations, the Museum's approach to collecting in this area has remained unusual and distinctive when compared with other institutions concerned mainly with the musical qualities of instruments.[23]

Perhaps the most important change in collecting policy was a growing emphasis on British, specifically English, furniture of the seventeenth and eighteenth centuries. Although this change gained momentum only in the first decade of the twentieth century, it began in the 1890s, a decade infused with a sense of romantic patriotism and nostalgia which saw, among other events, the founding of the National Trust for Places of Historic Interest or Natural Beauty (1895) and of the magazine *Country Life* (1897).[24] The earliest major exhibition of English furniture took place in 1896, not

19. For an early view of the distinction between the 'ornamental' and 'fine' arts, as well the values attributed to Renaissance furniture, see J. B. Waring, *A Handbook of the Museum of Ornamental Art in the Art Treasures Exhibition* (London: Bradbury & Evans, 1857), pp.2–3 and 45–6.

20. Ibid., pp.48–51.

21. See for example the comment, 'No furniture has ever excelled that made in France during the brilliant period of the reign of Louis the sixteenth', in *The Industrial Arts, Historical Sketches, Furniture* (London: Chapman and Hall for the Committee of Council on Education [1876]), p.21. The catalogue of the Jones Collection discussed the value of Jones's French furniture to a remarkable extent; see *Handbook*, op. cit., pp.1–3, 51, 56, 65–6, 89, 107–08. The Gore House exhibition (see note 14) was dominated by French pieces.

22. [C. Engel] *Catalogue of the Special Exhibition of Ancient Musical Instruments* (London: Science and Art Department, South Kensington Museum, 1872), p.xi. As early as 1869 an internal Museum report commented that 'the Department has now formed a really good collection of ornamental instruments but is deficient in violins' (*Robinson Reports*, pt II, 30 May 1868 – 1 January 1869).

23. P. Thornton, 'Caring for the National Collection', *Early Music Gazette* (January 1980), pp.1–3.

24. D. Watkin, *The Rise of Architectural History* (London: Architectural Press, 1980), pp.94–5, and J. Cornforth *The Search for Style, Country Life and Architecture 1897–1935* (London: André Deutsch, 1988), pp.19 ff.

25. *Catalogue of a special loan collection of English furniture and figured silks manufactured in the 17th and 18th centuries* (London: HMSO, 1896). An earlier Bethnal Green exhibition, 'A special loan collection of furniture' (1878), remains poorly documented.

in South Kensington but at the Bethnal Green branch of the Museum, located in the heart of the East London furniture-making district.[25] 'A Special Loan Collection of English Furniture and Figured Silks' signalled to the leading furniture trade journal 'the revival of interest on the part of the [Museum] authorities in our great East London furnishing industry', by virtue of its having made available for study 'furnishing treasures' of the seventeenth and eighteenth centuries.[26] The two approaches to objects – the 'manufactured' object intended to educate the craftsman and the aesthetically significant example of decorative 'art' – were thus brought together, much as they had been in the 1850s. That this exhibition was drawn from private collections rather than the Museum's own holdings highlighted its lack of English objects and, in particular, the lack of a permanent display 'of the periods of British taste which are most worthy of emulation'.[27] It equally demonstrated what in retrospect might be described as a limited understanding of the eighteenth century, one which would dramatically increase in sophistication within the next decade.

This new view of the importance of English furniture coincided with an era of self-examination and reorganization at the Museum. In 1899, during the final years of the reign of Queen Victoria, the South Kensington Museum was renamed the Victoria & Albert Museum and the foundation of a new building laid. An external Committee on Re-arrangement was appointed in 1908 and recommended that the new displays be organized by material. In fact, this mirrored the administrative structure founded in 1897 by the Director Caspar Purdon Clarke who had established a Department of Furniture, along with those devoted to Textiles, Sculpture and Ivories, Ceramics, and Metalwork. In 1909, when the new V&A building opened, the name was changed to Woodwork (or Woodwork, Furniture and Leather) and the departmental structure reaffirmed. These new departmental divisions were intended to nurture specialist scholars, and it is within this context that the new efforts at collecting English furniture must be placed. From 1911 onwards English furniture is repeatedly identified in V&A documents as the 'section of the collections which stands most in need of strengthening'.[28]

The V&A was not a pioneer in the collecting of seventeenth- and eighteenth-century English furniture; its efforts reflected numerous outside forces. Spurred on by the Aesthetic Movement and the 'Queen Anne' Revival, the late nineteenth century acquired a taste for the lighter forms and woods of mid- to late-eighteenth-century English furniture. This resulted in the reproduction of Adam-style furniture (p.164), the first reprints (1895–7) of the famous pattern books by Sheraton and Hepplewhite, and the active pursuit of original examples of mid- to late-eighteenth-century furniture in the marketplace, including objects from great country house sales as collector's trophies and not simply as decoration. Following on from the efforts of antiquaries who published from the 1830s, British furniture history emerged in the 1870s, and culminated in Percy Macquoid's four-volume *History of English Furniture* (London, 1904–08), the first history (as opposed to exhibition catalogue) illustrated with photographs rather than line drawings.[29] Although this publication lacked the close connection to the V&A that characterized subsequent books, it was a pioneering work which dominated the field for twenty years.[30] Had war not broken out in 1914, greater appreciation of the eighteenth century and the publication of the next generation of books would have been hastened rather than delayed until the 1920s.

Although the V&A recognized by 1914 that it was still 'deplorably deficient' in fine English furniture,[31] early acquisitions tended to be representative of furniture types

26. 'The Exhibition of Old English Furniture – first notice', *Cabinet Maker & Art Furnisher* (July 1896), p.26.

27. 'The Exhibition of Old English Furniture', *Cabinet Maker & Art Furnisher* (October 1896), p.86. The need for clear, well-organized, didactic displays – the taxonomic terms 'classification and arrangement' were often used – was a frequent subject of discussion among both visitors and Museum staff. See Burton, 'The V&A', op. cit., passim and, for an outside view, 'The Seventeenth-Century Room at South Kensington', *Cabinet Maker & Art Furnisher*, vol. XVIII, no. 215 (May 1898), p.289.

28. V&A, *Review of the Principal Acquisitions, 1911* (London: HMSO, 1912), p.58. Further research will undoubtedly establish an earlier date for this view. In 1909, when the new V&A buildings and galleries were opened, the *Cabinet Maker* (vol.XLII, no.513, 24 July 1909, p.106) commented that 'readers, who are of course in the position of connoisseurs as regards furniture, would doubtless be struck with the paucity of fine pieces of the work of the Chippendale and Sheraton period [in the V&A]…There is a vast amount of work of this period in the hands of private collectors and genuine pieces fetch such enormously high prices…'.

29. These topics have not yet received sufficient attention although the scene is set by J. Cornforth, op. cit. (note 24), pp.19–27. A more ambitious discussion of the collecting activities of William Lever (later, Lord Leverhulme), deals with many relevant issues: L. Wood, 'Lever's Objectives in Collecting Old Furniture', *Journal of the History of Collections*, vol.4, no.2 (1992), pp.211–26.

30. See D. Beevers, 'Percy Macquoid. Artist Decorator and Historian', *Antique Collector* (June 1984), pp.70–75, and *Antique Collector* (July 1984), pp.48–53; R. Edwards, 'Percy Macquoid and others', *Apollo*, vol.XCIV, no. 147 (May 1974), pp.332–9.

31. V&A Museum Advisory Council, Report No.4, 'Report on the Principal Deficiencies in the collections of the Victoria and Albert Museum…13 February 1914', p.5, Circ 1, V&A Archive.

and styles of design rather than pieces carrying firm evidence of their maker or with a documented history of ownership. Exceptions which have stood the test of time and are now regarded as among the most important objects in the collection acquired in these early years include the Turkey-work chair, with its covers dated 1649 (acquired in 1896, p.60), and the suite of painted furniture commissioned from Thomas Chippendale by the actor David Garrick (1917, p.120). The latter acquisition highlights the interest in objects owned by or associated with famous figures in British history, a category not officially recognized in V&A documents yet one which attracted attention in the inter-war years.

By the time the V&A entered the market actively, the increasing 'difficulty of obtaining good and unrestored examples' was noted both within the Museum and in the press.[32] Although funds for acquisition were very limited in the inter-war years, nonetheless, the 1920s brought some of the greatest treasures: the Chinese bed from Badminton House, originally thought to have been designed by Chippendale (1921, p.104); the celebrated cabinet designed by Horace Walpole and made to house his enamels and miniatures at Strawberry Hill (1925, p.96); and the chair long thought to have been used by Charles I at his trial (1928, p.68). The 1920s were also an unusually productive period for publishing the collection: between 1922 and 1931 eight volumes of furniture catalogues (including Japanese and Chinese lacquer) and seven picture books on English furniture appeared.[33]

Despite the desperate economic conditions, the Department continued to be active during the 1930s. Icons such as the 'Great Bed of Ware' (1931, p.48), Henry VIII's writing-desk (1932, p.30) and the Adam-Chippendale chair made for Sir Lawrence Dundas (1937, p.118) were purchased. By the outbreak of war a sufficient number of major pieces had been acquired to enable the V&A authorities to shift their complaints of deficiencies from English furniture as a whole to specific areas of the collection including 'Queen Anne and early Georgian gesso furniture' and domestic clocks.[34]

The collecting of British furniture in the inter-war period reflected a concern to provide a comprehensive teaching collection which echoed the first ideals of the Museum and complemented the continental collections established during the nineteenth century. The *History* and *Dictionary* of English furniture (pp.9, 15) had provided a challenge to the V&A to illustrate both the styles of furniture as laid out in the former and the types of furniture as categorized in the latter. In contrast to the exhibition pieces and highly ornate cabinets of the nineteenth century, the Museum now began to buy large quantities of typical seventeenth- and eighteenth-century British furniture – chairs, small tables, commodes. Many were anonymous as to designer, maker or original client. The extensively illustrated publications of Macquoid and Edwards had developed a practice of connoisseurship, in which the curator's role was to choose a good or even outstanding 'specimen' which well illustrated the Adam or Hepplewhite style. The emphasis on documentation, familiar to recent decades, was absent as archival work was in its infancy. Similar representative criteria were applied by the Circulation Department who were at the same time buying furniture for the express purpose of lending pieces to smaller museums and houses throughout Britain (see below, p.20). In 1977, on the closure of that department, those collections were absorbed into the Department of Furniture and Woodwork.

From the late nineteenth century onwards, the practice of furnishing houses with antiques had become increasingly prevalent. This taste affected the expectations and

32. V&A, *Review of the Principal Acquisitions, 1913* (London: HMSO, 1914), p.63.

33. A bibliography is appended to Jervis, op. cit. note 1, pp.129–31.

34. V&A, *Review of the Principal Acquisitions During the Year 1935* (London: HMSO, 1936), p.46.

perceptions of the V&A's visitors. No longer were the pieces exhibited primarily to inform and educate artisans, they were there to please a growing clientele of amateur connoisseurs. Hindsight might see this as a movement away from engagement with popularism, yet the great wave of publications which originated in the 1920s had a non-specialist readership in mind. It is difficult now to appreciate the extent to which the rediscovery of the virtues of plain oak, walnut and mahogany furniture was experienced as a liberation from what was perceived as the clutter and over-ornamentation of the Victorian period, and as an affirmation of national virtues shared by Art and Crafts pioneers, Neo-Georgian architects, and promoters of a more modern approach to design alike. Practicality, quiet dignity, solidity, high standards of craftsmanship and restraint were among the qualities most prized. What may in the 1990s seem dull and worthy seemed, in the 1920s, as fresh and handsome to connoisseurs and craftsmen alike.

A Picture Book of English Chairs, first published in 1925, started with an introduction which gave a brief social history of the form, in great contrast to the catalogues of the nineteenth century which been concerned with ornament and technique. Of the twenty examples illustrated, only four dated from earlier than 1650 and the last in the series was dated about 1800. Only three of this impressive range had been acquired before the end of the nineteenth century. Picture books on English chests, cupboards and cabinets (1926) English tables (1927) and English mirrors (1928) soon followed. In each case they mainly illustrated acquisitions of the twentieth century and were heavily weighted with eighteenth-century examples.

This new emphasis in collecting and publication by the V&A was paralleled by the development of a wide general literature on English furniture, not only books but articles in such periodicals as *The Connoisseur, Antique Collector* and *Country Life*.[35] One of the most prolific writers and strongest influences on taste among collectors, both personal and institutional, was the private dealer R.W. Symonds who published from 1922.[36] Like Macquoid, he not only wrote authoritatively but frequently acted as vendor and adviser to important collectors, including the V&A's benefactor Claude Rotch. His careful use of a wide range of sources in his writings, including contemporary newspaper reports and advertisements, challenged the V&A's curators to develop a more rigorous discipline of furniture history.

The broadly based connoisseurship apparent in V&A publications continued to be the main inspiration for acquisitions until after World War II. In 1924 Oliver Brackett (Keeper, 1926–35) had published *Thomas Chippendale, a Study of his Life, Work and Influence*, but this had remained an isolated monograph among books on furniture which generally treated periods and styles. V&A publications concentrated on catalogues and the popular booklets. It was twenty years later that the then Keeper, Ralph Edwards, published *Georgian Cabinet-Makers* (1944) with the prolific independent (and under-appreciated) scholar, Margaret Jourdain.[37] This made accessible information about more than sixty cabinet-making firms, finally dispensing with the old reliance on the magic names of Chippendale, Hepplewhite and Sheraton. By 1953, with the publication of Ambrose Heal's *The London Furniture Makers*, more than 2,500 makers in London alone were recorded. In 1958 the V&A itself published Peter Ward-Jackson's *English Furniture Designs of the 18th Century*, which revealed a sophisticated command of such themes as the history of design and ornament, the transmission of styles, set within a framework of hard facts about manufacture and patronage; appreciation was now backed up by analysis. The gifts of Brigadier Clark (1946–68, through the

35. S. Moore, 'Faith and Faultless Choice, Furniture in the Early Years of "Country Life"', *Country Life*, vol. CLXXXI, no.2 (8 January 1987), pp.72–5.

36. Ibid., pp.72–3 points out the small and overlapping worlds of dealers, writers, cabinet-makers and collectors, although this remains an under-researched subject. On Symonds's work see, C. Streeter and M. Baker, 'A Bibliography of Publications by Robert Wemyss Symonds', *Furniture History*, vol. XI (1975), pp.88–107.

37. Jourdain often wrote anonymously or under the name of others, e.g., she was the author of F. Lenygon's *Decoration and Furniture of English Mansions during the Seventeenth and Eighteenth Centuries* (London: T. Werner Laurie, 1909) and numerous *Country Life* articles. Her contributions as a co-author seem also to have been understated.

National Art Collections Fund) and the bequest of Claude Rotch (1962) effectively mark the finale of this wide, generalized collecting of English furniture.

Continental furniture was not neglected during the first half of the twentieth century, but the balance had swung firmly in the direction of English furniture. The collecting of the nineteenth century had endowed the Museum with rich continental holdings. Large-scale buying was no longer necessary. The purchase of an elaborately inlaid, early Augsburg German cabinet (1931, p.40) continued a pattern set in the nineteenth century, and the acquisition of the extravagantly Rococo ornamental casket now known to be by Piffetti (1946, p.94) seems, in retrospect, a bold move, standing very much apart from prevailing taste. The contrast with more recent collecting is clearly illustrated by the fact that the ownership of this splendid piece by Lionel de Rothschild earlier in the century was not recorded at all in the papers relating to its purchase. During the keepership of Delves Molesworth (1954–66), who came to Furniture from the Sculpture Department, important examples of continental furniture (pp.82, 152) were acquired to an extent not seen since the nineteenth century but these tended now to contribute to the more recently appreciated attributes of secure dating or known maker.

The keepership of Peter Thornton (1966–84), represented one of the most fruitful and interesting periods for collecting in terms of the range and quality of acquisitions.[38] Many of the new (or newly emphasized) motives for, and ideas about collecting crystallized at this time: the interest in architect-designed furniture (pp.122, 144), in dated, labelled and otherwise documented objects (pp.84, 148), and in a broader range of both British and continental furniture (pp.98, 142, 194). There was, in addition, a keen desire to look beyond the V&A itself to expand knowledge of furniture and its context. Contacts with country house owners increased, as did the use of county record offices, valuable repositories of documents on houses which had grown during the post-World War II period. These encouraged the growth of the Furniture Department's own Archive which had begun purely as a collection of photographs during Molesworth's keepership. Around these activities was a sense of novelty and excitement that revitalized the Furniture Department. By the mid-1970s especially the Department and the Furniture History Society became inextricably linked.

Following the steep rise in prices throughout the entire art market during the late 1970s and early 1980s, the price of major examples of furniture has, in relative terms, risen in comparison to run-of-the-mill objects. The promotional activities of the major auction houses have increased owners' expectations of securing high prices by selling at auction and the workings of the marketplace have changed. While significant objects now appear for public sale, it has likewise become harder for the V&A to secure objects privately, whether through gift or purchase. With a purchase grant frozen since 1985, it is difficult for a public institution to keep up with the marketplace, although it is doubtful that there has ever been a time when Museum officials have expressed satisfaction with their acquisition budgets. Although historic objects of great importance are still acquired (p.124), the V&A is very restricted in the number of such purchases it can make in a given year and depends largely on the generosity of funding bodies such as the National Art Collections Fund and National Heritage Memorial Fund.[39]

38. P. Thornton, 'A very special year. The Victoria and Albert Museum's furniture acquisitions in 1977', *Connoisseur* (June 1978), pp.138–45, and *Review of the years 1974–1978* (London: HMSO, 1981), pp.52–8. Thornton had transferred to Furniture from the Textiles Department.

39. C. Wilk, 'Recent Acquisitions of Furniture and Woodwork at the Victoria and Albert Museum', *Burlington Magazine*, vol.CXXXV, no.103 (June 1993), pp.443–8.

Nineteenth-century furniture

Regency furniture of the Sheraton or satinwood style had been included within the canon of acceptable English furniture as collected by the V&A and published in books such as Macquoid's *History* (1904–08) since the turn of the century; it fitted within the category of 'late Georgian'. However, despite an 1890s fashion for French Empire, the canon excluded 'eccentricities that characterised the later designs of Sheraton', and the 'ultra-classical affectation' of later Regency, especially the designs of Thomas Hope (p.138).[40] By the late 1920s, the view that 'nothing artistically original was produced after 1820' was old fashioned in advanced circles and 1830 became the point of no return; yesterday's eccentricities became 'the last consistent and recognizable style…before the Victorian breach in traditional design'.[41] The inclusion of later Regency furniture in several books by prominent writers on furniture[42] reflected this changed view and the V&A followed suit, especially during the 1930s, when much Regency furniture was collected, and the 1940s, when more significant pieces, bold designs which quite clearly broke with eighteenth-century traditions, were acquired. Influential collectors, including the American Edward Knoblock – who later bequeathed to the V&A important Thomas Hope furniture – and Lord Gerald Wellesley – who later, as the 7th Duke of Wellington, gave Apsley House to the nation (1949) – also encouraged the V&A's appreciation of this more robust and sophisticated, later Regency furniture.

The V&A's noteworthy acquisition of William Morris's 'St George's Cabinet' (p.158) in 1906 had little to do with any nascent interest in Victorian furniture; its purchase was a tribute to Morris's continuing stature a decade after his death, and to his close links with the V&A.[43] Although there was widespread antipathy to Victorian furniture among collectors and curators during the first half of this century, the V&A's stance was complex.

Nineteenth-century furniture, with the exception of 'Empire', was not mentioned in a report on the 'Principal Deficiencies in the Collections' (1914).[44] But the V&A's commitment to provide a complete view of the history of the decorative arts – reaffirmed at the turn of the century[45] – and the difficulties encountered in forming a representative collection of seventeenth- and eighteenth-century furniture, led curators to temper a natural reaction against Victorian furniture with an institutional pragmatism. A memorandum to Oliver Brackett, Keeper of Furniture, in 1921 read:

> Sooner or later we shall be obliged (if the collection is to be historically complete) to include characteristic pieces of Victorian furniture, provided, of course, that such pieces are reasonably good models of design and craftsmanship and if we delay too long we may find it difficult to acquire them at all.

The reply urged caution:

> As a matter of principle I agree that we must, very cautiously, take opportunities of acquiring really good examples of Early Victorian furniture…restricted to the earlier period.[46]

Victorian pieces were acquired by the Woodwork Department during the 1920s and not all were early examples, although many were gifts; objects made between the 1860s and 1880s were more likely to find favour if they had an association with the Pre-Raphaelite painters (with whom Morris was linked) which increased their significance

40. Percy Macquoid, *A History of English Furniture*, vol.IV, 'The Age of Satinwood' (London: Lawrence & Bullen, 1908), pp.241 and 247.

41. Ibid, p.249; M. Jourdain, *Regency Furniture* (London: Country Life, 1934), p.xiv.

42. For example, M. Jourdain, *English Decoration and Furniture of the Later XVIII and Early XIXth Centuries* (London: Batsford, 1923), and Jourdain's *Regency Furniture*, op.cit., the first book on the subject.

43. An internal memo argued that the cabinet 'would be a valuable link in the history of English furniture, as being from the hand of William Morris himself'. Memo from A.B. Skinner to Mr Ogilvie, 6 July 1906, Christie's Nominal File, V&A Registry. The V&A's loyalty to Morris remained steadfast. In 1934, when a centenary exhibition was held at the V&A and co-organized by V&A staff, the 'neglect, even in certain quarters… contempt' felt for his work was mentioned. J.W. Mackail in *Century of William Morris, Catalogue of Exhibition* (London: Curwen Press, 1934), p.8.

44. Victoria & Albert Museum Advisory Council, Report No.4, 'Report on the Principal Deficiencies in the Collections of the Victoria and Albert Museum…13 February 1914', p.5, Circ 1, V&A Archive.

45. See, for example, V&A, 'The Purposes and Functions of the Museum', proof of printed leaflet, 5 November 1912, p.2, no.7, Ed84 papers, V&A Archive.

46. Memo, CS [H. Clifford Smith] to Oliver Brackett, 25 August 1921; undated reply, W.P. Watt Nominal File, V&A Registry.

and acceptability in the V&A context.[47] In general, however, the official view was expressed by Brackett:

> I am…of the opinion that there is hardly anything in Victorian furniture which would be useful to modern craftsmen in design etc. – in fact a great deal of it is frankly bad.[48]

This view did not rule out acquisitions – a papier-mâché bedstead was acquired in 1931 as a 'remarkable example of mid-Victorian taste';[49] yet despite a clear understanding that eventually the tide of taste would move in favour of the Victorian age,[50] it was not until the 1950s and, above all, the active involvement of the V&A's Circulation Department, that the V&A embarked on an active programme of acquisitions.

The principle that V&A objects should be exhibited around the country for the benefit of students, designers and craftsmen who could not travel to London was established as early as 1853.[51] A Circulating Museum was created by 1855 with its own collection of objects and, following decades of successful operation, the Circulation Department was founded in 1909 to lend objects and exhibitions to 'provincial' museums. This development arose from the opening of the new V&A building and the re-organization of the collections in 1909. 'Unique pieces, or masterpieces of international importance' were excluded from the Circulation Collection, so the new department steered clear of the traditional areas of collecting; equally, it avoided objects difficult to transport, especially large or fragile ones, and those of great value (in excess of £1,000 in 1950). Instead of allowing itself to be confined to secondary material, Circulation, staffed by a generation younger than most other departments, turned to neglected periods and the eminently affordable, newly made object and put together collections of great interest in their own right.

It was Circulation that between 1953 and 1968 collected most of the Victorian and later furniture,[52] and it was Circulation that organized the ground-breaking exhibition, 'Victorian and Edwardian Decorative Arts' in 1952. Well in advance of the main thrust of the Victorian revival, this remarkable exhibition emphasized originality in design and insisted on the 'twin criteria of date and attribution', with the aim of 'drawing attention to, and thus…preserving for posterity, important…relics that would otherwise have been lost'.[53] The Keeper of Circulation and exhibition organizer, Peter Floud (Keeper c.1947–60), argued that such an exhibition offered an unparalleled opportunity to 'obtain for the permanent collections material which will, in the long run, have to be acquired anyway'.[54] He was proved right: pieces were acquired during the preparation for the exhibition (pp.178, 180), during the exhibition itself (p.168) and later, as a result of research begun for the exhibition (p.192).

In the decades that followed, the Victorian and Edwardian collections moved from strength to strength. The highpoint of later years was undoubtedly the furniture given by and purchased from the family of Charles (1916–71) and Lavinia Handley-Read (d.1971), astute and dedicated collectors of nineteenth- and twentieth-century objects, with whom the Furniture Department had a close association (p.140).[55] Their collecting, which had begun in the early 1960s, favoured architect-designed pieces, including those by Pugin, Burges, and Godwin, and museums throughout Britain benefited from their generosity.

In recent years the size and quality of the British nineteenth-century collections have confined acquisitions to exceptional documented pieces (pp.172, 176) and the focus has shifted to previously under-represented continental and American furniture

47. It is worth noting that the major mid-nineteenth century pieces acquired by the Woodwork Department – including the 'King René's Honeymoon Cabinet' (w.10-1927), designed by Philip Webb for Edward Burne-Jones, a cabinet painted by H.S. Marks, RA (w.10-1933), and Burne-Jones's own painted sideboard (w.10-1953) – were prized for their painting. Two exceptions, cabinets by Collinson and Lock (Misc.127-1921) and Bruce Talbert (w.44-1953), were long-standing loans from the Commissioners of the 1851 Exhibition, converted to gifts.

48. Memo, Brackett to Director, 7 June 1931, W.P. Watt Nominal File, V&A Registry.

49. V&A, *Review of the Principal Acquisitions During the Year 1931* (London: Board of Education, 1932), p.42. It should be noted that this bed (w.63-1931) was a gift from H.M. Queen Mary.

50. See, for example, the attitude expressed in 1947, when the re-installation of the Bethnal Green branch was discussed: 'If the perplexity of taste of the 19th c [is] of interest in future, some care would, I feel, be exercised in regard to what now seems odious'. Memo, W.A. Thorpe [Woodwork Department] to Ralph Edwards [Keeper], V&A Registered Papers, 47/1018a, Bethnal Green General, V&A Registry.

51. B. Morris, *Inspiration for Design, the Influence of the Victoria & Albert Museum* (London: V&A, 1986), pp.56–64, writes that this began in 1853; 'V&A Museum Circulation Department, Its History and Scope', V&A booklet [early 1950s], cites 1850 as well as the establishment of a Circulation Department in 1852. It has not yet been possible to corroborate either version in the V&A Archive.

(pp.146, 148, 156, 170, 184). Even now, however, British nineteenth-century pieces form the most comprehensive and consistently high-quality part of the furniture collection.

Twentieth-century and contemporary furniture

Between 1872 and 1900 the Museum acquired very little newly designed furniture. The Donaldson collection (see above), today considered a high point, was the exception to this rule and the collecting of twentieth-century furniture, whether historic or contemporary, continued to be exceedingly infrequent during the first half of this century. Although Circulation began to form a teaching collection of contemporary decorative arts in 1909, it did not initially include furniture. Before the 1960s, acquisitions were restricted to British furniture in both the Circulation and Woodwork Departments. Circulation resumed collecting turn-of-the-century British Arts and Crafts in the 1950s and, in the 1960s, French, German and Austrian Art Nouveau pieces. The acquisition of continental furniture of the 1920s and 1930s – including Modernist and Art Deco examples – began in 1965. However, with no dedicated gallery these objects were rarely displayed at South Kensington, and in 1964 an observer was concerned that it would be 'another 50 years perhaps before the whole [twentieth-century] collection goes on show'.[56]

The exhibition 'Modern Chairs 1918–1970' (1970), organized by Circulation, represented a watershed.[57] A large amount of furniture was collected for this exhibition during the late 1960s, including classic designs of the pre- and immediate post-World War II period, as well as many contemporary designs including the latest examples of plastic furniture (p.216). The whole of the twentieth century (albeit with a Modernist bias) then became accepted as a proper field for collecting. The focus was sharpened in 1975 by the dedication imposed by Director Roy Strong (1974–87) of a portion of the V&A's annual purchase fund to twentieth-century objects, and, during the 1980s, the approach increased in sophistication and expertise. This decade saw the acquisition of a major collection of thirty-eight examples of Viennese furniture of about 1900 (p.194), much 1920s furniture (p.198), as well as the purchase of iconic furniture of the 1950s (p.212). In 1983 the V&A's first twentieth-century gallery at the South Kensington site finally opened and by the late 1980s the V&A had begun to apply rigorously to modern furniture the principles that had, especially in recent decades, guided the collecting of historic furniture – an emphasis on provenanced and documented examples and, in a move to cease the anomalous practice of acquiring later reproductions or 're-issues' of modern classics, a strict policy of collecting original period objects only. It is precisely this continuity of approach to historic and to modern objects that makes the V&A's furniture collection so rich and exceptional.

Today there is a concern that the collecting of newly designed furniture – which serves to fulfil the V&A's original mission to educate students and designers – should achieve the right balance with the acquisition of objects with a history of ownership, with some life before the Museum. The V&A attempts to make up for the lack of history of new objects by recording – through interviews and through documentation – the story of their design, manufacture and marketing. This approach is exceedingly rare in today's museum world, where the collecting of modern objects is restricted, firstly, to icons, and, secondly, to the finished and largely decontextualized object. The emphasis on design process, provenance and documentation will undoubtedly make the V&A's collection even more valuable in decades to come.

52. Administrative changes meant that from 1968 the Department of Furniture & Woodwork formally acquired nineteenth-century furniture, although a shift had begun in 1966 with the appointment of the first Assistant Keeper with specific expertise for nineteenth-century furniture, Simon Jervis. Circulation remained responsible for most twentieth-century collecting until it was closed in 1977, although expensive objects or those deemed unsuitable for travelling (e.g. the Eileen Gray screen illustrated on p.200) were acquired by the Furniture Department.

53. V&A, *Exhibition of Victorian and Edwardian Decorative Arts, Catalogue* (London: HMSO, 1952), p.5. The view of Floud, exhibition organizer, tended to exclude commercial productions and revivalist furniture which were collected by the Furniture Department.

54. Memo, Peter Floud to Director, 8 October 1949, V&A RP 225/B/8, 'Victorian and Edwardian Decorative Arts, Policy and Accounts', V&A Registry (file missing), cited by C. Hay, 'An investigation of acquisition and display policies...' (Museums Association Diploma Thesis, 1988), p.21.

55. *Victorian and Edwardian Decorative Art, the Handley-Read Collection* (London: Royal Academy, 1972). See also S. Jervis, 'Victorian Decorative Art at the Royal Academy, Charles Handley-Read's collecting achievements', *The Connoisseur*, vol.179, no.270 (February 1972), pp.89–8, and J.M. Crook, *William Burges and the High Victorian Dream* (London: John Murray, 1981), pp.5–14.

56. Fiona MacCarthy, 'Planning for Posterity', *Guardian* (11 July 1964).

57. *Modern Chairs 1918–1970* (London: Whitechapel Art Gallery, 1970), introduction by Carol Hogben (exhibition curator).

Collecting and the V&A's advisory role

Since the end of World War II, the V&A's collecting activities have been much influenced by the increased consciousness of what is now referred to as the national 'heritage' and, specifically, by the various roles Museum experts play advising the government on matters related to furniture and its historic setting. The sense of 'losing' aspects of national history and culture, and of further losses to come, gave rise to new organizations, laws and mechanisms aimed at preserving that history.

The sale of great country houses and, more commonly, the dispersal of their contents, had been a serious problem since the agricultural failures and the Depression of 1873; but it was only after World War II, in response to the sad but sustained crescendo of demolition of important town and country houses (1920–55), that a broad range of initiatives was adopted.[58]

In 1948 Ham House and, in 1949, Osterley Park House were given to the National Trust by their owners; the contents – including the extraordinarily well-documented seventeenth-century furniture at Ham and the large collection of Adam-designed furniture at Osterley – were purchased by the nation, and, because contents could not be given to the Trust and the National Land Fund could not be used to buy contents, the administration of the houses was assigned to the V&A.

Concern over the fate of such houses led to the Gowers Report of 1950 which considered what steps might be taken not only to preserve 'houses of outstanding historic or architectural interest' but, equally the 'house and its contents as a unity'.[59] In 1952, the steady flow to other countries of important objects from historic houses and private collections led to the establishment of the Reviewing Committee on the Export of Works of Art. Although based on an arcane foundation of currency control, the effect of the system was to institute the requirement of an export licence for objects that had been in the country for more than 50 years and were valued over a certain amount (originally £250 for furniture, at the time of writing £39,600). The Keeper of Furniture (since 1989, the Curator), along with other national museum colleagues, has served as expert adviser to the Committee from its inception.

In 1953 the terms of the National Land Fund were extended beyond the original remit to allow for the purchase of chattels and works of art associated with houses in 'certain ownership' (mainly National Trust), thus providing another method of keeping contents in their original setting, although museums were not part of this process. An additional means to the same end, albeit with far wider application, was the Finance Act of 1956. Aimed specifically at encouraging the retention of import-ant objects within the United Kingdom, the Act enabled 'the acceptance [by the Treasury] in satisfaction of death duties of works of art of pre-eminent aesthetic merit or historical value irrespective of any association with particular buildings'. Acceptance in the early years was limited. Suitable objects, mainly pictures, were initially lent, and then allocated directly to national and regional museums, as well as to bodies such as the National Trust and English Heritage. Subsequent changes in policy led to broader acceptance criteria (objects of local or national importance could he accepted and could be allocated also to houses vested in charitable trusts), as well as acceptance in lieu of capital gains tax. Of even greater significance to museum collecting was the eventual decision (1980) to allow such objects to remain in their historic settings, rather than being removed to museums. Although it was paintings rather than decorative arts which were the main object of these various legislative acts, all were to have an impact on the V&A's collecting of furniture.

58. J. Harris in R. Strong et al., *The Destruction of the Country House 1875–1975* (London: Thames & Hudson, 1975), pp.15–16. Notable earlier campaigning was sporadic but had included editorials in *Country Life*, e.g., 'The National Heritage' (25 January 1930), Lord Lothian's famous address to the National Trust urging it to concentrate its efforts on country houses rather than open spaces (1934), and the foundation of the Georgian Group (1937). See also Cornforth, op. cit., note 24, pp.82–5.

59. HM Treasury, *Report of the Committee on Houses of Outstanding Historic or Architectural Interest* (London: HMSO, 1950), p.1.

The underlying significance of these varied events was highlighted for the general public when in 1974, during European Architectural Heritage Year, the V&A put on the exhibition, 'The Destruction of the Country House'.[60] Both exhibition and accompanying book dramatically illustrated the extent of past losses while also suggesting positive action for the future. The Furniture and Woodwork Department of the V&A under Peter Thornton had, through its custodianship of Ham and Osterley, begun a revolution in the interpretation of historic interiors, especially conspicuous in the arrangement of furniture. Highly practical exercises in furniture-moving were nothing less than experiments in authenticity, eventually returning interiors such as the Gallery at Osterley more nearly to their appearance in the eighteenth century, underlining the critical relationship of furniture to interior architecture, and rescuing the fine seat furniture in particular from its role as 'extras' in the crowd scenes of Victorian and later room arrangements. Although the idea of displaying historic houses in their 'first generation' guise has itself become the object of revisionism, at the time it represented an innovative reaction against the lived-in look of many historic houses, including those of the National Trust. These successful experiments, supported by increasing academic research in this new aspect of furniture studies, led to an advocacy role which rapidly turned into an advisory one as an increasing number of private house owners, local museums, government departments (especially the Department of the Environment) and the National Trust turned to the V&A for assistance in evaluating, re-decorating and interpreting historic interiors and their contents.[61] Underpinning these activities was the recognition that furniture was most appropriately seen within its original historic setting.

These various post-war efforts at 'saving' houses and objects of national importance were potentially in conflict with the V&A's desire to acquire for its galleries pieces of the first rank, including those from great houses. However, this conflict seems never to have existed in fact. Until the 1960s, most V&A purchases of English furniture were made from dealers; these objects had already been sent into the market by owners or as a consequence of the break-up of houses. The V&A could frequently solace itself that it was 'saving' items that might otherwise go abroad. It was only after World War II that tax mechanisms were available to discourage the dispersal of collections. Until that time the owner's decision to sell had to be accepted and the only option open to the V&A was to step in with the remedy of purchase. The changed circumstances of post-war legislation led to the acquisition of a small selection of the important furniture from Mentmore Towers, Buckinghamshire, the Rothschild country house which had descended to the Earls of Rosebery. Although the Government would not agree in 1977 to accept Mentmore and its contents in satisfaction of death duties, as advocated by the V&A among others – lack of an endowment was the main stumbling-block – it accepted five pre-eminent pieces of furniture (p.98) and allocated them to the V&A.[62] Nevertheless, by the 1970s, the position was clear: 'the museum has ample scope for collecting among those objects whose context has been destroyed and, when an historic ensemble survives, should encourage its retention intact rather than attempt to extract the plums'.[63]

Not only does the V&A not wish to contribute to the denuding of great houses, but in recent years it has been in the position of lending back furniture to historic houses (open to the public) when previous owners have elected to sell off their furniture (p.90). The V&A is rare among museums in that it now sometimes acquires furniture with the intention that, should a particular house be opened to the public,

60. The exhibition coincided with discussion surrounding the Capital Transfer Tax Bill which, from 1975, allowed historic houses and their contents to be vested in private charitable trusts.

61. P.Thornton, 'Furniture Studies – The National Rôle', *Burlington Magazine* (May 1978), pp.279–84 and 'Saving the contents', in Strong *et al.*, op. cit. (note 58), pp.142–61.

62. The V&A was one of the strongest advocates of maintaining the house and its contents, and purchased an additional seven objects at the sale; see K. R.[oberts], 'Mentmore and the V&A', *Burlington Magazine*, vol. CXX, no.902 (May 1978), p.316.

63. Thornton, 'Furniture Studies', op. cit., pp.280–83.

it will be returned on loan (p.114). Such action is in accord with its view that the national collection extends in a broader sense beyond South Kensington to embrace all museums and historic houses, at least those open to the public, where proper standards of care can be maintained. This policy has been actively encouraged by the National Heritage Memorial Fund which has done much to keep houses and their contents together.

The denial of export licences by the Reviewing Committee on the Export of Works of Art (see above) for objects deemed to be of national importance can on occasion lead to acquisitions of an unexpected nature (p.156). The case for stopping export is made to a formal Reviewing Committee hearing by the Curator of Furniture (acting as the government's expert adviser, rather than on behalf of the V&A). The Committee itself then makes a recommendation to the Secretary of State for National Heritage who makes the decision. If a licence is temporarily withheld, a UK institution willing to attempt to raise the funds necessary to purchase the object within a strict time limit is sought, and in some instances the V&A itself steps forward. This is particularly the case when non-British furniture is in question, because few institutions in Britain collect in this field. Rare as such purchases are, they often bring to attention objects of major significance. There are, however, export-stopped objects which slip through the net because of lack of purchase funds – perhaps the most famous furniture example was the monumental *pietre dure* cabinet from Badminton House (1726–8, sold in 1990). However, with the existence of National Lottery money since 1995, it is likely that a larger proportion of export-stopped objects will remain in the UK.

Although the Victoria & Albert Museum has collected furniture for nearly one hundred and fifty years, it is worth noting that nearly half of the hundred objects in this book were acquired during the last thirty years. However, it must be pointed out that many of the acquisition criteria that we now value most – the need to represent fully British design, a desire to be broadly international, an emphasis on documented examples that are, at the same time, touchstones of design, and the requirement that furniture of our own time be collected – were neither imagined, let alone embraced by many of our eminent predecessors. Taste, value systems and the meaning of objects change over time. If the same exercise is undertaken in another hundred years, our successors will undoubtedly make a very different selection which will, equally, favour their own more recent acquisitions.   c.w.

Note to the text

The heading for each object follows the same form. The omission of any particular line of information (e.g. name of maker or markings) indicates that this is unknown.

Object type: The name of the object type is given, followed by the name in the original language when this is a widely used term in furniture writing or a term used for a particular piece of furniture at the time of its making. Only in one historical instance is a title used, for 'The Great Bed of Ware' which earned this title soon after it was made. Titles for recent furniture, assigned by manufacturers or designers, are given.

Nationality and date(s): The nationality of the object refers to the country, using its modern name, and, when known, the place of manufacture. Dates are of design and manufacture, except where qualified in the heading or text.

Designer and/or maker names: These are always indicated when known. In some cases, it has been possible to attribute an object to a region or city in the line above even though evidence for the designer or maker has not been found. Birth and death dates are included when known.

Commission: If the object was made for a known client, a particular building or exhibition, this is indicated.

Materials: These are generally given in descriptive order, the most apparent listed first, the carcase wood given last. It has not always been possible to confirm identification by microscopic analysis. Upholstery is original unless otherwise noted.

Marks: These generally relate to manufacture.

Measurements: Largest dimensions (i.e. the highest, widest or deepest) are always noted, unless otherwise indicated.

Museum number: This indicates the year of acquisition and is prefixed by a number indicating its sequence within a particular year, e.g. 7654-1861 was the 7694th object acquired in 1861, and w.28-1954 was the twenty-eighth object acquired in 1954. Since 1909 V&A departments have maintained separate acquisition sequences. The prefix 'Circ.' indicates that the object was acquired by the Circulation Department, 'w.' that it was acquired by the Woodwork (or Furniture and Woodwork) Department.

Source and method of acquisition: Gifts or purchases from private individuals are indicated by the use of title (e.g. Sir, Mr, Mrs or foreign equivalents). Dealers and firms are otherwise indicated.

There is no bibliography as it would have been necessarily vast. The notes indicate the most accessible publications, in English where possible, and serve as a general guide to essential sources, including those leading to yet further reading.

All photographs were taken by the V&A photo studio unless otherwise indicated. For items from other institutions or houses, copyright of the photos belongs to the listed institution unless otherwise indicated. Sources are indicated in the photo captions.

Contributors

Frances Collard (FC) Catherine S. Hay (CSH) Eleanor John (EJ) Sarah Medlam (SM)
Tessa Murdoch (TM) Carolyn Sargentson (CS) Christopher Wilk (CW)
Gareth Williams (GW) James Yorke (JY)

Chest

Italian (Florence or Siena): circa *1350*

Poplar carcase, covered with canvas, painted
red and blue, decorated with tin leaf and gesso
figures, and reinforced with iron bands

H: 54.5 cm; W: 142 cm; D: 58.5 cm
Museum No. 317-1894
Purchased from the firm of Stefano Bardini, Florence

Fig.1. Detail of cassone *decoration*

This brightly coloured chest with gesso decoration is a
rare survival from medieval Tuscany, and is thought to
have come originally from the hospital of Santa Maria
Nuova in Florence[1]. It may have been a marriage chest,
used to store the bride's clothes, linen and other valuables:
the initials punched on the iron straps may have referred
to the families involved. However, it could also have been
a *coffano di donazelle* or 'damsels' chest', probably called thus
because it was decorated with young girls, and not necessarily connected with marriage. Francesco di Marco Datini,
'The Merchant of Prato', had a number of *coffani di donazelle* listed in his inventory of 1363.[2]

The V&A's example is decorated with slender Gothic
figures, characteristic of Tuscan *trecento* paintings, either
standing at the *fonte d'amore* (fountain of love) or riding on
horseback, partaking in the *caccia d'amore* (hunt of love).
Love themes from medieval romances were often represented on more luxurious household objects from about
1300 (fig.1). The figures wear garments with sleeves that
trail at the elbows. These would have been at the height of
fashion during the 1350s but somewhat old fashioned by
about 1360.[3] The dragons at the sides, placed in Gothic
quatrefoils, may have been purely decorative but they may
also have been the owner's personal cipher, a feature often
found on Italian *cassoni*. The back is painted with coarse
criss-cross patterns, and was not originally intended to
be seen.

Chests were the most important form of domestic
storage during the Middle Ages, and are often illustrated
as placed along the sides of a bed. Two similar examples,
one blue and one red, both with flattened iron bands, are
depicted in *The Miracle of the Blessed Agostino* by Simone
Martini (*c.*1284–1344) (fig.2). These bands would have
served to reinforce a chest, which would have stored
valuables. Writing from Avignon in May 1384, Francesco
Datini ordered a pair of chests from Florence, 'painted on
a vermillion or azure ground, according to what you can
find. Let them be handsome and showy… Spend on them
7 or 8 florins a pair, as you think best; the finer and better
they are, the better I can sell them.'[4] He may well have
had in mind something similar to the V&A chest.

The figures are made of gesso (a mixture of powdered
chalk and animal glue) cast in a stone mould, which was
often lined with several layers of yellow or white tin foil, in
imitation of silver or gold. A large number of figures could
be produced from these moulds, hence the repetitive
nature of the decoration. They were then applied to the
chest without extra glue, as there was enough left from the
moulding process to allow them to adhere to the surface.
The process is described at length by Cennino Cennini
in his *Il Libro dell' Arte* (a handbook for craftsmen), which
would imply that such decoration was common in Tuscany
during the Middle Ages and part of what the artist was
expected to do.[5]

Precious few examples of painted furniture have survived from the Middle Ages, and this is the only known
chest with this distinctive decoration in a public collection
outside Italy.   J.Y.

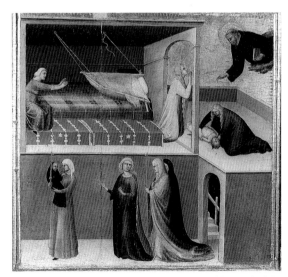

Fig.2. The Miracle of the Blessed Agostino *by Simone Martini
(Pinacoteca Nazionale, Siena)*

1. W. Bode, *Die italienischen
Hausmöbel der Renaissance*
(Leipzig: Hermann Seeman
Nachfolger, 1902), p.6. In
1894, the V&A paid
£338 5s 0d for this *cassone.*
There is a similar one in
the Castello di Vincigliata,
outside Florence, and one
in the Fondazione Cini, in
Venice, formerly part of
the Barsanti Collection in
Rome. According to
Wilhelm Bode, a number of
similar chests lay in store in
the hospital of Santa Maria
Nuova in Florence, before
entering the art market at
an unspecified time, presumably not long before the
V&A bought its example.

2. I. Origo, *The Merchant
of Prato, Francesco di Marco
Datini* (London: Jonathan
Cape, 1960), p.40.

3. F. Zeri, Mauro Natale
and Alessandra Mottola,
*Dipinti toscani e oggetti d'arte
dalla collezione Vittorio Cini*
(Vicenza: Neri Pozzi, 1984),
p.59.

4. I. Origo, op. cit., p.40.

5. C. Cennini, *The Craftsman's Handbook*, trans. D.V.
Thompson, Jr. (New York:
Dover Publication, 1960),
pp.110–11, 'How to do
Chests'; P. Young, J. Darrah,
J. Pilc and J. Yorke, 'A
Sienese Cassone at the Victoria and Albert Museum',
The Conservator, no.15 (1991),
includes a diagrammatic
explanation of Cennini's
instructions.

Cassone

Italian (Siena): circa *1430*

Pinewood with gilt gesso decoration.
Impressed into gesso surface of the three
frontal panels: 'Credo in uno deo…'

H: 61 cm; W: 160 cm; D: 56 cm
Museum No. 7815-1862
Purchased from an unknown source

Fig.1. Cassone, *Italian, c.1430, gilt gesso (Danske Kunstindustrimuseum, Copenhagen)*

Fig 2. Cassone, *Italian, c.1430, gilt gesso (Prince of Liechtenstein Collection, Schloss Valuz, Liechtenstein)*

This chest is a fine piece of Italian gilt furniture in the late-Gothic style and a rare surviving example of a *cassone* with liturgical rather than marriage connotations. Until the object was acquired by the South Kensington Museum in 1862, it had been used for storing ecclesiastical vestments in an unspecified private chapel.[1] The liturgical inscription on the *cassone* would suggest that it served such a purpose when it was first made. It could have been intended as a gift to a Sienese church from a member of the Chigi family, whose coats of arms are prominently displayed on the front. They were not only very successful as bankers but also closely involved with the church. By 1400, the Chigi family could boast of at least two ancestors who had been beatified – *il Beato* Giovanni da Lecceto and *la Beata* Angela. It was their charitable work in the hospitals of Siena that qualified them for this holy honour, which was often a step towards canonization.

There is a similar chest in the V&A with gilt Gothic gesso decoration (Museum No. 247-1894), as well as other examples in Copenhagen (fig.1) and in the Prince of Liechtenstein Collection, formerly in Vienna (fig.2).[2] Of the four, only the Chigi *cassone* has retained anything approaching the original punched decoration on its lid: rosettes, framed in foliate patterns and seraphim (angels), with semi-circles round the edges. However, the noticeable differences between the various patterns on the lid and those on the sides, and the metallic quality of the gilding of the lid, suggest that this section may have been heavily restored or 'improved' at a later date. At the back are painted twenty shields on a dark background, arranged in two tiers and left blank, without any trace of early coats of arms.

Gilt *cassoni* appear from time to time in inventories of the early decades of the fifteenth century,[3] and enough were being produced in Venice for a sumptuary law to be passed in 1489 to control expenditure on luxury goods by banning the making or use of *chasse dorate* (gilt chests).[4] Because it was intended to resemble gold as closely as possible, gilding was a highly expensive process; another

sumptuary law (1530) declared that nothing consumed money as effectively. The Chigis had less cause to worry about expenses than most, and in presenting a church with a gilt *cassone*, they no doubt thought they were 'storing up treasures in Heaven'.

The gilding was laid on a layer of gesso, which – if sufficiently thick – would often be stamped with wooden moulds into repetitive patterns or fashioned into relief figures. Vasari claimed that Donatello performed such work.[5] The various ornaments and animals are decoratively punched in a manner that anticipates the *pastiglia* decoration of boxes from Venice and Ferrara of the 1480s onwards (p.34). The Chigi *cassone* is inscribed with the opening line of an abbreviated version of the Nicean Creed. The inscription, a mixture of Latin and medieval Tuscan, reads 'CREDO IN UNO DEO PATRE ONIPOTENTE FATORE CIEL[I?] E TER[RAE?] ED IN SIBIUIO(?) ONIO ED IN UNU DOMINO CIESO CRISTO FILIU DEI UNICIE FILIU EO ES PSTRI NATO ANTE ONIA', and translates 'I believe in one God, the Father Almighty, the maker of Heaven and Earth, and in all things visible and invisible, and in our Lord Jesus Christ, the Son of God, begotten of the Father before all things'. The religious inscription may have served to ward off evil or simply as decoration suitable for ecclesiastical furniture. J.Y.

1. J. Pollen, *Ancient and Modern Furniture and Woodwork* (London: Chapman and Hall, 1874), p.126.

2. P. Schubrig, *Cassoni; Truhen und Truhenbilder der Italienischen Früirenaissance, ein Beitrag zur Profanmalerei im quattrocento* (Leipzig: Karl W. Hiersemann, 1915), fig.1.

3. A. Schiaparelli, *La Casa Fiorentina e i suoi arredi nei secoli XIV e XV* (Florence: Casa Editrice Le Lettere, 1983, reprint of 1908 edition), p.259.

4. P.K. Thornton, *The Italian Renaissance Interior 1400–1600* (London: Weidenfeld & Nicolson, 1991), p.196.

5. W.L. Hildburgh, 'On Some Italian Renaissance Caskets', *Antiquaries Journal*, vol. XXVI (1946), pp.124 ff.

Writing-desk

British: 1525–7

Walnut and oak, lined with painted and gilded
leather, painted decoration by Lucas Hornebolte
(*c*.1490–1544); outer covering of shagreen added
in eighteenth century

H: 24.5 cm; W: 40.5 cm; D: 29.2 cm
Museum No. w.29-1932
Purchased from Durlacher Bros, London, with the
aid of the Murray Bequest

*Fig.2. Hans Burgkmair, Woodcut of
Mars, c.1510 (British Museum, London)*

*Fig.3. Hans Burgkmair, Woodcut of
Venus, c.1510 (British Museum, London)*

The coat of arms of Henry VIII (reigned 1509–47)
together with the heraldic badges of his first queen,
Catherine of Aragon (1485–1536), painted on this portable
writing-desk, indicate that it is a rare survival of luxury
furniture made for royal use. Such small writing-desks
or writing boxes were used on tables, and it was not until
the late seventeenth century that the desk developed as a
specialist form of table with drawers. Similar desks appear
in the royal inventory taken on Henry's death in 1547.
They were not described in sufficient detail to make
identification possible, though their contents were listed.
In a closet next to the King's privy chamber at Greenwich
Palace were three desks covered with leather, one of
which was 'furnysshed with boxes withoute Counters with
a penne knyfe and a payer of sisorres'.[1] This desk has a
tray for papers within its inner lid, and several small
compartments and drawers for writing implements.

Tudor taste demanded luxurious furnishings; the inner
surfaces of the desk are lined with leather, lavishly decorated with gilding and painting of the highest quality.
Heraldic devices are framed by early Renaissance ornament, newly introduced to England by continental artists.
The outer lid (fig.1) is decorated with interlaced strap-work
enclosing Tudor badges including the portcullis and
Tudor rose, Henry's badge (the fleur-de-lys) and Catherine's personal badge (a sheaf of arrows). Heraldic
imagery, which provided a ready repertoire of colourful
motifs for Tudor craftsmen but also carried powerful
messages of ownership and allegiance, was used extensively at the court of Henry VIII for furnishings, liveries
and as architectural decoration; the decoration of Hampton Court Palace, Surrey, well illustrates this.[2]

The painted decoration on the desk can be attributed
to the King's painter, Lucas Hornebolte of Ghent, who
first appeared in the royal accounts in September 1525.[3]
The figures and profile heads, painted against a blue
ground in roundels, bear a strong resemblance to the
portrait miniatures introduced by Hornebolte when he
arrived at the English court. The desk must therefore date
from between 1525 and 1527, when Henry began proceed-
ings for divorce from Catherine.

The underside of the inner lid shows Henry's coat of
arms with, on either side, figures of Mars in armour and
Venus with Cupid, after woodcuts by the celebrated
German artist Hans Burgkmair, published around 1510
(figs 2–3). Six other small paintings appear on the lids of
the interior compartments: a medallion head of Christ,
surrounded by grotesque ornament; St George, patron
saint of England, with the dragon at his feet; male and
female profile heads amid scroll-work designs; and the
heads of Paris and Helen, inscribed 'Paris de Troy' and
'Helen de Greci' flanked by arabesques. Even the lids of
the interior drawers are decorated with dragons and
greyhounds, badges of the Tudor family.

There is a Latin inscription in classical lettering
(much rubbed), around the edge of the paper tray, which
may be reconstructed as: 'DEUS REGNORUM EC[CLESIAE]
CHRISTIAN[A]E MAXIMUS PROTECTOR IMPERII DA SERVO TUO
HENRICO OCT[AVO] REGI ANGLIAE DE HOSTE
TRIUMPHUM M[AGNUM]', or 'God of King-
doms great Protector of the authority of
the Christian Church give to your servant
Henry VIII King of England a great
victory over his enemy'.

The original exterior covering of
the desk is not known, but might
have been leather or velvet,
with an outer leather travelling case. The present
covering of shagreen (shark
or ray-skin), with metal
mounts, dates from the
eighteenth century and indicates the historic ven-
eration with which
the desk was treated
even at that time.

C.S.H.

1. Harley MS 1419 f. 45v.,
British Museum, London.

2. S. Thurley, *The Royal
Palaces of Tudor England*
(New Haven/London: Yale
University Press, 1993),
pp.98–102.

3. R. Strong and V.J.
Murrell, *Artists of the Tudor
Court* (London: Victoria &
Albert Museum, 1983), p.34.

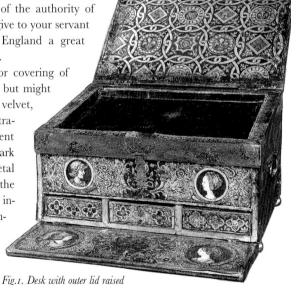

Fig.1. Desk with outer lid raised

Frame

Italian (Ferrara): 1502–19

Walnut, carved and partly gilt
Diam: 48.2 cm
Museum No. 7694-1861
Purchased from the Managers of the
Guarantee Fund for purchasing the
Collection of Monsieur Soulages
of Toulouse

Fig.1. Madonna and Child with Angels, *Florence, c.1450*
(V&A, Museum No. 7694a-1861)

Fig.3. Detail of eagle and hare

This elaborately carved walnut frame, highlighted with gilding, has traditionally been accepted as the looking-glass of Lucrezia Borgia (1480–1519). The glass is a modern replacement of a gilt-bronze relief of the *Madonna and Child with Angels* (fig.1), the back of which served as the mirror plate when acquired by the Museum.[1] Originally, both objects could well have formed – either together or separately – parts of an *ancona* or icon, and would probably have been placed in the owner's chamber as a private object of worship.

The frame is decorated with a number of Renaissance signs and emblems, emanating from the letter 'Y', or Greek letter *Upsilon*, at the base. This was the Pythagorean symbol for the choice between the life of Virtue or of Vice. The scattered letters on the left half of the mirror make up the word *bonum* (good) and those on the right *malum* (bad). The figures represented at the top of the mirror are an angel, who represents eternal salvation, and a skeleton, the symbol of death and damnation. The 'good' emblems include the lion for Fortitude, the unicorn for Chastity and a maiden fending off a dragon. The 'bad' include the satyr for Pride, the hog for Gluttony, the porcupine for Ferocity, the monkey for Lust and the wolf for Cruelty. Such moralizing themes would have been appropriate for the frame of an *ancona*.

The frame bears the flaming bombshell *impresa* or emblem (fig.2) of Alfonso I d'Este, 3rd Duke of Ferrara (1486–1534), who was renowned for his expertise in artillery and gunpowder, at a time when it was a relatively newfangled invention. The hidden message of his military prowess might be further reinforced by the inclusion of an eagle carrying off the hare (fig.3); a similar omen (albeit with two eagles) was described by the Athenian poet Aeschylus in the *Agamemnon* (458 BC) to predict the destruction of the ancient city of Troy.[2] In 1502 Alfonso married Lucrezia Borgia, the illegitimate daughter of Pope Alexander VI. She died of a haemorrhage, following childbirth in 1519. If she did possess this frame and use the reverse of

the *ancona* as a mirror, then it would have been made between those two dates. The quality of the carving is extremely high, and may well have been made in the royal workshops, or *Cantieri*, attached to the Palazzo Ducale of Ferrara. Recent researches have produced names of carvers such as Paolo Dallolio, who sculpted gilded wooden rosettes for Lucrezia Borgia's chamber, and even a supplier of mirrors by the name of Lazzaro.[3] Indeed Alfonso had his own small workshop, in which he could pursue his royal hobby of turning wood.[4]

The frame and bronze disc formerly belonged to Jules Soulages, a prosperous lawyer from Toulouse. His important collection of Renaissance furniture was exhibited at Marlborough House between December 1856 and January 1857 and was purchased for the nation in instalments between 1859 and 1865 for the price of £11,782. When acquired for the considerable sum of £150, this object was listed as a mirror of 'burnished metal', possibly owing to its bright polished surface and to the gilding on the *ancona*.[5] At a later (unknown) date, the disc was removed and displayed separately.   J.Y.

1. J. Hungerford Pollen, *Ancient and Modern Furniture* (London: HMSO, 1874), pp.185–7.

2. Aeschylus (transl. H. W. Smyth), *Agamemnon* (London: Heinemann, 1971), p.15: '…the kingly birds… devouring a hare with brood unborn checked in the last effort to escape'.

3. G. Manni, *Mobili in Emilia* (Modena: Artioli Editore, 1986), p.97.

4. Ibid., p.100.

5. Science and Art Department of the Committee of the Council of Education, *List of Objects in Art Division, South Kensington Museum, acquired During the Year 1861* (London: HMSO, 1862), p.25.

Fig.2. Detail of the 'Bombshell' impresa *of Alfonso I d'Este*

Casket

Italian (Venice or Ferrara?): 1530–38

Alderwood, gilding and white lead *pastiglia*

H: 9.5 cm; L: 23 cm; W: 13 cm
Museum No. 777-1891
Purchased from Lord Zouche, Parham, West Sussex

There exists in various public collections a distinct group of Italian boxes, gilded and decorated with *pastiglia*, a substance made of white lead bound with egg.[1] The only surviving example which can be dated with any certainty is this example; it bears the coat of arms of Cardinal Bernardo Cles (1485–1539), Bishop of Trento between 1514 and 1538. His coat of arms on the lid includes the cardinal's hat, which he had been entitled to include since 1530, but not the paschal lamb, which he added on becoming Bishop of Bressanone in 1538. His personal *impresa*, a bundle of sticks tied with a cord, inscribed 'UNITAS', is also placed on the lid of the box (fig.1). The front and back of the box are decorated with equestrian battle scenes and the Rape of Lucretia: the former on the right and the latter on the left side of the box. In the nineteenth century, a lock was fitted and a blue velvet lining was added to the inside of the box.

The *pastiglia* figures and motifs were shaped in a metal mould or matrix and then glued to the gilt surface of the box. The use of such implements explains why the same figures and patterns reappear in different scenes and on several boxes. The surface is decoratively punched – no doubt to improve the adhesion of the *pastiglia*. In Ferrara the gilding of such objects was usually done by miniaturists, including even the renowned painter from that city Cosimo Tura.[2] The lead paste was frequently referred to locally as *pasta di moscho* (musk paste). These scented boxes were often decorated with scenes from love stories and may have served, among other things, as small wedding presents.

It has been suggested that this type of decoration may have originated in France and that Giancarlo di Monlione (or Carlo da Bretagna, the name which most frequently recurs in Ferrarese accounts) brought the technique from his home in Brittany. However, by 1524, when Margaret of Austria's inventory was being compiled, these boxes were very much regarded as Italian. Seven *coffrets* were described as made of 'pâte cuite à la mode d'Italie, bien ouvres et dorez' (paste prepared in the Italian manner, finely worked and gilded).[3] She also possessed one such box, decorated with the arms of the Dukes of Burgundy, and another decorated with figures and a rosette on the lid.[4] The inventory of Bianca Maria di Challant, drawn up in Milan on 12 February 1522, refers to 'Cassete cinque alla venetiana dorate' (five small boxes decorated in the Venetian manner).[5] These could refer either to *pastiglia* or gilt gesso decorations.

As well as being made in Ferrara, these boxes could also have been produced in Venice. The latter city controlled the lead monopoly in Italy and was also an important centre for publishing books and woodcuts which were used as sources for the decoration on the boxes. Scenes on the boxes are copied from such woodcuts as Jacobus Argentoratensis' *Triumph of Caesar* (Venice, 1504) or illustrations of Livy's *Roman History*. J.Y.

1. P. de Winter, 'A little-known creation of Renaissance decorative arts: the white lead pastiglia box', *Saggi e Memorie di Storia dell' Arte*, no.14 (1984), pp.9–131.

2. G. Manni, *Mobili in Emilia* (Modena: Artioli Editore 1986), pp.39–40.

3. H. Michelant, *Inventaire des Vaiselles, Joyaux, Tapisseries, Peintures, Livres et Manuscrits de Margeurite d' Autriche, Régente et Gouvernante des Pays-Bas (1523)* (Brussels: F.Hayez, 1870), p.71.

4. Ibid., p.77.

5. L. Vaccarone. *Bianca Maria di Challant e il suo corredo* (Turin: Francesco Casanova, 1898), p.8.

Fig.1. Detail of the lid

Cabinet

Italian (Mantua or Ferrara?): circa *1530; with restorations and stand* circa *1880*

Walnut inlaid with various woods. Inscribed on the inside of the fall-front: 'PLUS OULTRA'

H: 81.3 cm; W: 134 cm; D: 44.4 cm
Museum No. 11-1891
Purchased from the firm of Stefano Bardini, Florence

Fig.1. Detail of inside of lid

This cabinet, said to have belonged to the Holy Roman Emperor Charles V (reigned 1519–55), is perhaps the earliest surviving cabinet to have been made in Italy.[1] The inside of the fall-front is decorated with a device of pillars (fig.1) and the inscription 'PLUS OULTRA' (there is more beyond), the *impresa* or emblem created for Charles V in 1516, before he became Holy Roman Emperor.[2] This emblem was devised by Aloysius Marliano, Bishop of Tuy, to celebrate the Spanish conquests in the New World in the year in which Charles became King Designate of Spain. The emblem refuted the received wisdom that the rocks of Calpe and Abyle, placed by Hercules on either side of the Straits of Gibraltar (and known as the Pillars of Hercules), marked the ends of the earth.

The cabinet is reported to have come from the Gonzaga palace of Custozza, between Verona and Mantua.[3] It is thought to have been presented to the Emperor Charles V by his lieutenant Ferrante Gonzaga (1507–57) at Tournai in 1531, a year after Gonzaga had been received into the Order of the Golden Fleece.[4] The Emperor visited Mantua and celebrated the feast of St Andrew there on 30 November 1532; the saint's cross, repeated on the inside of the fall-front, may well have referred to this event. Although Charles V had become Holy Roman Emperor in 1519, his device is still depicted beneath a ducal crown (he had been Duke of Burgundy before becoming King of Spain in 1517). The Italian craftsmen responsible may well have been working from an earlier model. Nevertheless, the links between the cabinet and the Order of the Golden Fleece are reinforced by the biblical story of Gideon (*Judges*, VI, 36–40, VII, 1–7, 19–21) on the outside of the fall-front. Gideon was told by God to leave a fleece out overnight, and if the ground was dewy but the fleece remained dry, then victory would be his over the Midianites.

The drawers of the cabinet are mostly decorated with inlaid putti, scrolls and sea-monsters. It is possible that the letters 'DM' on the top middle drawer stand for *Domus Mantuae* – the House of Mantua. The two large side drawers in the middle tier are decorated with intarsia still-lifes of books and writing implements, subjects well suited to the more intimate and scholastic atmosphere of the princely *studiolo*. The cabinet may originally have had a moulded base, removed at a later date. The stand was probably assembled not long before the cabinet was acquired by the Museum, but the high quality of the carving of the brackets suggests that they were taken from an earlier piece of furniture.

Intarsia was a highly skilled form of inlay made up from woods of natural colours and with different stains. First developed in Tuscany from about 1300, it reached high levels of sophistication, in the hands of Baccio Pontelli and Giuliano da Maiano from Florence from about 1430[5] and Lorenzo and Cristoforo Canozi of Ferrara from about 1460.[6] However, as lavishly carved furniture became more fashionable by about 1520, still-life intarsia decorations, which owed so much to the perspectival discoveries of the 1430s, gradually disappeared. An interesting example of late work (about 1550) is a cabinet (fig.2) attributed to Leone Leoni and thought to have been made for Ferrante Gonzaga, towards the end of his life.[7] The abundance of strapwork and arabesques shows strong influence of Mannerist ornament, associated with Augsburg. However, the *Plus Oultra* cabinet, with its still-lifes in intarsia and richly carved cornice in the antique style, marks something of a transition from perspectival *trompe l'oeil* decoration to lavish carved adornment. J.Y.

Fig.2. Leone Leoni, cabinet, c.1550, probably made for Ferrante Gonzaga (Galleria Estense, Modena)

1. W.A. Thorpe, 'The *Plus Oultra* Cabinet at South Kensington', *Connoisseur*, vol. CXXVIII (July 1951), pp.24–8, 56.

2. E. Rosenthal, '*Plus Ultra, Non Plus Ultra* and the Columnar device of Emperor Charles V', *Journal of the Warburg and Courtauld Institute*, vol. XXXIV (1971), pp.204–28.

3. W. Bode, *Die italienischen Hausmöbel der Renaissance* (Leipzig: Hermann Seemann Nachfolger, 1902), p.66. The cabinet was bought by the V&A in 1891 as part of a job lot costing £2,450.

4. W.A. Thorpe, op.cit., p.27.

5. M. Haines, *The 'Sacrestia della Messe' of the Florentine Cathedral* (Florence: Cassa di Risparmio, 1983), passim.

6. P.L. Bagatin, *L'Arte dei Canozi Lendinaresi* (Trieste: Edizioni Lint, 1990), passim.

7. G. Manni, *Mobili in Emilia* (Modena: Artoli Editore, 1986), pp.229–33; Graziano Manni, 'Précieux cabinet italien du 16e siècle', *l'Estampille*, no.223 (March 1989), pp.28–31.

Cabinet

South German, 1550–80; stand: British?, 1800–20

Marquetry of various woods, boxwood carvings;
carcase of oak; ash drawer linings

H: 139.5 cm; W: 95 cm; D: 61 cm
Museum No. 27-1869
Purchased from the firm of Durlacher, London

Table cabinets of this form were produced in South Germany in the second half of the sixteenth century. The style and quality of this piece indicate that it may have been made in Augsburg, one of the commercial centres where the luxury trades, especially cabinet-making and goldsmithing, flourished during this period.[1] Such cabinets developed from travelling writing cabinets, but the form of the present piece, with two doors rather than a drop-front writing flap, indicates a shift in function towards cabinets to be used primarily for housing precious objects or 'curiosities', collections of a broad range of both natural and man-made objects intended to represent the world in microcosm. Such collections might be housed in cabinets which reflected in their decoration both virtuosity and complex iconography.[2]

Whereas the exterior of this cabinet is decorated with intense and violent battle scenes, the interior carvings (fig.1), sometimes accompanied by moral maxims in Latin, strike a more contemplative tone: for example, a ruler is urged to listen to the advice of Age, and Time leads Youth from ignorance to understanding.

The marquetry and carved decoration are likely to have been adapted from printed sources. The four carved battle scenes on the exterior show some similarities to engravings by Jost Amman (1539–91), who settled in Nuremberg in 1561.[3] The strapwork grotesques on the interior are similar to the work of such Netherlandish designers as Cornelis Bos (1506–64) and Cornelis Floris (1514–75) from the 1540s and 1550s.[4] The boxwood carvings on the drawer fronts are probably largely adapted from the engravings of Virgil Solis (1514–62), who was also working in Nuremberg, although only one design which may be linked to the carvings has been identified to date (figs 2–3).

Fig 1. Detail of interior showing distribution of drawers

OCE·OCVLIS·ALIS·TOTI·SVM·COGNITA·MVNDO

Fig.2. Engraving of Fame, c.1550–70, workshop of Virgil Solis (V&A Museum No. 18971)

The cabinet is made of quartered oak (an expensive cut of a high-quality wood), the boxwood carvings applied to the drawer fronts are finely detailed, and the inner compartments are either lined with arabesque marquetry or carefully selected ash veneer, reminiscent of watered silk. Such cabinets were one of the forms of furniture to be collected by antiquarian connoisseurs in the early nineteenth century. Many pieces were re-built and embellished for these wealthy enthusiasts; the extent of such work, as on this piece, remains a matter of debate.

The cabinet, and probably the stand, was in the extensive and eclectic collection of William Beckford (1760–1844) at Fonthill Abbey during the first quarter of the nineteenth century.[5] The cabinet is described in the catalogue of the abortive 1822 sale of his collection as being 'from the PALACE at WHITEHALL, and executed from designs of HOLBEIN for KING HENRY the VIIIth'. The stand was almost certainly commissioned by Beckford.[6] It was clearly designed to accompany the cabinet, having similar though less fine arabesque marquetry decoration (perhaps from another piece of early furniture), and also bearing portcullis and Tudor rose marquetry motifs, heraldic emblems associated with Henry VIII which make reference to the claimed provenance. E.J.

Fig.3. Detail of interior showing boxwood carving of one of the drawer fronts

VOCE·OCVLIS·ALIS·TOTI   SVM·COGNITA·MVNDO

1. L. Möller, *Der Wrangel-schrank und die Verwandten Süddeutschen Intarsienmöbel des 16. Jahrhunderts* (Berlin: Deutschen Verein für Kunstwissenschaft, 1956), pp.101–05.

2. D. Alfter, *Die Geschichte des Augsburger Kabinettschranks* (Augsburg: Josef Bellot, 1986), pp.42–6.

3. Philippus Lonicerus, *Icones Livianae succenctis versibus illustratae* (Frankfurt: G. Coruinum and V. Galli, 1572).

4. R. Berlinner and G. Egger, *Ornamentale Vorlageblätter des 15. bis 19. Jahrhunderts*, vol. 1 (Munich: Klinkhardt & Biermann, 1981), pp.67–8 and vol. 2, figs 626 and 638–42.

5. *Magnificent Effects at Fonthill Abbey Wilts to be sold by Auction by Mr Christie… October 1, 1822…*, lot 43 of fifth day's sale, p.41.

6. C. Wainwright, 'Some Objects from William Beckford's Collection now in the Victoria & Albert Museum', *Burlington Magazine*, vol. CXIII, no.818 (May 1971), p.258.

Cabinet

German (Augsburg): 1560; stand: 1850–1900

Designed by Hieronymus Wolf (1516–80?). Made by the 'HS' Master. Marquetry of walnut, plum, maple, birch and other woods; carved boxwood drawer fronts; carcase of pine.
Inscribed: 'HS 1560'

H: 59.5 cm; W: 96.5 cm; D: 42.5 cm
Museum No. W.24-1931
Presented by Mrs A.W. Hearn, Menton, France

Fig.2. Hyeronymus Cock, Praecipua aliquot romanae Antiquitatis ruinarum monumenta *(Antwerp, 1551)*

Fig.1. Chest on chest, 1565 by 'HS' (Schweizerisches Landesmuseum, Zurich)

This *Schreibschrank* (writing cabinet) is dated and inscribed with the initials of its maker, HS. It is perhaps the earliest dated, inlaid Augsburg cabinet, although the stand was made for it only in the nineteenth century when the cabinet was restored. Although HS remains unidentified, a chest on chest by him is known, dated 1565 and decorated with architectural fantasies (fig.1).[1] The cabinet is an illustration of the manner in which decorative motifs spread rapidly once printed designs became available. Furthermore it could be regarded as the herald of that prestigious type of furniture of the early seventeenth century, the Augsburg *kunstschrank* (art cabinet).

The outside of the fall-front is decorated with Classical ruins, based on Hyeronymus Cock's series of engravings (fig.2). The top and sides of the cabinet are decorated with arabesques, a form of pattern which spread through Germany from Italy, particularly Venice, with the help of the engravings of Virgil Solis, published between about 1540 and 1570.

The interior consists of a series of drawers decorated with marquetry scrolls and carved plaques. The upper row depicts the Five Senses and the lower, the Eight Planets. These are derived from engravings by Virgil Solis (fig.3).[2] Like Spanish *escritorios* (p.54) from about 1550, the interior is decorated with elements of Classical architecture, such as aedicules (framed openings flanked by columns supporting broken pediments) and a colonnade. Such decoration testified amply to the wide, Classically based education of the original owner, as well as the popularity of Classically inspired engravings amongst craftsmen. It has been suggested that the scheme of decoration may have been devised by Hieronymus Wolf (1516–80), librarian and secretary to the banker Hans Jakob Fugger.

After Charles V became Holy Roman Emperor in 1519, his domains covered both Spain and parts of Germany,

Fig.3. Virgil Solis, Jupiter, c.1550 (V&A, Museum No. E.2527-1913)

including Augsburg. The writing-desk or *Schreibschrank* was derived from the Spanish *escritorio*; two examples appeared in the 1546 inventory of Anton Fugger, the imperial banker.[3] Among the more famous craftsmen from Augsburg was Hieronymus Strohmair, whose patrons included Philip II of Spain. Though such cabinets had originated in Spain in about 1570 they were increasingly imported into Spain from Augsburg and regarded as highly prestigious pieces of furniture.[4]

Although described as *eingelect* (inlaid), the Augsburg techniques were more similar to marquetry: pieces of veneer were glued to the surface rather than cut into solid wood. The abundance of architectural engravings produced in Nuremburg and Augsburg by Virgil Solis, Lorenz Störer, Peter Flötner and Hans Vredeman de Vries provided craftsmen with many motifs and ideas. The combination of outstanding technique and abundance of ornamental sources assured Augsburg of a dominant position in the making of furniture in Europe. J.Y.

1. H. Kreisel, *Die Kunst des deutschen Möbels*, vol.I (Munich: C.H. Beck, 1970), pp.68–70.

2. I. O'Dell-Franke, *Kupperstiche und Radierungen aus der Werkstatt des Virgil Solis* (Wiesbaden: Franz Steiner, 1977), pls 39–41.

3. D. Alfter: *Die Geschichte des Ausburger Kabinettschranks* (Augsburg: Josef Bellot, 1986), pp.21, 104, n.60.

4. T. Sánchez Pinilla, 'Importación de muebles de Ausburgo en 1584', *Archivo español de Arte*, vol. XXXIX (1966), pp.324–5; M.Paz Aguiló Alonso, *El Mueble en España siglos XVI–XVII* (Madrid: Ediciones Antiqvaria SA, 1993), pp.103–04.

Spinet

Italian (Venice): circa *1570*

Painted cypress wood case and soundboard, parchment rosette, ebony and certosina keys; original cypress jacks. Inscribed (back of nameboard): 'Restored by Andrew Douglas/ Oxford 1961'. Range of fifty notes, GG/BB–c3

H: 18.4 cm; W: 159.5 cm; D: 40.4 cm
Museum No. 19-1887
Purchased from Revd Nigel W. Gresley, Milbourne St Andrew, Blandford, Dorset

Fig.2. Looking-glass with stand, Italian (Venice), about 1590 (V&A Museum No. 506-1897)

Fig.3. Detail of the keys of the spinet

This instrument is one of the few surviving objects which can be linked with any certainty to Queen Elizabeth I (reigned 1558–1603).[1] Although known for the past two centuries as 'the Queen Elizabeth Virginals', it is in fact a spinet, a polygonal instrument, the strings of which run diagonally to the keys. It bears the royal coat of arms of the Tudors and the falcon with the sceptre, the device of Elizabeth's mother, Queen Anne Boleyn. Although unsigned and undated, it closely resembles the spinet from Venice by Benedictus Florianus of 1571 (fig.1) and was almost certainly made in that city around that time.[2]

The decoration of the case consists of blue and red moresques (interlaced scrolling) on a gilt background, a form of decoration widely used on small Venetian objects such as boxes and looking-glasses (fig.2). From about 1530 such motifs were copied from objects imported from the Middle East, as was the *certosina* decoration on the sharps and flats (fig.3), geometric patterns made up from minute pieces of bone or ivory and exotic woods and deriving its name from an association with Carthusian monks. The rosette is Gothic and, as is characteristic of Italian keyboard instruments of the time, the soundboard is left undecorated. The case, which is thought to date from the 1680s, is covered with red velvet lined with yellow silk and decorated on the inside with gilt floral patterns on a black background, in imitation of Japanese lacquer. The original case may well have been covered with crimson velvet: there are a number of references in the Lord Chamberlain's accounts to the supplying of this material for the covering of virginals' cases, including a delivery in May 1560 to William Treasorer 'maker of our instruments'.[3]

Queen Elizabeth's skills as a player were recorded by Sir James Melville (1535–1617), Mary Queen of Scots' Ambassador. We are told that she 'played excellent well…she used not to play before men, but when she was solitary, to shun melancholy'.[4] Keyboard instruments were considered more lady-like than the lute, since the player did not risk developing rounded shoulders.

A number of keyboard instruments are recorded in the inventories of King Henry VIII, including a claviorgan 'painted with grene Rabeske [Arabesque] woorke'.[5] However, owing to this instrument's similarity to the Florianus spinet and its absence from the royal inventories of King Henry VIII, it is thought that this spinet was never in the King's possession. In 1620 Richard Connock, Prince Henry's agent in the Duchy of Cornwall, bequeathed to his godson Richard Vivien 'my best virginals rounded with crimson velvet, being sometime the virginals of the late Queen Elizabeth…'.[6] From then on until 1798 nothing is known of this instrument (assuming it was this that actually belonged to Connock). According to Jonah Child, a painter from Dudley (Worcestershire), Lord Spencer Chichester bought it that year from an unknown source in London, and kept it at Fisherwick, his family seat, until 1805. Child bought it at a house sale that year and wrote a letter to the *Gentleman's Magazine* in 1815 describing this very instrument and offering to pass it on 'to a more suitable possessor'.[7] It was later acquired by the Revd Nigel Gresley, of Milbourne St Andrew, Blandford, Dorset, who finally sold it to the V&A for £125 in 1887. J.Y.

1. R. Russell, *Victoria & Albert Museum, Catalogue of Musical Instruments*, vol.1, *Keyboard Instruments* (London: HMSO, 1968), pp.36–7; H. Schott, *Victoria & Albert Museum, Catalogue of Musical Instruments*, vol.1, *Keyboard Instruments* (London: HMSO, 1985), pp.29–31.

2. D.H. Boalch, *Makers of the Harpsichord and Clavichord 1440–1840*, 2nd edn (Oxford: Oxford University Press, 1974), p.44.

3. F. Hubbard, *Three Centuries of Harpsichord Making* (Cambridge, Mass: Harvard University Press, 1972), p.137.

4. R. Russell, *The Harpsichord and Clavichord – An Introductory Study* (London: Faber & Faber, 1959), p.67, quoted from *Memoirs of Sir James Melville*, ed. by G. Scott (London, 1683).

5. Russell (1959), op.cit., p.156.

6. Transcript of Connock's will, Calstock Community Archive, Cornwall, supplied by Peter Mayer.

7. *Gentleman's Magazine*, LXXXV, part I (1815), p.593.

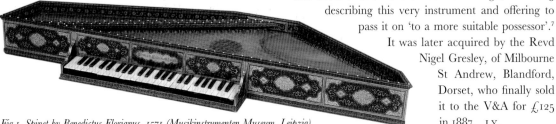

Fig.1. Spinet by Benedictus Florianus, 1571 (Musikinstrumenten Museum, Leipzig)

Spinet

Italian (Milan): 1577

Made by Annibale Rossi (active *c*.1542–77). Cypress case and soundboard, boxwood and ivory ornaments, inlaid with pearls, amethysts, lapis lazuli, jasper, agate, turquoise and other precious and semi-precious stones.

Inscribed: 'ANNIBALIS DE ROXIS MEDIOLANENSIS MDLXXVII'

H: 27 cm; W: 54.5 cm; L: 148 cm
Museum No. 809-1869
Purchased from the firm of Castellani, Paris

Fig.1. Detail of keyboard (satyr with splayed legs)

Fig.3. Detail of rosette

This remarkable jewelled spinet is perhaps the most lavishly decorated keyboard instrument to survive.[1] It is adorned with some 1,928 precious and semi-precious *cabochon* stones, including pearls, garnets, lapis lazuli and jasper.[2] It is the last known instrument executed by Annibale Rossi[3] but it is a very early example of *pietre dure* (hardstone) decoration, an art practised in Rome from about 1550 and Florence from 1588, which remained popular during succeeding centuries.

A contemporary account mentioning Rossi appeared as early as 1595:

> this skilful maker constructed among other works a clavichord [*clavicordo*] of uncommon beauty and excellence, with the keys all of precious stones and with the most elegant ornaments. This instrument was sold for 500 crowns, and is now in the possession of the learned and refined nobleman Signor Carlo Trivulzio.[4]

Given the vagueness of terms then used for keyboard instruments, Trivulzio's 'clavichord' could well have been the jewelled spinet. The fact that such an instrument was mentioned in a book on the nobility of Milan clearly demonstrates that these bejewelled instruments would have added greatly to the status of the owners.

The front of the case (fig.1) is decorated with a series of ivory cartouches, boxwood masks and satyrs with splayed legs, in the manner of Cornelis Bos (1506–56) (fig.2). The decoration is strongly influenced by the strapwork ornament first developed by Rosso Fiorentino in the Galerie François I at Fontainebleau (1535–9), and widely circulated through prints by Bos, Lorenz Störer and others.[5] A style of ornament which originated in Italy, this returned there by means of engravings printed in France, the Netherlands and Germany. Unlike the many Gothic examples of this period (p.42), the rosette on the soundboard of the instrument (fig.3) is decorated with strapwork cartouches, winged grotesques in the style of Bos and an antique bust of a putto in the centre. The jack-rail is held in position by slots modelled to resemble the mouths of a monster and a lion, and is adorned with four miniature statues along the top: one putto playing a lute, another playing a hurdy-gurdy, another a viol and another a *lyra da braccio* (a Renaissance violin). At each end of the keyboards stands a boxwood statuette – Venus and Cupid on the left and Mars on the right. The keyboard has a range of fifty notes, C/E–f3.

But for the contemporary reference to him, Rossi would remain a very obscure figure. His son, Ferrante, carried on his father's business, and surviving examples of his work date from 1580 to 1590.[6] The V&A owns another spinet, formerly a claviorgan (Museum No. 156-1869), by Annibale Rossi, dated 1555, but this is far less ornate. The jewelled spinet was part of the collections of Antoine Louis Clapisson (1808–66), a French composer, and after being exhibited at the Paris Exposition Universelle of 1867 was acquired by the Museum in 1869 for £1,200, a price unprecedented for any musical instrument it had previously purchased and nearly equal only to that paid for a statue of Cupid (Museum No. 7560-1861) acquired in 1861 for £1,000 and then thought to be by Michelangelo.[7]   J.Y.

Fig.2. Cornelis Bos, engraving of seated satyr with splayed legs (V&A Museum No.23090.22)

1. C. Engel, *A Descriptive Catalogue of the Musical Instruments in the South Kensington Museum* (London: G.E. Eyre and W. Spottiswoode, 1874), pp.272–5; R. Russell, *Victoria & Albert Museum, Catalogue of Musical Instruments*, vol.1, *Keyboard Instruments* (London: HMSO, 1968), pp.35–7; H. Schott, *Victoria & Albert Museum, Catalogue of Musical Instruments*, vol.1, *Keyboard Instruments* (London: HMSO, 1985), pp.36–9.

2. C. Engel, op.cit., p.273–4.

3. D.H. Boalch, *Makers of the Harpsichord and Clavichord, 1440–1840* (Oxford: Oxford University Press, 1974), pp.127–8.

4. P. Morigi, *La Nobiltà di Milano* (Milan, 1595) cited by C. Engel, op. cit., pp.273–74.

5. A. Gruber (ed.), *L'Art décoratif en Europe. Renaissance et Maniérisme* (Paris: Citadelles & Mazenod, 1993), passim.

6. D.H. Boalch, op. cit., pp.127–8.

7. Science and Art Department of the Committee of Council of Education, *List of Objects in Art Division, South Kensington Museum, acquired During the Year 1861* (London: HMSO, 1862), p.35.

Claviorgan

British (London): 1579

Built by Lodewyk Theewes (active 1561–79).
Painted oak, spruce soundboard, embossed paper
lining. Inscribed on the inside of the lockboard:
'Ludowicus Theewes me fecit 1579'
Harpsichord: H: 23 cm; W: 213 cm; D: 89 cm
Organ: H: 104 cm; W: 230 cm; D: 102 cm
Original keyboard range probably C,D-c3
Museum No. 125-1890
Given by Mrs Luard-Selby, Igtham Mote, Kent

The Theewes Claviorgan is the earliest surviving dated
keyboard instrument to have been made in England.[1] It is
a cross between a harpsichord and an organ, with organ
pipes originally fitted below; only the outer case and a few
fragments of the original workings, including one key, one
pipe and several jacks, survive. As the instrument is both
painted and dated, it is an important piece of furniture in
its own right. Painted furniture is recorded in inventories
but precious few examples have survived. Indeed the very
survival of this claviorgan enhances the view that sophisticated furniture was produced in London during this
period and that sixteenth-century interiors were far more
colourful than has widely been thought.

The lower case of the instrument is a massive sepul-
chral structure, decorated with strapwork cartouches which
frame *trompe-l'oeil* paintings of gemstones. The case is
articulated with Ionic pilasters, the shafts of which imitate
grained marble, one of the earliest examples of such
painting to survive. The upper part of the case is
decorated with coats of arms within Classical paterae-in-
rectangles. When the casework was cleaned in 1947 the
arms of the Roper family were revealed beneath those of
Sir Edward Hoby, of Bisham, Berkshire, and his wife
Margaret, daughter of Henry Carey, 1st Baron Hunsdon,
who married in 1582.

Fig.1. Detail of inside lid

The harpsichord is covered with tooled calf-leather,
and decorated with concentric rectangles, somewhat
crudely imitating wooden moulding. The lid (fig.1) carries
Theewes's inscription and is decorated with a cartouche of
Orpheus, embellished with sphinxes, monkeys and fruit
within a strapwork framework. The monkeys amid the
strapwork are similar to those in a series of playing cards,
engraved by Virgil Solis (fig.2).[2] As one would expect on
an instrument from a workshop of a Fleming (albeit one
based in London), sprigs of flowers are painted in tempera
onto the soundboard – one of the earliest-known examples
of this decoration. The rosette on the soundboard no
longer survives.

Lodewyk Theewes came from Antwerp, where he
became a member of the Academy of St Luke in 1561.
Both his father, Jacob, and his uncle, Lodewijk, also made
keyboard instruments. In 1571 he was recorded as a
'virginall maker, a Dutchman' living in the parish of St
Martin-le-Grand, London.[3] No other instruments by him
have been traced. No dated English keyboard instrument
made between the Theewes claviorgan and the 1622 John
Haward harpsichord (Knole, Kent) has survived. Nevertheless, a number of claviorgans are mentioned in the
inventories of Henry VIII, such as a 'single Virginall and
single Regall withe a Stoppe of timbre pipes'.[4] Only three
sixteenth-century claviorgans (or former parts of claviorgans) are known to have survived: the 1555 Rossi spinet
(p.44), the Theewes claviorgan, and an unsigned and
undated example made
between about 1550 and
1600 in the collections
of the Kunsthistorisches
Museum in Vienna. The
instrument in the V&A
remained largely undis-
turbed and, as far as is
known, unrecorded, for
many years in the chapel
at Ightham Mote, Kent,
until being presented along
with the 1725 harpsichord
made by Thomas Hitch-
cock (Museum No. 126-
1890) to the Museum in
1890. J.Y.

1. R. Russell, *Victoria &
Albert Museum, Catalogue of
Musical Instruments*, vol.1,
Keyboard Instruments (London:
HMSO, 1968), pp.48–9;
H. Schott, *Victoria & Albert
Museum, Catalogue of Musical
Instruments*, vol.1, *Keyboard
Instruments* (London: HMSO,
1985), pp.40–42.

2. I. O'Dell-Frank,
*Kupferstiche und Radierung aus
der Werkstatt des Virgil Solis*
(Wiesbaden: Franz Steiner,
1977), figs f84–f93.

3. D.H. Boalch, *Makers of
the Harpsichord and Clavichord,
1440–1840* (Oxford: Oxford
University Press, 1974),
p.178.

4. F. Hubbard, *Three
Centuries of Harpsichord Making*
(Cambridge, Mass: Harvard
University Press, 1972),
p.134.

*Fig.2. Virgil Solis, design for a
playing card, c.1550
(V&A Museum No.12841.2)*

The Great Bed of Ware

British: 1590–1600, with later additions

Oak, carved and originally painted, with panels of marquetry
H: 267 cm; W: 326 cm; D: 338 cm
Museum No. w.47-1931
Purchased from Frank Partridge & Sons, London, with the assistance
of the National Art Collections Fund

Fig.1. Henry Shaw, Specimens of Ancient Furniture (London: William Pickering, 1836), pl. XXXVII

One of the best-known pieces of English furniture, this bed has been famous since it was made in the late sixteenth century. Known as the 'Great Bed of Ware' since at least 1609, it epitomizes the flamboyantly carved and painted beds of the late Elizabethan period, although its fame rests primarily on its unusually large size, almost twice that of a normal bed.[1]

Its name derives from the town of Ware in Hertfordshire where, until 1870, it passed through the ownership of several inns. Surprisingly, the origins of the bed are unclear. It has been suggested that it was made for a local house, Ware Park, which was built for Thomas Fanshawe in 1588–90, though there is no evidence to support this.[2] It is more likely that it was made as a curiosity or early form of advertisement to attract customers to stay at one of the inns in the town, as Ware was then a day's journey from London on the road north and a convenient place for travellers to stop.

The earliest reference to the bed is by a German visitor, Prince Ludwig of Anhalt-Köhten, who in 1596 mentioned in his diary a bed at Ware in which four couples could sleep side by side.[3] The bed's fame must have spread quickly as it is referred to in Shakespeare's *Twelfth Night*, first performed in 1601: Sir Toby Belch describes a sheet as 'big enough for the bed of Ware'.[4] The bed continued to be mentioned in bawdy tales and by writers and travellers through to the nineteenth century. By then antiquarian interest had resulted in published illustrations, such as that in Henry Shaw's *Specimens of Ancient Furniture* (fig.1), which increased the bed's fame.[5]

In 1870 the bed was bought by a hotel owner who displayed it in a small museum in the grounds of the Rye House Hotel at nearby Hoddesdon until the 1920s. It was sold to a local brewery and then bought by a leading antique dealer from whom it was purchased by the V&A.[6]

Though its dimensions far exceed those of any other known bedstead, on stylistic grounds the bed is comparable to other beds of the same period. The woodwork is profusely carved with anglicized Renaissance patterns, acanthus leaves and strapwork. The carving of the human figures on the headboard, and the panelling on the underside of the tester, or wooden canopy, show traces of paint and would have originally have been brightly coloured, as was much Elizabethan furniture. In the arches of the headboard, the two marquetry panels which show architectural scenes in perspective (fig.2) are typical of the work introduced by German craftsmen settling in London in the late sixteenth century, and are strongly influenced by designs of Hans Vredeman de Vries (1527–1604), the Dutch artist.[7]

The appearance of the bed has altered with the passage of time: the paintwork has almost vanished, the height of the bed has been reduced by approximately 30 cm by shortening both the posts and the legs, and comparison with Shaw's illustration and early photographs shows that the frieze and cornice around the top of the tester are replacements. Hangings would originally have been suspended from the tester on three sides to provide privacy and warmth, with mattresses and bed-clothes laid over cords threaded through the holes in the bed-stock, concealing the lower half of the headboard.   C.S.H.

1. Ben Jonson referred to 'the great bed at ware' in his 1609 play *Epicoene; or the Silent Woman*, Act V Scene 1.

2. W.A. Thorpe, 'The Great Bed of Ware and Harry Fanshawe', *Country Life*, vol.XC, no.2326 (15 August 1941), pp.286–90.

3. Ibid, p.288.

4. W. Shakespeare, *Twelfth Night*, Act III Scene 2.

5. By tradition, those who slept in the bed carved their initials in the headboard, or left impressions of their ring in wax seals, which can still be seen on the bed-posts.

6. In 1864, J.C. Robinson, then responsible for buying exhibits, had rejected the bed as 'a coarse and mutilated specimen' (Robinson Reports, vol.II, part III, Minute no.14604), reflecting the contemporary scorn for British pieces which were compared unfavourably with continental examples. By 1928 the pendulum had swung.

7. B.M. Forman, 'Continental Furniture Craftsmen in London 1511–1625', *Furniture History*, vol.VII (1971), pp.94–120.

Fig.2. Detail of the marquetry on the headboard of the bed

Cabinet

Italy (Naples): circa *1600*

Probably made by Iacopo Fiamengo (active 1594–1602). Ivory plaques and ebony veneer on a carcase of pine and cedar

H: 97.7 cm; W: 104.8 cm; D: 51.7 cm
Museum No. w.36-1981
Purchased from P. & D. Colnaghi, London

Fig.1. The cabinet, photographed at IVa Esposizione Nazionale di Belle Arti, *Turin, 1880*

This unsigned cabinet is a fine example of the ebony-veneered furniture decorated with ivory plaques, made mostly in Naples and Spain from the mid-1590s until the 1640s. The provenance of this piece remains unknown but it was exhibited at the *IVa Esposizione Nazionale di Belle Arti* at Turin in 1880 (fig.1). Since then, the original top has been lost – the presence of drawers hidden inside what is now the uppermost moulding suggests that the original top section slid out as the current top panel now does – and the lock on the right door replaced by an engraved ivory disc, originally on the inside of that door.

These cabinets were made of costly materials, and could perhaps be regarded as Southern Europe's answer to the ebony and silver-mounted versions made in Augsburg during the same period. Just as Northern European cabinets were fitted with many artfully concealed compartments, this Neapolitan example contains some seventy-seven drawers, many of which lie hidden behind sliding panels, to either side of a central section. The abundance of these hidden drawers served to conceal important documents and valuables. The luxurious decoration displayed the status of the owner and demonstrated the virtuosity of the cabinet-maker, who often came from Flanders or Germany, bringing his native techniques with him.

The only known Neapolitan cabinet-maker of this period identified so far is Iacopo Fiamengo, who presumably came from Flanders, as his name (the Fleming) suggests.[1] The ivory plaques which covered these cabinets were executed by specialists in Naples, some native and some from Northern Europe like Petrus Pax, described as *alemanus intagliatore* (German engraver).[2] One extant cabinet of 1597 (fig.2) bears the signatures of Gennaro Picicato and Jacopo de Curtis. Antonio Spano (active 1579–1614), a Neapolitan engraver, established himself in Madrid, and produced plaques for a signed but undated cabinet (Varez Fisa Collection, Madrid) depicting scenes from the history of Naples, including the triumphant entries of the Emperor Charles V and Philip II.[3]

In the early seventeenth century Naples was under Spanish rule, perhaps its most important overseas pos-session in Europe. After annexing Portugal in 1589, Spain secured the monopoly of importing from Goa ebony and ivory, both highly prized materials. Ivory engraving became a speciality of Naples, but during this period there were also Spanish cabinet-makers who executed similar pieces.[4] Examples decorated with engraved *historias* (scenes) are found in inventories of the time.[5] *Historias* on cabinets often depicted Roman legends, battles and hunting scenes. Artists could look to a number of printed sources, hunting scenes such as *Venationis piscationis et avcupii typi* (Antwerp, 1582) by H. Bol and F. Galle, Marteen van Heemskerk's series of battle prints *Divi Caroli V...Victorias* (Antwerp, 1556) or illustrations to Ovid's *Metamorphoses* by Antonio Tempestà (Antwerp, 1606).[6] The illustrations on this cabinet include episodes from the life of Romulus, the first King of Rome, engraved by Giovanni Battista Fontana and published in 1575. Philip II tried to emulate Romulus, and this may have been partly the reason for the choice of subject on both this cabinet and the example illustrated in fig.2.[7] J.Y.

Fig.2. Mappa Mundi *cabinet with plaques by Picicato, De Curtis and others (Museum für Kunst und Gewerbe, Hamburg)*

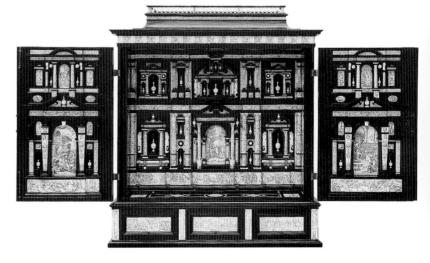

1. A. González-Palacios, 'Giovanni Battista de Curtis, Iacopo Fiamengo e lo stipo manierista napoletano', *Antologia di Belli Arti*, no.6 (May 1978), pp.136–48.

2. Ibid., pp.136, 138.

3. M. Paz Aguiló Alonso, 'La Exaltación de un reino. Nápoles y el mobiliario de lujo a la vuelta del siglo XVI', *Arquivo Español de Arte*, vol.LXV (1992), pp.179–98.

4. M. Paz Aguiló Alonso, *El Mueble en España – Siglos XVI–XVII* (Madrid: Ediciones Antiqvaria, 1993), p.114.

5. Ibid., pp.112–13.

6. *Meubles d'apparat des Pays-Bas Méridioneaux* (Brussels: C. Coessens, 1989), p.86.

7. D. Altfer, 'Ein neapolitan-ischer Kabinettschrank des Giacomo Fiammingo', *Pantheon*, XXXVII (April/June 1979), p.135–41.

Chair

British: circa 1625

Carved oak, painted.
Design attributed to Francis Clein
(1582–1658)
H: 110.5 cm; W: 69.2 cm; D: 66 cm
Museum No. w.9-1953
Purchased from Christie, Manson & Woods Ltd,
London

Fig.1. Section through the Great Chamber or Gilt Room, Holland House, from C.J. Richardson, Architectural Remains of the Reigns of Elizabeth and James I (London: privately printed by the author, 1838–40), vol.I, plate IV

This form of chair was introduced to England in the second decade of the seventeenth century, influenced by continental prototypes. Based on the Italian *sgabello*, a trestle-stool with cartouche-shaped board supports and back, fixed with mortise-and-tenon joints to a seat with a circular depression, this chair has arms, the shape of which recalls French *caqueteuse* armchairs.[1] The dominant shell-shaped back and the swags and pendant mask on the front were appropriate for the Classical interiors designed for English court circles by the architect Inigo Jones (1573–1652).[2]

Like Jones, Francis Clein spent several years in Italy before working for Christian IV of Denmark on the decoration of the Royal Castle at Rosenborg. He was recommended to Charles, Prince of Wales (Christian IV's nephew), in 1623 by Sir Arthur Anstruther, the English Ambassador in Copenhagen, and was appointed designer to the Mortlake tapestry manufactory in London. Clein returned to England in 1625 and was granted a pension by Charles I. He designed a triumphal arch to celebrate the arrival of Queen Henrietta Maria from France in 1625 and the façade of Wimbledon House, Surrey, which became a royal residence. In addition he designed interiors for Bolsover Castle, Carew House, Ham House, Holland House for Henry Rich, 1st Earl Holland, and Stoke Bruerne for Sir Francis Crane, founder of the Mortlake tapestry manufactory. He also published several sets of ornamental engravings in London in the 1640s and 1650s.[3]

This chair has no history of ownership but is attributed to Clein by comparison with a similar chair from the Gilt Chamber at Holland House, Kensington, redecorated in the mid-1620s.[4] Horace Walpole described this room (fig.1) as 'a beautiful Chamber, with a ceiling in grotesque, and small compartments on the chimneys, in the style and not unworthy of Parmagiano. Two chairs, carved and gilt with large shells for backs, belonged to the same room, were undoubtedly from his [Clein's] designs; and are evidence of his taste.'[5] A later writer noted that these chairs 'are painted white, and partly gilt. A large bench, formed by three of these chairs placed together, with one arm only at each end, was discovered some years ago, in a lumber-place over the stables'.[6] The shell-shaped back of the chairs and bench echo the shell-decorated niche above the central door in the Gilt Chamber.

The design was inspired by furniture seen during Clein's Italian visit and the work of Inigo Jones, with whom he was closely associated. A pair of similar chairs are shown in the Picture Gallery at Arundel House in the Strand, shown in the portrait of the Countess of Arundel, painted by Daniel Mytens in 1618 (fig.2).[7] This Gallery was designed by Inigo Jones shortly after his return from Italy with the Earl of Arundel in 1614. By 1670 such chairs were no longer fashionable and those designed by Clein for the Long Gallery at Ham House appear as garden furniture in Henry Danckerts' painting of King Charles II being presented with a pineapple at Ham.[8] This chair is a rare survival of courtly furniture from the early seventeenth century.[9] T.M.

Fig.2. Detail from Alathea Talbot, Countess of Arundel by Daniel Mytens, c.1618 (National Portrait Gallery, on loan to Arundel Castle)

1. P. Thornton, *Seventeenth Century Interior Decoration in England, France & Holland* (New Haven/London: Yale University Press, 1978), pp.93, 186, 340–41.

2. J. Harris, S. Orgel and R. Strong, *The King's Arcadia: Inigo Jones and the Stuart Court* (London: Arts Council, 1973).

3. S. Jervis, *The Penguin Dictionary of Design and Designers* (London: Penguin/Allen Lane, 1984), pp.114–15.

4. Two chairs from the same set came to the V&A in 1984; a further two had been acquired by the Birmingham Museum and Art Gallery in 1955.

5. *Anecdotes of Painting in England*, ed. R.N. Wornum (London: Henry G. Bohn, 1849), vol.II, p.375.

6. S.C. Hall, *The Baronial Halls and Picturesque Edifices of England* (London: Chapman & Hall, 1848), vol.II, p.7.

7. *Treasure Houses of Britain* (Washington: National Gallery of Art, 1985), no.50 and cat. nos 57, 59.

8. Marquess of Cholmondeley, Houghton Hall, Norfolk.

9. S. Jervis, '"Shadows, not substantial things", Furniture in the Commonwealth Inventories', in A. Macgregor (ed.), *The Late King's Goods* (London/Oxford: Alistair McAlpine/Oxford University Press, 1989), pp.277, 291.

Vargueño

Spanish (Salamanca?): circa *1630;*
stand circa *1850*

Walnut, giltwood, bone; iron locks, handles
and ornaments on a red velvet backing

H: 145 cm; w: 115.5 cm; D: 46 cm
Museum No. Circ.178a&b-1955
Bequeathed by Sir Victor Wellesley, KCMG, London

Fig.1. Detail with central door opened

If Spain has made one vitally important contribution to
European furniture, it is the cabinet. From the *escritorio* (or
vargueño, to use the later and more familiar term) evolved
such prestigious pieces as the ebony Augsburg *Kunstschrank*
of the seventeenth century with silver mounts and the
Florentine *stipo*, embellished with *pietre dure* (hardstone)
plaques. The *escritorio* derives from the Catalan *hembra*, a
bridal chest with two large doors at the front each concealing a series of drawers.[1] As the Spanish name suggests,
the *escritorio* served as a writing-desk, which could also
store papers and implements. In the earlier decades of the
sixteenth century, these pieces were inlaid with geometrical Arabic motifs in bone, in a style known as *Mudéjar*.
However, as Spanish craftsmen became more familiar
with Classical architecture and ornament, largely through
Francisco de Villalpando's translation of Sebastiano
Serlio's treatise *L'Architettura* (1552), the insides of these
writing cabinets were frequently decorated with Classical
ornament. They also relied on gilding, bright colours and
pieces of bone decorated with Indian ink.

This *escritorio* is similar to those made in Salamanca
from about 1620.[2] The inside is arranged in an architectural manner, with Baroque aedicules (framed openings
flanked by columns, supporting a broken pediment) placed
in the centre of the upper tier and the left and right sides
of the lower tier. The walnut drawer-fronts are decorated
with vermilion paint, white moresques (scrolling patterns)
and pieces of bone, inscribed mostly with abstract patterns
in Indian ink and arranged geometrically (fig.1). The
craftsmen of Salamanca concerned themselves with gaudy
surface decoration of the interior, aimed to impress the
moment the piece was opened up. The outer cases were
simple cuboid structures, without carving or even
moulding. However, a number of surviving examples were
decorated on the outside with flower-vase patterns in
pieces of inlaid bone. More, including this one, were
lavishly covered with iron ornaments and locks on velvet
grounds (fig.2), no doubt to create an impression of both
security and dignity.

Escritorios have been known as *vargueños* since about
1870. Juan Riaño somewhat fancifully suggested that such
pieces originated from the town of Vargas, hence their
name.[3] Although stands (or rather 'feet') are referred to in
sixteenth-century inventories, almost all surviving stands,

including this example, were made during the nineteenth
century. *Escritorios* and related pieces of furniture are
illustrated in a number of Spanish paintings of about 1650,
such as *The Vocation of St Matthew* by Juan de Pareja
(Museo Nacional del Prado, Madrid) and a *Still-Life with
Sweets, Vessels and an Ebony Chest* by Antonio de Pareda
(State Hermitage Museum, St Petersburg). Only one
design for an *escritorio* has survived: a somewhat austere
architectural example by Juan de Villanueva, dated 1597
(Archivo Histórico Provincial de Cuenca, Cuenca).[4]

The *escritorio* as a form of furniture was adopted with
enthusiasm throughout Europe, but was superceded in
status in Spain by foreign versions which had derived from
it, made in Naples, Antwerp and southern Germany.
Indeed, so sought after were the foreign cabinets and so
depressed were the prices of *escritorios* that Philip III felt
compelled to ban 'all types of chests [*bufetes*] from Nuremburg' in 1603 in order to protect the trade.[5]   J.Y.

1. G.H. Burr, *Hispanic Furniture* (New York: Archive Press, 1964), p.32.

2. M. Paz Aguiló Alonso, *El Mueble en España* (Madrid: Ediciones Antiqvaria, 1993), pp.107–10.

3. J. Riaño, *Classified and descriptive catalogue of the objects of Spanish production in the South Kensington Museum* (London: HMSO, 1872), p.2.

4. M. Luz Rokiski Lázaro, 'Dibujo de un Bargueño del Siglo XVI', *Boletín del Seminario de Estudios de Arte y Arqueología* (1979), pp.452–4.

5. S. Jervis, 'A tortoiseshell cabinet and its precursors', *V&A Bulletin*, no.4 (October 1968), p.134.

Fig.2. Outside of *vargueño*

Wassail Table and Furnishings

British: 1640–80

Lignum vitae with ivory decoration

Table: H: 76 cm; W: 89 cm; D: 58.5 cm

Bowl: H: 50 cm

Candlestands: H: 93 cm

Candlesticks: H: 24 cm

Museum No. w.8-k-1976

Purchased from Spink & Son, London

This suite of furniture was originally used for the serving of wassail, or spiced ale – the word derives from the Anglo-Saxon 'wes haeil', or 'health to you' – which was traditionally offered at Christmas and on other feast days. The small, footed bowl rising from the lid of the large bowl would have held the spices essential for the concoction, and the silver-rimmed dipper cups could be inverted to dry after use on the decorative knobs surrounding the spice box. Other wassail bowls survive with sets of dipper cups, but this set is uniquely elaborate in having a matching table, candlestands and candlesticks.

The entire set is lavishly enriched with turned decoration on both the ivory and the wood. The lid of the bowl, the tops of the candlestands (fig.1), and the ivory roundels set into the top of the table are decorated with virtuoso examples of rose engine turning, in which decoration is incised into the flat plane of the material while it is spun on a lathe.

Lignum vitae, imported from the West Indies since the early sixteenth century, has a dark colour and dense, even grain particularly suited to turning, and was often used for wassail bowls. Its high oil content made it resistant to liquids; in addition it was reputed to have medicinal properties which could pass into the liquid it held; this made it a particularly favoured wood for bowls, goblets and other utensils used for eating or drinking.[1] Ivory, an expensive and highly prized material, provided an ideal contrast to the dark lustre of the *lignum vitae*.

This group of objects was passed down through generations of the same family until it was acquired by the V&A in 1976. By family tradition the set was given to Sir Charles Cokayne, the first Viscount Cullen (1602–61), by Charles I after the Battle of Naseby in 1645, during the English Civil War. Cokayne's seat, Rushton Hall, Northamptonshire, was close to the site of the battle. The set was always known by the family as 'King Charles' Wassail table'.[2] Recent assessment, however, suggests a more complex origin.

On stylistic grounds, the table and candlestands are thought to date not from the 1640s but from the 1670s, when their spiral twisted supports and delicate silhouette

Fig.2. Henry Shaw, Specimens of Ancient Furniture *(London: William Pickering, 1836), pl. XXII*

would have been newly fashionable.[3] Matching tables and candlestands were frequently placed between window piers and the candlelight was reflected in a mirror hung above the table; it is possible that this set was intended for a similar location. The wassail bowl itself is of a type made throughout the century. It is possible that the bowl and cups date from the 1640s, while the table, candlestands and candlesticks were added later to complete the set. The quality of the craftsmanship is worthy of royal connections; it may have been acquired by the 2nd Viscount's wife, Elizabeth, who was a noted beauty at the court of Charles II, and was Lady of the Bedchamber to Queen Catherine of Braganza.

The set first came to public notice in 1826 when it appeared in an engraved view of the great hall at Rushton, in J. P. Neale's *Views of the Seats of Noblemen and Gentlemen* (London, 1826). In 1836 it was illustrated in Henry Shaw's *Specimens of Ancient Furniture* (fig.2), as ranking amongst the most important sets of early furniture in the country.   C.S.H.

1. E. H. Pinto, *Treen and other Wooden Bygones* (London: G. Bell & Sons, 1969), p.33.

2. From 'Rushton Hall and its owners', *Northamptonshire Notes and Queries*, vol.VI (1896), p.59, quoted in P. Thornton and S. Jervis, 'King Charles's Wassail Table', *The Connoisseur*, vol.192, no.772 (June 1976), p.138.

3. Thornton and Jervis, ibid.

Fig.1. Detail of top of candlestand showing rose engine turning

Cabinet on Stand

French: 1640–50

Ebony on a carcase of oak and pine, with carved decoration illustrating the story of Diana and Endymion. Inscribed inside left door: 'L'Endimion'

H: 197.3 cm; W: 176 cm; D: 61 cm
Museum No. 1651-1856
Purchased from an unknown source

Fig.1. The scene carved on the left door of the cabinet

Fig.2. Diana and her Nymphs espy Endymion, *from Book II of* L'Endymion, *by Jean Ogier de Gombauld (Paris, 1636) (London Library)*

During the seventeenth century the exquisite small table cabinets which had become important objects of status during the sixteenth century throughout Europe (p.50), began to develop into larger pieces for galleries and grand state apartments in royal and courtly interiors. They were provided with their own stands to allow the fine workmanship of the cabinet to be presented at a convenient height.

In France the first imports of timber from the Far East and South America had begun in the late sixteenth century but it was not until the middle of the seventeenth century that the trade became established and allowed the development of a consistent fashion in the use of the new woods. Ebony was the first to be taken up, following its established use in the workshops of Augsburg, the Low Countries (Belgium and the Netherlands) and Italy. For this reason cabinet-makers (who made veneered furniture in exotic woods) began to be called *ébénistes* in France in the later years of the century, in contrast to *menuisiers* (who made carved furniture for gilding or painting).

Many parallels for this cabinet exist. The form became popular in French court circles by about 1640. What gives this group of cabinets their identity is the subject of the carvings, taken from a narrative source, either biblical or literary.[1] On this cabinet the story told is that of the goddess Diana and her pursuit of Endymion, after a prose romance by the writer Jean Ogier de Gombauld (c.1576–1666) published in 1624, which achieved great fame. The panel inside one door is inscribed with the title. Several of the carved scenes on the cabinet are derived from the illustrations to the book, most of them by Crispin de Passe the Younger (1593–1670) (figs 1 and 2).[2] One of the patrons of the writer was Louis XIII's queen, Anne of Austria, who became Queen Regent for the young Louis XIV in 1643. She exercised much power and many of the known cabinets are associated with her court circle. The use of engravings as sources for decoration on furniture was common practice from the sixteenth century (p.30). Craftsmen both copied them directly and used them as sources for their own drawings.

This cabinet follows an already established tradition by which the decoration became richer as the cabinet was opened. The carving continues on the interior. The doors present further episodes of the Endymion story, and the drawer fronts are carved with scenes of the Labours of the Months (probably also from engravings, though these are so far unidentified). In the centre is a small cupboard which, when opened, presents a theatre set of richly coloured marquetry and mirror glass, contrasting strongly with the ebony (fig.3).

Despite the sophistication of the design no firm identification of the craftsmen involved has yet been possible. At one time such cabinets were ascribed to the cabinet-maker Jean Macé (c.1602–72), a native of Blois who had been trained in the Netherlands. He was certainly listed as one of the most noted *menuisiers en ebeyne* (furniture makers in ebony) and he was known to have worked for the Queen Regent, but it has not proved possible to identify him as the maker of any cabinet of this type.[3] A similar cabinet in the Ashmolean Museum, Oxford, is said to be inscribed 'G. Marot 1644', although this inscription has not been found in recent examinations; it may refer to Girard Marot, father of Jean Marot (1640–1701) and grandfather of Daniel Marot (c.1663–1752).[4] S.M.

1. Th.H. Lunsingh Scheurleer, 'Novels in Ebony', *Journal of the Warburg Institute*, vol.XIX (1956), pp.259–68. Cabinets with comparable iconography are found in many public and private collections. They were widely collected in the mid-nineteenth century.

2. J. Ogier de Gombauld, *l'Endimion* (Paris, 1624; second edition 1636). Crispin de Passe the Younger provided more than half of the engravings for the book; others are anonymous; two are inscribed 'L. Gaultier' for Léonard Gaultier (1561–1641); one is inscribed 'I Picard fecit' for Jacques I Picard (active 1608–28). Carved details are taken from engravings from all three artists and from the anonymous plates.

3. Daniel Alcouffe, 'Les Macé, Ebénistes et Peintres', *Bulletin de la Société de l'Histoire et de l'Art français* (1971), pp.61–82.

4. Nicholas Penny, *Catalogue of European Sculpture in the Ashmolean Museum, 1540 to the Present Day* (Oxford: Clarendon Press, 1992), no.287, vol.II, pp.49–51.

Fig.3. Detail of interior

Chair

British: the covers 1649, the associated frame contemporary

Beech frame with upholstery of knotted woollen pile (Turkey-work). Back cover dated 1649 with the initials 's G C', possibly of the original owners

H: 83.2 cm; W: 46.4 cm; D: 38.8 cm

Museum No. 428-1896

Purchased from H. Horne & Sons, Yorkshire

This back-stool is of a type developed in the early seventeenth century, when upholstered chairs were becoming popular. The frames were usually of oak, but beech was sometimes used as it was cheaper (fig.1). Such chairs had padded seats and a low padded back, and were covered with warm, hard-wearing woollen upholstery inspired by knotted wool carpets imported from Anatolia (Turkey). Turkey-work chairs were common in seventeenth-century inventories but few of the surviving examples are dated; the inclusion of a date and initials in the upper panel is unique.[1] A set of four similar covers on oak frames, now at Holyroodhouse, were acquired in London in 1668.[2]

It was accepted practice to acquire the Turkey-work covers and have the chairs made up for them; such covers were also easily exported to the American colonies. As early as 1601 the household inventory of Hardwick Hall, Derbyshire, lists 'twelve Covers for Stooles of turkie work' stored in the Low Wardrobe.[3] Ironically, the V&A covers were acquired on a later oak chair frame, but were transferred to a contemporary beech frame.[4] The lower ends of the legs on the present frame have been shortened (or heavily worn) as the stretchers would originally have been about four inches from floor level.

Turkey-work was first made in Britain in the second half of the sixteenth century. The imported 'carpets' which inspired the chair covers were more often used as table or trunk coverings, window and wall hangings. They were occasionally cut up and re-used as panels of upholstery on chairs. The one-piece cover of an early seventeenth-century armchair in the V&A was probably cut down from a table carpet (fig.2), whereas the dated panels on this chair were specially woven to shape on the loom, with a chequered selvedge. It is now thought that Turkey-work was the product of professional weavers working in one centre in England, possibly Norwich.[5] At first British designs were inspired by the abstract patterns of Turkish carpets but they soon adapted the embroidery patterns of the Stuart period. This design, inspired by contemporary embroidery, consists of a naturalistic floral pattern in coloured wools. Turkey-work covers were still in demand in the last decade of the seventeenth century.

Turkey-work was woven with a strong linen or hemp warp and weft. The worsted, long-staple wool knots were added alternately with the weft, or after every two wefts. The knots were then cut to produce an even pile. Before these covers were conserved the large missing areas of pile had been painted on the canvas to which the covers had been stuck during an earlier restoration. Remarkably the covers retained their original wool braid from which the fringe was hung, although the fringe itself was incomplete. The covers were applied to a new linen backcloth (fig.3) before being applied to the chair frame.

Before they were acquired by the Museum, the covers passed through the hands of the dealer S.W. Wolsey who recognized their importance and mounted them on a later frame. His attitude reflects the growing awareness in the late nineteenth and early twentieth centuries of the importance of surviving early textiles.[6]   T.M.

1. Other examples of dated, British, Turkey-work include a carpet with the arms of Montagu, 1585, in the Buccleuch Collection and a table carpet in the V&A bearing the arms of Molyneux impaling those of Rigby of Lancashire and the date 1672 (Museum No. T.132-1924).

2. M. Swain, 'The Turkey-Work Chairs of Holyroodhouse', E.S. Cooke (ed.), *Upholstery in America and Europe from the Seventeenth Century to World War I* (New York: Norton, 1987), pp.51–63.

3. Ibid., p.58. Also cited is an inventory of Caerlavrock Castle, Dumfriesshire, 1640: '7 covers of Turky work for Stules and a Cushion'.

4. G. Owens, 'Now You See It, Now You Don't: The Conservation of a Turkey-Work Chair', *V&A Conservation Journal* (July 1994), pp.7–10.

5. M. Swain, op.cit., p.54.

6. S.W. Wolsey and R.W.P. Luff, *Furniture in England, The Age of the Joiner* (London: Arthur Barker Ltd, 1968), pp.76–7.

Fig.3. Turkey-work covers during conservation

Fig.1. Chair before re-upholstery, showing the beech frame

Fig.2. Armchair with Turkey-work cover, cover not original to chair (V&A Museum No. W.30-1923)

Cabinet

Italian pietre dure *plaques, 1644;*
cabinet, probably French (Paris), circa
1650; modified in Britain circa *1820*

Pietre dure panels by Domenico Benotti
(active 1640–53); lower bronze plaques
after models by Francesco Fanelli
(*c*.1609–42). Commissioned by John
Evelyn (1620–1706). Veneered with
ebony on a pine carcase, with oak
drawer linings; inlaid with panels of
Florentine *pietre dure*; contemporary
and later bronze mounts

H: 167.5 cm; W: 19.2 cm; D: 39.5 cm
Museum No. W.24-1977
Purchased from Christie, Manson &
Woods Ltd, London

Fig.1. Detail of Orpheus panel inside the central door

Fig.3. Evelyn cabinet on its later stand

This cabinet was commissioned, possibly in Paris, by the diarist John Evelyn, to incorporate the nineteen Italian *pietre dure* plaques which he purchased from their maker, Domenico Benotti, in Florence in October 1644 during his first European tour.[1] Two other cabinets listed at Evelyn's house, Wotton, Surrey, in 1702 may also have been acquired on the continent.[2] *Pietre dure* panels, showing formal motifs or naturalistic designs of animals, birds, flowers or landscapes, in an inlay of semi-precious stones and marbles, were later often brought back by Grand Tourists in the eighteenth century. Such decoration was produced from the Renaissance onwards in court workshops in Florence, Rome, Milan, Naples, Paris and Prague.[3]

The cabinet was enlarged and embellished in the early nineteenth century after the manuscript of Evelyn's diary was published for the first time.[4] The cabinet then acquired greater significance as a family heirloom. The later alterations indicate a change in attitude brought about by the newly acquired fame of the cabinet's original owner. The bronze mounts provide evidence of these changes. They form three groups.[5]

The first group is of Italian manufacture and contemporary with the *pietre dure* panels. It consists of the capitals and bases of the pilasters, all the keyhole escutcheons, the swags flanking the topmost escutcheon and the two armorial shields on the bottom drawer, one of which bears Evelyn's crest, the *passant* griffin. As the bottom drawer is considered to be a nineteenth-century addition, the two armorial shields must originally have been in a different position, probably surmounting the cabinet.

The second group, cast in a leaded brass, consists of the relief of Orpheus singing to the beasts, mounted on the inside of the central door (fig.1) and eight smaller reliefs set into the bottom drawer. Originally thought to have

been modelled by the Italian sculptor Fanelli[6] and thus contemporary with the *pietre dure* plaques, it is now known that Fanelli died in London in 1642 before Evelyn's visit to Italy,[7] but his models were passed to one of his studio assistants and were thus available for later use. A similar group of bronzes can be seen on an English cabinet recently acquired by Pallant House, Chichester (fig.2).

The third group is distinguished by a reddish tinge in the gilding and consists of the ring-handles at the sides, four corner straps, half corner straps and four female masks on the pilasters. These, like the gallery on the uppermost section, probably date from the early nineteenth century. The five-legged ebonized stand may be of twentieth-century manufacture (fig.3). T.M.

1. E.S. de Beer (ed.), *The Diary of John Evelyn* (Oxford: Oxford University Press, 1955), vol.II, p.191.

2. Inventory of 1702 compiled by John Evelyn himself, ms. at Christ Church, Oxford. Information provided by J. McIntyre. One cabinet, made in Paris, is at the Geffrye Museum, London.

3. A.M. Giusti, *Pietre Dure* (London: Philip Wilson, 1992).

4. Discovered in one of the cabinets at Wotton in 1813; see de Beer, op. cit., vol.I, pp.53–4.

5. A. Radcliffe and P. Thornton, 'John Evelyn's Cabinet', *The Connoisseur*, CXCVI (April 1978), pp.254–61.

6. In 1959, the V&A acquired a set of thirteen brass reliefs of the same type (V&A Museum No. A.29-29l-1959).

7. Information provided by P. Wengraf.

Fig.2. Cabinet with Orpheus reliefs at Pallant House, Chichester

Cabinet on Stand

Flemish (Antwerp): 1650–60

Marquetry of tortoiseshell, ebony and ivory,
with composition including mother-of-pearl, on
a carcase of oak; the mounts of lacquered brass.
Unmarked

H: 167.5 cm; W: 141.5 cm; D: 49 cm
Museum No. w.8-1965
Purchased from J.A. Lewis & Son, London

Fig.1. Detail of front of one of the interior drawers

In our own time we understand clearly the subtle grading
of furniture, from the highest quality made by an artist-
craftsman for a particular patron, through the ranks of
good-quality production furniture made for the well-to-do
customer, to the cheapest of 'flat-pack' kits. It is harder to
understand such a hierarchy in earlier furniture and yet in
all eras there were notable differences in the quality of
furniture from different centres and for different markets.

In the Low Countries in the middle decades of the
seventeenth century there was a huge trade in cabinets for
a rich merchant society and for a wide export market. The
trade developed to rival the cabinet-making skills of the
Italian cities (p.50) and of Augsburg, which had catered to
the most luxurious courtly market.[1]

The *laque incrusté* (inlaid lacquer) which decorates
this showy and ambitious cabinet became a speciality of
Antwerp.[2] The use of tortoiseshell (laid on a red ground)
was a precursor of boulle marquetry (p.78). The areas
of ebony veneer on the drawer fronts and inside the cupboard doors (figs 1–2) were lightly engraved with scrolling
flower designs, the engraving filled with a resinous composition in bright colours, which was scattered with
minute chips of marble.[3] This technique was probably
intended to imitate *scagliola* (p.70), but use of mother-of-
pearl fragments in the framing bands is also reminiscent
of the *raden* technique of Japanese lacquer.[4] During the
seventeenth century such lacquer was highly prized in
Europe. The mounts of lacquered brass add to the
sumptuous colouring but close inspection reveals that they
are not finished with the fine chiselling found on gilt-
bronzes made for royal or courtly patrons.

The records of the Antwerp merchant family Forck-
hondt detail a large export trade in such cabinets, small
tables, boxes, mirrors etc. to Austria, Holland, Spain,
Portugal, France and England in the mid-century.[5] A
number of cabinet-makers are recorded as supplying
them, but it is not yet possible to attribute particular pieces
to individual workshops. In 1655 the invention of the
technique was claimed by Jaspaert de Vleeshouwer.[6]

It is unusual for such a cabinet to retain its stand. More
unusual yet is its survival with a table decorated en suite
(fig.2). Both come from the collections of the Craven

family and may have been purchased by the Earl of
Craven (1606–97). The Earl was a close friend and sup-
porter of Elizabeth of Bohemia, the sister of Charles I. He
was with her in the Low Countries during periods of exile
between 1649 and 1660 and it is possible that he bought
the cabinet and table during those years or that they
formed part of the Queen's bequest to him on her death
in 1662. Certainly they were recorded together in the
Green Damask Bed Chamber at Combe Abbey at the
time of the 1769 inventory.[7] S.M.

Fig.2. Detail of cabinet with the central doors open

Fig.3. Table en suite with the cabinet (V&A Museum No. W.7-1965)

1. S. Jervis, 'A Tortoiseshell Cabinet and its Precursors', *Victoria & Albert Museum Bulletin*, no.4 (October 1968), pp.133–43.

2. W.G. De Kesel, 'Laques flamandes du XVIIe Siècle', *L'Estampille*, 223 (March 1989), pp.28–39; W.G. De Kesel, *Vlaams Barok Meubilair in Lak* (Drongen: Tectavit Publicaties, 1991), pp.61–79.

3. Ibid., p.39.

4. B. von Ragué, *A History of Japanese Lacquerwork* (Toronto and Buffalo: University of Toronto Press, 1976), passim.

5. J. Denucé, *Art-Export in the 17th Century in Antwerp. The Firm Forchoudt* (Antwerp: Edition 'De Sikkel', 1931). The spelling of the name took various forms, but was misread by the earlier scholars.

6. De Kesel, op. cit., pp.32, 37.

7. Craven Papers, Craven 293 Bodleian Library, Oxford: 'A Curious Cabinett Inlaid with Tortishell/Pearl, Ivery, & Ornamented with Brass/A Ditto table'. A 1739 inventory (Craven 300) lists what may be the same pieces, but in separate rooms.

Cabinet on Stand

French (Paris): 1660–71

Attributed to Pierre Gole (*c.*1620–84).
Pine, veneered with ivory, tortoiseshell and floral marquetry of various woods with green-stained ivory; drawers of walnut; brass mounts and ebony mouldings

H: 126 cm; W: 84 cm; D: 39 cm
Museum No. W.38-1983
Purchased from Didier Aaron & Cie, Paris

Exotic materials have always been sought for the furnishings of royalty, both for their intrinsic beauty and as indicators of wealth and political power. The expense of such materials frequently restricted their use to small details of decoration, but this cabinet is a rare example of the most lavish use of ivory in French cabinet-making.

In the inventory of 1653 of the possessions of Cardinal Mazarin in Paris, the list included a cabinet veneered with tortoiseshell and with ivory borders and a table veneered with panels of tortoiseshell and ivory.[1] This cabinet is much rarer in using ivory as a ground for marquetry of flowers. The panels of marquetry are highly stylized, perhaps with the intention of imitating *pietre dure* panels, which were also used on the grandest furniture of the time (p.62). The contrast of colour is also reminiscent of porcelain, a highly fashionable luxury from the Far East during the seventeenth century.

The cabinet is attributed to the Dutch-born cabinet-maker, Pierre Gole. Gole was born in Bergen in Holland and came to Paris in about 1643. By 1656 he was described as cabinet-maker to the King.[2] Though much is known of his work from documentary evidence, pieces which can be confidently attributed to him are few. The surviving cabinets on stands attributed to him are all of high quality and have in common strong similarities of style, though not necessarily of construction; they are all veneered with exotic materials, including ebony, tortoiseshell and ivory (fig.1).

In 1662–4 he supplied for Versailles a suite of furniture in ivory and floral marquetry consisting of a cabinet, tables and *guéridons* (candlestands). A small table veneered in ivory and blue-stained horn (fig.2) is almost certainly one supplied by him in about 1674 for the small pavilion at Versailles known as the Trianon de Porcelaine, which was entirely decorated in blue and white.[3] A larger cabinet on stand with ivory marquetry in the collections of the Dallas Museum of Art is attributed to Gole as the best-known user of this material.[4]

Though the V&A's cabinet is contemporary with Gole's royal commissions of the 1660s, it is one of only two cabinets known to have been made on this miniature scale. Whereas the tops of larger cabinets were left plain, on this piece the top is decorated with floral marquetry, though elsewhere the expensive ivory is used carefully and the backs of the legs are veneered with walnut.

The cabinet is thought to have been made for Henriette Anne (1644–70), daughter of Charles I of England. She was married to the duc d'Orléans (brother of Louis XIV) in 1661, and lived in the Palais Royal, Paris. The inventory drawn up after her death in 1670 includes a description which mirrors this cabinet in detail.[5] In the absence of any other surviving cabinet of this small size, it is suggested that this is the one described. Gole acted as the expert adviser in the making of that inventory, which may suggest further that he had had earlier commissions in the household and may well have been the maker of this elegant piece. C.S.

Fig.1. Detail showing marquetry inside the central cupboard

1. Th. H. Lunsingh Scheurleer, 'The Philippe d'Orléans ivory cabinet by Pierre Gole', *Burlington Magazine*, CXXVI (June 1984), pp.333–9; 'Pierre Gole, ébéniste du roi Louis XIV', *Burlington Magazine* CXXII (June 1980), pp.380–94.

2. A. Pradère, *French Furniture Makers. The Art of the Ebéniste from Louis XIV to the Revolution* (London: Sotheby's Publications, 1989), pp.45–51.

3. G. Wilson, 'Two newly-discovered pieces of Royal French furniture', *Antologia di Belle Arti* (new series) nos 27–8 (1985), pp.61–6.

4. V.J. Vinson, 'Louis XIV Marquetry Cabinets in the Reves Collection', *Dallas Museum of Art Bulletin* (Spring/Summer 1988), pp.6–10.

5. Scheurleer, op. cit., p.334.

Fig.2. Table probably supplied for the Trianon de Porcelaine at Versailles in about 1674 (J. Paul Getty Museum, Malibu)

Chair and Footstool

British (London): 1660–61

Made by John Casbert (active 1660–76) for the coronation of Charles II, 1661. Beechwood, covered with purple velvet, trimmed with silver and gold fringes

Chair: H: 127 cm; W: 83.8 cm; D: 68.5 cm
Footstool: H: 50.2 cm; W: 55.2 cm; D: 36.8 cm
Museum No. W.12&13-1928
Purchased from Moreton-in-Marsh Cottage Hospital with the assistance of the National Art Collections Fund

This X-frame ceremonial chair is of an unusual Italian form first introduced into England in the mid-sixteenth century. Such chairs were made for royal ceremonies and used in palaces, cathedrals and the houses of leading courtiers to proclaim the status of the monarch or his representative. An early example survives in Winchester Cathedral and is associated with the marriage of Queen Mary I in 1554.[1] Another is at Knole, Kent. As such upholstered chair frames were usually constructed of beechwood, which is vulnerable to woodworm, this chair is an extremely rare survival.

The V&A chair is connected with William Juxon (1582–1663) who, as Bishop of London, attended King Charles I on the scaffold at his execution in 1649. When the chair was first published in the late eighteenth century, two family traditions were aired.[2] It was said to have been the chair King Charles I sat in at his trial in Westminster Hall in 1648, a tradition which is repeated in an inscription on a mid-nineteenth century drawing by George

Wallis (fig.1). It was also said to have been used by William Juxon, as Archbishop of Canterbury, at the Coronation of Charles II in Westminster Abbey in 1661.[3]

It is the second of these stories which has proved to be the correct one. After the death of Charles I, Juxon retired initially to Fulham Palace. He was imprisoned at the outset of the Commonwealth, but was released in 1649 and retired to his manor house at Little Compton, Gloucestershire, until 1660. The chair was recorded there shortly after Juxon's death in 1663.[4]

At the Restoration of Charles II, Juxon became Archbishop of Canterbury and officiated at the annointing and crowning of the new monarch in Westminster Abbey on 23 April 1661. 'A chair of Purple Velvett' was provided 'for the Arch-Bishop to sit in on the North-side of the Altar opposite to the King'.[5] There is no evidence that an earlier chair was refurbished for the occasion; on the contrary, the Lord Chamberlain's accounts for King Charles II's coronation confirm that John Casbert, upholsterer, was paid £4 for 'making a rich purple velvet Chaire of State for the Bishop wth a foot stoole and seat cusshion suitable: fringed with gold fringes and double gilt nailes with cases of Bayes', and that Ralph Silverson 'Fringe maker' was paid over £29 for the gold trimmings (fig.2).[6] For the coronation, Casbert also supplied other chairs of state upholstered in '[s]ad', 'dove' and 'skie' colours in addition to providing embroidered altar cloths, a crimson velvet canopy of state, His Majesty's standard and thirty-six banners. John Casbert, possibly of French extraction, is recorded as an upholsterer in London between 1660–76, when he supplied furnishings for royal palaces on an extensive scale as well as fittings for the royal yachts.[7] This may be the only surviving documented example of Casbert's work. T.M.

1. C. Graham, *Ceremonial and Commemorative Chairs in Great Britain* (London: Victoria & Albert Museum, 1993), pp.44–7, fig.56.

2. *Gentleman's Magazine*, vol.LXIII (July 1794), p.618; vol.LXIV, Part I (17 December 1794), pp.506–07, fig.3; vol.LXVIII, part II (November 1808), p.969 illus. (figs 6–7) drawings by Charles Pye.

3. R. Edwards, 'The "Charles I" Chair', *Country Life*, vol.LXIII, no.1621 (11 February 1928), pp.176–7.

4. It descended in the Juxon family until 1792, then through the Sands family to Moreton-in-Marsh Cottage Hospital.

5. Sir Edward Walker, *A Circumstantial Account of the Preparations for the Coronation* (London, 1820) cited by C. Beard, 'King Charles I's Chair: a New Theory, *The Connoisseur*, LXXX, no.320 (April 1928), pp.228–31.

6. Lord Chamberlain's Accounts, LC2/8. Public Record Office. I am grateful to James Yorke for discovering these documents. John Casbert's bill is undated but the batch of bills associated with the coronation are dated 'From Mich 1660 to Lady Day 1661'. Ralph Silverson charged for '87 oz of gold & passamaine Lardr & fringe at vis viiid per oz. 029: 01: 08'.

7. G. Beard and C. Gilbert, *Dictionary of English Furniture Makers, 1660–1840* (Leeds: W.S. Maney & Son/Furniture History Society, 1986), p.149; P. Thornton, *Seventeenth-Century Interior Decoration in England, France and Holland* (New Haven/London: Yale University Press, 1978), pp.198, 225.

Fig.1. Drawing by George Wallis inscribed 'The Chair in which Charles I sat during his Trial' (V&A Museum No. E.390-1928)

Fig.2. Back view of the Juxon chair

Table

Probably British: circa *1675*

From Warwick Castle, Warwickshire.
Pine carcase with *scagliola* top and legs
H: 80 cm; W: 116.5 cm; D: 76.2 cm
Museum No. W.12-1968
Purchased from Mallet & Sons Ltd, London

This table was made in imitation of the costly *pietre dure* objects (p.62) produced in leading European court workshops. *Scagliola* (the term derived from *scaglia*, Italian for scales or chips of marble) is made of selenite, a crystalized sulphate of lime, which is heated, ground into a very fine powder, mixed with colouring matter, then worked into a paste. *Scagliola* as a medium had obvious advantages over *pietre dure*. It was cheaper and the materials could be more easily transported than hardstone. Moreover, the technique could be easily imitated in England both by foreign and native craftsmen inspired by Italian examples.

Examples of *scagliola* have been found in Classical Roman decoration, but it was revived in sixteenth-century Italy and developed there in the seventeenth century by the master mason Guido del Conte (1584–1649).[1] There is evidence that *scagliola* was being imitated in Northern Europe by the early seventeenth century; by 1618 the German Aleman Haneman was working for the French court producing 'marbre de touttes couleurs contrefaitz' (counterfeit marble in all colours).[2]

John Evelyn, during his travels in Italy in 1644, questioned why *scagliola* had never been used in England 'for cabinets'. The earliest dated example of the use of *scagliola* in England, *c*.1673–5, is in the Queen's Closet at Ham House, Surrey, where black panels inlaid with naively rendered flowers and birds and green foliage ornament are used as the surround to the fireplace; the hearth stone *en suite* bears the Duke of Lauderdale's cipher and coronet[3]. These have recently been attributed to Baldassare Artinia, an Italian plasterer working in London.

The design of this table top – incorporating a central vase of flowers and at the corners paired cornucopiae filled with flowers, lemons, turnips, tomatoes, cherries and wheatsheaves – is much less sophisticated than contemporary Italian productions.[4] Yet this table is the only example where the decorations of the top and supporting structure are so closely integrated (figs 1–3). Clearly it was the product of an important workshop, actively

Fig.1. Detail of table top

Fig.2. Detail of stretcher

experimenting in the newly imported technique. The stretcher is similar in form to that of a Flemish table of the mid-seventeenth century in the V&A (Museum No. W.7-1965), indicating that it was probably made in a Dutch or Flemish workshop.

This table came from Warwick Castle where it was recorded in the Green Drawing Room.[5] It may have been acquired by Francis, 1st Earl of Warwick (1719–73), for in 1757 Dr Richard Pococke recorded that 'there are some beautiful marble tables in the castle brought from Italy by the present Earl'.[6] However it is not mentioned in the 1815 description of the contents of the castle,[7] and as Henry, 3rd Earl of Warwick (1816–53), bought a sixteenth-century *pietre dure* Florentine table from the Grimani Palace in Venice, the *scagliola* table may have been acquired in the nineteenth century.[8]   T.M.

1. R.B. Wragg, 'The History of Scagliola', *Country Life*, vol.CXXII, no.3169 (10 October 1957), pp.718–21.

2. H. Havard, *Dictionnaire de l'Ameublement*, vol.IV (Paris: Maison Quantin, n.d.), p.1083, in the article on 'Stuc'.

3. P. Thornton, 'The Furnishing and Decoration of Ham House', *Furniture History*, vol.XVI (1980), p.149.

4. A.M. Giusti, *Pietre Dure* (London: Philip Wilson, 1992), fig.70.

5. Christie's, 21 March 1968, lot 116.

6. Quoted by M. Binney, 'Warwick Castle Revisited – IV', *Country Life*, vol. CLXXII, no.4453 (23 December 1982), pp.2023–6.

7. W. Field, *The Town and Castle of Warwick* (East Ardsley, Wakefield: SR Publishers, 1969, reprint of 1815 edition).

8. *Warwick Castle Guide Book* (York, n.p., 1990), pp.12–13. A.H. Malan, *Famous Homes of Great Britain and their Stories* (New York /London: Putnam & Sons, 1902), pp.354–5, describes several tables in *pietre dure* and *scagliola* at Warwick Castle.

Fig.3. Detail of frieze

Harpsichord

French (Paris): 1681

Made by a member of the Vaudry family. Japanned walnut case, spruce soundboard, walnut bridges. Painted on the jack-rail: 'Vaudry à Paris 1681'. Restored to original range (fifty notes) GG/BB (short octave)-c3

H: 94 cm; W: 81 cm; L: 219 cm
Museum No. W.12-1974
Purchased from Ronald A. Lee Works of Art, London, with the assistance of the vendor

Fig.1. Detail of harpsichord

This harpsichord is one of the very few French keyboard instruments and japanned objects to have survived from the reign of Louis XIV (1651–1715).[1] Although at least two harpsichords by a maker called Vaudry (as well as one by a certain Vaudrez) are listed in an inventory of the workshop of the later harpsichord maker Jacques Bourdet (c.1660–1737), this instrument, signed on both the jack-rail and the underside of the harpsichord, is the only known surviving example by this maker.[2] The Vaudry family included Jean-Antoine (d.1750), who in 1718 claimed the title 'seul maître faiseur d'instruments de musique du Roi à la suite du grand conseil' (only master maker of musical instruments to the King attendant upon the Grand Council).[3] Presumably, he was a younger relation of the Vaudry who made the 1681 instrument.

Soon after it was built, this harpsichord is said to have been delivered to Savigny-les-Beaune (Burgundy), the property of le comte de Migieu. According to family tradition, it stood in the room occupied by Louis-Bénédicte de Bourbon, la duchesse du Maine (1676–1753), who was briefly interned there in 1719 after the failure of the Cellamare Conspiracy against the *Régence* of 1718. The duchesse was fond of music, and it played an important part in her lavish *Divertissements* at her country residence at Sceaux, in the Île-de-France. Her room at Savigny was adorned with Chinese-inspired motifs or chinoiseries, and the case of this harpsichord certainly would have matched it.[4]

In decorating her room in the Chinese taste she would have been closely following one of the most innovative European fashions of the time. The importation of porcelain, lacquer and silks by the several East India companies established in the maritime countries of north-west Europe in the seventeenth centuries created a luxury market in rare and marvellous objects. Their designs were soon copied by European craftsmen. The inventory of Louis XIV's furniture included 'un cabinet de Chine à neuf étages en piramide' (a Chinese cabinet with nine shelves like a pyramid).[5] From about 1710 pieces with chinoiserie decoration were produced in large numbers, and in 1713 Claude III Audran was granted a royal privilege to establish 'une manufacture de verny pour le moins

aussy beau que celuy de la Chine' (a factory to make varnish at least as fine as the Chinese).[6] Nevertheless, few such pieces have survived.

The most widely known designs for chinoiserie (John Stalker and George Parker's *A Treatise of Japanning*) were not published in Oxford until 1688, seven years after the harpsichord was built. In France no chinoiserie pattern book was published before Jean-Antoine Fraisse's *Livre de Desseins Chinois* (1735). The decorator did not use Jan Nieuhof's *Embassy from the East-India Company of the United Provinces to the Grand Tartar Cham, Emperor of China* (Paris, 1665) but seems to have copied buildings directly from imported porcelain and lacquer and figures from the European sources of Jacques Stella's *Pastorales* (Paris, 1667) and Jacques Callot's *Varie Figure Gobbi* (Florence, 1619), adding Chinese hats to transform them (figs 1–2).

Following the Netherlandish custom, the harpsichord soundboard is decorated with naturalistic flowers. The parchment rosette (the soundboard hole) is decorated in the Gothic style, as are the arcadings of the keys.

Numerous modifications have occurred to this instrument. The frontmost pair of spiral legs have quarters cut away to accommodate a box containing organ pipes; the harpsichord was at some stage played as a claviorganum (i.e., a harpsichord-cum-organ). It underwent a widening of the keyboard in the eighteenth century in order to accommodate three and later six extra notes.   J.Y.

Fig.2. Jacques Callot, Gobbi (V&A Museum No. 24586-5)

1. D. Adlam, 'Restoring the Vaudry', *Early Music*; vol.4, no.3 (July 1976), pp.255–65; and H. Schott, *Victoria & Albert Museum, Catalogue of Musical Instruments*, vol.1, *Keyboard Instruments* (London: HMSO, 1985), pp.63–5.

2. F. Hubbard, *Three Centuries of Harpsichord Making* (Cambridge, Mass: Harvard University Press, 1965), p.299.

3. Schott, op. cit., p.64. As there was only one specialist in each category 'à la suite du grand conseil', Vaudry was making more of his status by adding to his title 'seul...faiseur' (only... maker). Information kindly supplied by Jean-Dominique Augarde.

4. Adlam, op. cit.

5. J. Guiffrey, *Inventaire général de mobilier de la courone sous Louis XIV* (Paris: J. Rouam, 1885), p.69.

6. M. Sonenscher, *Work and Wages – Natural Law, Politics and the Eighteenth-century French Trades* (Cambridge: Cambridge University Press, 1989), pp.221–2.

Desk

French (Paris): 1685–1700

Attributed to Bernard I Vanrisamburgh (d.1738, master before 1722). Marquetry of brass, ebony, ivory, mother-of-pearl and clear tortoiseshell or horn with painted paper beneath; carcase of pine

H: 78 cm; W: 119.5 cm; D: 71.2 cm

Museum No. 372-1901

Given by Mrs J.A. Bonner, Brighton

Fig.1. Detail of the top

As early as the sixteenth century, furniture associated with writing had acquired high status and was often decorated with materials of great luxury and fine workmanship. Such pieces were highly personal to the owner and were important indicators of rank. This form of desk, which became fashionable in France at the end of the seventeenth century, is often called a 'bureau Mazarin'. The term clearly attempts to link the form with the statesman Cardinal Mazarin (1602–61), but it was not used before the nineteenth century, though since that time it has become a convenient shorthand for these writing-tables with eight legs and drawers to either side of a kneehole.[1]

The earliest-known table of this form was made in about 1669 and is first documented in the Journal du Garde-Meuble (a register of furniture supplied to the French royal households) in 1676. That table is attributed to the royal cabinet-maker, Pierre Gole (p.66).[2] Although such tables are generally thought to have been used as desks, several late seventeenth-century engravings show them in use as dressing-tables.[3] This example is dated towards the end of the seventeenth century by virtue of the complexity of its form and surface ornament (fig.1).

This desk also forms part of a smaller group of such tables, linked closely by their form and decoration, and all of the highest sophistication of design. One of these (fig.2) is known to have been made after 1692 for the Elector of Bavaria, Maximilian II Emanuel (1662–1726), who spent years of exile in France. His purchases of furniture and, in particular, of pieces decorated with boulle marquetry (of tortoiseshell, brass and other exotic materials – p.78), were an important factor in the development of similar specialisms in cabinet-making in the German states (pp.82–4). Another desk, in the Royal Collection at Windsor, bears the arms of the duchesse de Retz.[4] A fourth, very close in form to the V&A desk, was on the art market in the 1960s.[5]

Though there are differences of form between these pieces, the use of highly coloured boulle marquetry in *contre-partie* (on a brass ground – p.78) unites the group. Several of the coloured areas of the marquetry, including the elaborate baskets of flowers and the areas coloured green, were made by gluing painted paper to the back of clear horn. This allowed the cabinet-maker to bring into

his piece some of the brightest colours, which were otherwise only available in *pietre dure* (p.62). Unlike furniture veneered with wood, which inevitably fades and discolours over the years, these desks retain much of their original, brilliant colouring, which would have contributed so importantly to their first, fashionable impact in courtly interiors.

There are many parallels within the group in the design and disposition of the figures, flowers and exotic birds. Perhaps most striking is the repetition on the recessed centre panel of each desk of the motif of an obelisk wrapped in a garland of ivy. Other details of the marquetry are repeated on this group and on other types of furniture, suggesting that they form the output of a single workshop.[6] A likely candidate as maker of this desk is Bernard I Vanrisamburgh (c.1660–1738). Born in Groene, Holland, he was the first of a dynasty of three cabinet-makers working in Paris in the late seventeenth and eighteenth centuries (p.102). A recently discovered inventory of his workshop includes objects of comparable type and a stock of materials for such veneers.[7] C.S.

Fig.2. Desk, French, 1692–1700, made for the Elector of Bavaria (J. Paul Getty Museum, Malibu)

1. N. de Reyniès, *Le Mobilier domestique* (Paris: Imprimerie Nationale, 1987), vol.I, pp.378–9. For a variant form see vol.II, pp.1088–90.

2. Ibid., vol.I, p.378.

3. P. Thornton, *Seventeenth Century Interior Decoration in England, France & Holland* (New Haven/London: Yale University Press, 1978), p.231, n.25.

4. Almost certainly for Paul-Françoise Marguerite de Gondi (1655–1716), the duchesse de Retz and of Lesdiguières.

5. Sotheby's, London, 12 July 1963, lot 177.

6. G. Himmelheber first linked the V&A piece with the Elector's desk in 'Puch-weiser, Boulle und die Boulle-Möbels für München', H. Glaser (ed.), *Kurfürst Max Emmanuel, Bayern und Europa um 1700* (Münich: Hirmer Verlag/Bayerisches National-museum, Schloss Lustheim, 1976), vol.I, p.250–63.

7. J-N Ronfort and J-D Augarde, 'Le Maître du bureau de l'Electeur', *L'Estampille*, no.243 (January 1991), pp.42–75.

Cabinet on Stand

Dutch (Amsterdam): 1690–1710

Attributed to Jan van Mekeren (1658–1733).
Marquetry of kingwood, ebony, rosewood, olive,
sycamore and other woods on a carcase of oak.

H: 206 cm; W: 172 cm; D: 60.5 cm
Museum No. w.5-1986
Purchased from Mr L.P.M. van Aalst, Breda

Marquetry, the decoration of surfaces with veneers of
woods chosen for colour or grain, developed from the
intarsia (inlay) practised in the Italian states from the
fourteenth century (p.36). In the seventeenth century it
received new impetus from the import of exotic timbers
and, in the last twenty years of the century, reached a
standard of technical perfection scarcely surpassed since.
Parisian cabinet-makers were the most expert and in particular André-Charles Boulle (1642–1732), cabinet-maker
to Louis XIV, whose workshop excelled in creating panels
showing naturalistic flowers, animals, birds and butterflies,
as much as in the specialized work in brass and tortoiseshell which bears his name (p.78).[1]

The technique was also developed to a high degree in
the Netherlands. The status of the cabinet on stand as an
important item of formal furniture had been established
by the 1640s in Paris (p.58) and by the middle of the
century smaller cabinets on stands veneered in tortoiseshell and ebony were highly prized in the Low Countries
(p.64). They gradually became simpler and larger, with
flat surfaces showing the fashionable marquetry. Their
outward appearance was all-important and the interior
fittings were sometimes very simple (fig.1). Cabinets were
often made *en suite* with tables and candlestands, sometimes (though rarely in the Netherlands) with a mirror.

Dutch marquetry was noted for its naturalistic flowers
in highly formal arrangements. The sources of such
designs were flower paintings like those of Jean-Baptiste
Monnoyer (1636–99), engraved by the painter or by other
engravers and published by Nicolas de Poilly (1626–96) or
Jacques Vauquer (1621–86) (fig.2). Such plates were widely
used by craftsmen either as direct sources or for inspiration for their own drawings.

Woods were used both in their natural colouring and
stained in bright colours. Fading has usually obliterated
the bright reds, blues and greens, but traces sometimes
remain along the glue lines. Once cut, individual pieces
might be scorched on the edges by dipping in hot sand, to
give a three-dimensional appearance of shading, while
such details as leaf veins were added by finely engraved
dark lines (often obliterated by careless later restoration).

This cabinet is attributed to a cabinet-maker from Tiel,
Jan van Mekeren, who set himself up in Amsterdam

Fig.1. Interior of the cabinet

probably around 1687.[2] Five other cabinets are so closely
similar in form and marquetry that they must be from the
same workshop and one of these bears his signature. His
workshop must have included craftsman with the very
highest skills.[3] Nothing is known of his own training but
it is possible that he had passed some time in a Parisian
workshop (another important early exponent of floral
marquetry in Paris, Pierre Gole, was a native of The
Netherlands – p.66). Van Mekeren was clearly successful
in his trade. In 1704 he was mentioned as one of Amsterdam's eleven best cabinet-makers and in 1710 he shared
the honour with eighteen fellow craftsmen. Archival records
of property bought testify to his material success and the
surviving cabinets tell of his technical excellence.   S.M.

1. A. Pradère, *French Furniture Makers. The Art of the Ebéniste from Louis XIV to the Revolution* (London: Sotheby's Publi-cations, 1989), pp.92–9.

2. Th.H. Lunsingh Scheur-leer, 'Jan van Mekeren, een Amsterdamsche meubel-maker uit het einde der 17de en begin der 18de eeuw', *Oud Holland*, 58 (1941), pp.178–88.

3. Th.H. Lunsingh Scheur-leer, 'Amerongen Castle and its furniture', *Apollo*, vol.80 (1964), pp.360–67;
R. Baarsen, *Nederlandse Meubelen 1600–1800* (Amsterdam: Rijksmuseum, 1993), nos 25 and 26.

Fig.2. Title page of a set of plates of flowers engraved by Jean-Baptiste Monnoyer, published by Nicolas de Poilly, Paris, c.1665 (V&A Museum No. E.541-1950)

Armoire (Cupboard)

French (Paris): circa *1700*

Ebony veneer with marquetry of engraved
pewter and brass; panels of clear horn over
blue pigment; carcase of oak
H: 256 cm; W: 161 cm; D: 61.5 cm
Museum No. 1026-1882
Bequeathed by Mr John Jones, London

Fig.1. Drawing for an armoire, *attributed to André-Charles Boulle. Red chalk on paper, with ink additions (Musée des Arts décoratifs, Paris)*

Fig.2. Detail of one upper panel of armoire

Such large cupboards had long been in use in France before the form was adapted in the late seventeenth century as a *meuble d'apparat*, a piece of furniture designed primarily for its impressive appearance in state rooms. This *armoire* is exceptional for its monumental scale and fine decoration and especially for the quality of the design and workmanship of the panels of engraved marquetry.

The maker is unknown, but it is clearly the product of a highly-skilled workshop. Marquetry composed of a combination of tortoiseshell, horn, brass and other metals is known as 'boulle' marquetry, after André-Charles Boulle (1642–1732), cabinet-maker to Louis XIV.[1] Boulle was only one of several first-rate cabinet-makers to develop such marquetry in Paris; his status as royal cabinet-maker is likely to have ensured that it was his name that became synonymous with the technique. Boulle marquetry was termed '*première partie*' when the brass decoration was inlaid into a dark ground (usually of tortoiseshell or ebony) and '*contre partie*' when the ground was of metal and the decorative inlay of tortoiseshell or other contrasting material.[2]

A drawing attributed to Boulle's workshop, and possibly by his hand, shows two alternative designs for a cupboard on this scale (fig.1). Though a number of *armoires* of this date are attributed to Boulle (some also including panels of marquetry in wood for which he was also noted), the decoration of the panels on the V&A piece shows no similarities to boulle marquetry firmly associated with his workshop. The maker remains anonymous but the quality of the craftsmanship suggests a workshop of similar sophistication to that of Boulle; in particular, the engraved detail in the brass of the figures is especially fine (fig.2). Such engraving has often been lost in later cleaning or restoration and with it the sense of three-dimensional modelling to the figures which gives the best work such liveliness. A most distinctive feature on this *armoire* is the very large oval panels in the centre of each door, veneered with horn over a blue pigment, and with a device of interlaced 'L's (one reversed) in brass. This may be the cipher of the Grand Dauphin (d.1711), grandson of Louis XIV. The same cipher appears on a book binding supplied by Boulle for Louis XIV (fig.3).[3]

Boulle marquetry remained in high esteem throughout the eighteenth and nineteenth centuries (p.100) and was one of the first enthusiasms of the early nineteenth century collectors of antique French furniture. This *armoire* came to the Museum in 1882 as part of the exceptional bequest of furniture, porcelain and metalwork from Mr John Jones. Its earlier history is not known, but it is likely that the present cornice was made at the time that it was sold to him, probably to replace a lost one, and that new, adjustable shelves were fitted inside, above lockable strongboxes. C.S.

1. A. Pradère, *French Furniture Makers. The Art of the Ebéniste from Louis XIV to the Revolution* (London: Sotheby's Publications, 1989), pp.67–109.

2. G. Wilson, 'Boulle', *Furniture History*, vol.VIII (1972), pp.47–69.

3. Bibliothèque Nationale de France, Paris, MSS. fr.6695.

Fig.3. Book binding with interlaced 'L's, supplied to Louis XIV by André-Charles Boulle (Bibliothèque Nationale, Paris)

Cabinet

British: circa *1700*

Walnut veneer with marquetry decoration; carcase of pine

H: 239.5 cm; W: 144.7 cm; D: 61 cm
Museum No. w.136-1928
Given by Mr H.T.G. Watkins, Richmond, Surrey

This cabinet was made in about 1700 to commemorate the marriage of Margaret, daughter of Edward Trotter of Skelton Castle, to George Lawson, of Harlsey Castle, Yorkshire.[1] The outer doors bear the couple's monograms 'GL' on the left and 'ML' on the right, while the arms of the two families appear on the door of the inner cupboard (figs 1–2), with the Lawson crest on the inner side of the door.

The cabinet has a complete and interesting history. It passed to Margaret Lawson's sister, Mrs Catherine Bower, of Bridlington, who in turn left it to her son, Henry, in her will dated 21 April 1742 with the words: 'Item, I give to my son Henry Bower as a token of my Gratitude for his particular affection & care over me during my many and long illnesses, my Silver Tea Kettle and lamp and my large inlaid cabinett with china Jarrs thereto belonging which were my late sister Lawson's'. The cabinet was passed down from generation to generation until it was given to the V&A in 1928.

The unusual and imposing double pediment has four small plinths rising from the top, which may have been designed to display the Chinese porcelain which was associated with the cabinet. The fashion for showing Chinese porcelain imported by the Dutch East India Company, at its height in the 1680s and 1690s, was popularized by William and Mary and their court architect Daniel Marot (*c.*1663–1752), who brought the taste from Holland. The sparseness of contemporary furnishings limited the possibilities for exhibiting porcelain, which was consequently often placed on cabinets, overdoors or mantelpieces.

The cabinet represents the finest of late seventeenth-century marquetry, a technique which shortly afterwards fell from favour and was not revived until the middle of the following century. The maker of this cabinet is as yet unknown. British marquetry cabinets on this scale are extremely rare; a cabinet made for William Bowes of Gibside and Streatlam, Co. Durham, and his wife Elizabeth Blakiston, who married in 1691 (fig.3), is, however, so closely similar, as to suggest that both were made by the same local cabinet-maker. The lower drawers have strikingly similar sprays of berries (or possibly the dried seed pods of the honesty flower) tied with true-lovers' knots.[2]

While decidedly British in overall form and style, the cabinet has elements in its decorative detailing which suggest an awareness of continental forms. The high

Fig.2. Detail of cabinet with inner door open, showing the Lawson crest

Fig.3. Cabinet made for William Bowes (Metropolitan Museum of Art, New York)

pediments, with their intricate mitring or 'pleating' of the cornice mouldings, suggest a German influence, while the marquetry of birds and flowers is reminiscent of Dutch craftsmanship (p.76). The crossed 'L's on the doors (for Lawson) may be a deliberate and flattering reference to the monogram of the French king Louis XIV (p.78), the leader of all European fashions.

The elaborate marquetry decoration includes, on the inside of the doors, the subtle use of burr woods to suggest the marble tops of console tables which support Classical urns containing flowers. The composition follows decoration on contemporary Dutch cabinets (p.76). Flowers are also present on the inner drawer fronts and include roses, tulips, lilies, anemones and pinks. The respect with which the cabinet has been treated by the same family explains its superb condition. It retains its high-quality brass drop handles, though bracket feet have replaced the original bun feet. C.S.H.

1. Information provided by the donor in 1928. The exact marriage date is unknown, although Margaret was born in 1670 and died in 1728. George (d.1726/7) was the son of Godfrey Lawson, a wealthy Leeds woollen merchant. The Trotter and Lawson families were evidently closely connected as George's sister, Elizabeth (b.1663), married Margaret's eldest brother, John (b.1659).

2. The cabinets are compared in R. Edwards, *The Dictionary of English Furniture* (London: Country Life, revised edition, 1954), p.169, and in Herbert Cescinsky, 'Four English Marquetry Cabinets', *Burlington Magazine*, vol.IV, no.CCCXXI (December 1929), pp.277–84.

Fig.1. Detail of cabinet interior, showing the arms of the original owners

Cabinet

Probably Austrian (Vienna): 1715, with modifications circa 1735 and later

Marquetry of tortoiseshell, mother-of-pearl, brass, copper and silver on a carcase of oak; mounts of gilt-copper; drawers lined with printed paper, possibly Augsburg. Cartouche on main panel engraved: 'MDCCXV'; cresting with the arms of Johann Franz Anton Khevenhüller, Bishop of Wiener-Neustadt 1734–41

H: 73.5 cm; W: 120 cm; D: 47 cm
Museum No. W.17-1958
Purchased from Gerald Kern Ltd, London

Fig.1. Detail of the arms of Johann Franz Anton, Graf Khevenhüller

Though the form of this cabinet is derived from architecture, and the perspective marquetry is monumental in aspiration, the scale suggests a very personal use. More important than architecture in its design are the highly developed skills of fine metal-working and the use of luxury materials (tortoiseshell and mother-of-pearl with fine engraving), which had been developed over two centuries in the cities of the south German states and particularly in Augsburg, often in the making of snuff-boxes and such small luxury items.

The coat of arms (fig.1) indicates the early ownership of the cabinet by Johann Franz Anton, Graf Khevenhüller who, in 1734, became Bishop of Wiener-Neustadt, a city just south of Vienna. The arms must date from after that time because they include a pontifical hat.

The cabinet may once have stood on a similarly decorated stand. A table composed of elements of closely similar marquetry and mounts (fig.2) has been on the art market twice in the last forty years.[1] It is clear that it was made in the same workshop. Whether it could have been made from parts of an original stand for this cabinet is less certain. The cross-stretcher of the table carries the monogram 'CF' but this has not been plausibly identified.

The cabinet remains without a firm attribution despite its high quality.[2] Boulle marquetry (pp.74, 78) was made in workshops in several cities of the German-speaking states in the early eighteenth century. It is difficult to distinguish the work of individual workshops, both because of a sophisticated international taste amongst patrons which meant that styles were imitated and because of the widespread mobility of craftsmen who might work in several centres as part of their post-apprenticeship training.[3] Some of the earliest pieces using the boulle technique outside France were made in Künzelsau in Swabia, in the workshops of Johann Daniel Sommer (active

1666–92),[4] including a cabinet made for the Prince Bishop of Würzburg, and it has been demonstrated that furniture associated with writing, and thus with high intellectual status, was frequently decorated with boulle marquetry for rulers in the southern German states.[5] Bishops and high-ranking prelates frequently wielded temporal power quite as great as secular princes and in matters of artistic patronage were extremely influential.

The sources for the decoration have not been traced but the architectural fantasy of the main panel, the drawer fronts and the figures on the side panels are reminiscent of engraved designs by Paul Decker (1677–1713), published in Augsburg and Nuremberg in the early eighteenth century.[6]

Both the extensive use of mother-of-pearl and the elaborately sculpted mounts relate the cabinet to a number of similarly decorative tables and stands.[7] Some of these have been attributed to Augsburg because of their fine metal mounts but clearly Vienna, as the imperial capital, is likely also to have been an important centre for the manufacture of such sophisticated pieces.   S.M.

1. Sold most recently Paris, Picard, 21 December 1994, lot 140.

2. H. Kreisel and G. Himmelheber, *Die Kunst des Deutschen Möbels*, vol.III (Munich: C.H. Beck, 1970), p.149 first suggested a Viennese origin.

3. H. Graf, 'Southern German Writing Furniture in the Boulle Technique: Johann Puchwiser (*c.*1680–1744) and His Workshop in Munich', *Studies in the Decorative Arts*, vol.I, no.I (Fall 1993), pp.51, 53.

4. G. Himmelheber, 'Die Möbel des Johann Daniel Sommer' in Fritz Kellermann (ed.), *Die Künstlerfamilie Sommer* (Sigmaringen: Jan Thorbecke Verlag, 1988), pp.121–40. The cabinet is illustrated figs 21–23.

5. Graf, op. cit., pp.49–72.

6. S. Jervis, *Dictionary of Design and Designers* (London: Penguin/Allen Lane, 1984), p.142.

7. G. de Bellaigue, *The James A. de Rothschild Collection. Furniture and Gilt Bronzes* (Fribourg: Office du Livre, 1974), nos 114 and 115, with further pieces noted there.

Fig.2. Table, incorporating marquetry and mounts which must have come from the same workshop (H. Blairman & Sons, London)

Writing Cabinet

German (Würzburg): 1716

Made in the workshop of Servatius Arend (1673–1729), court cabinet-maker, by Jacob Arend and Johannes Wittalm, for Johannes Gallus Jacob von Hohlach. Cipher and arms of owner on the doors and his name in the marquetry of the writing flap. Marquetry of walnut and various woods with tortoiseshell, ivory, pewter and brass on a carcase of pine; the drawers lined with coloured, embossed paper

H: 180 cm; W: 165 cm; D: 78 cm

Museum No. w.23-1975

Purchased from Mrs E. Gibbons, Worcester

From the late seventeenth century, France led fashions in European furniture. In particular, the technique of boulle marquetry (pp.74, 78) was widely copied, though in the case of this cabinet the luxurious technique was combined with simpler wood marquetry.

Writing cabinets had become by the early eighteenth century an important indicator of status in a gentleman's study or library. In Würzburg such a double-tiered writing cabinet was called a *Trisur*, a term relating to 'treasure'.[1]

This piece would have represented the highest achievements of the luxury trades. Large size, ebullience of shape and complexity of construction (with three writing compartments, many apparent drawers and some 'secret' ones) announce it as a piece for admiration. The curved surfaces challenge the skill required for its extensive and

Fig.1. Interior of the writing flap showing the pewter inlay 'Gallus Jacob'

ambitious marquetry. The incorporation of the name and arms into the marquetry (figs 1 and 2) underlines the cabinet's importance to its owner, Johannes Gallus Jacob von Hohlach, who was at that time an official at the court of the Prince Bishop of Würzburg.[2]

Since the nineteenth century craftsmanship has been so revered that it is difficult to appreciate how anonymous were the men who made even the grandest furniture in previous centuries. Even if we know the name of the patron and the master cabinet-maker, the man at the bench is normally anonymous. In this case, a letter found inside the structure offers a rare, wide-ranging yet very personal view of the lives of the two makers.[3] The paper, signed by Jacob Arend of Koblenz and Johannes Wittalm of Vienna is dated 22 October 1716. In the German states at this time it was the practice for young men newly out of their apprenticeship to spend time working in other centres. The two young men were much concerned with their poverty: they record that it was a lean year 'when cabbage and corn were often the best food we could obtain' and when the only solace was to get 'right drunk', though 'the vines have not grown well these last four years'. Part of the problem was 'the big war in Hungary against the Turks'. Jacob Arend carefully records on the back of his lament 'I…have invented this cabinet on my own, and have drawn and marked it out. I have cut it [the marquetry] with a fret-saw and shaded it'.

The full history of the cabinet is not known. It was bought in England on 31 August 1843 by John Gibbons for £160 and remained in his family until it was bought by the V&A. In 1846 it was recorded in a Gibbons family group (fig.3) painted by Charles Robert Leslie (1794–1859). When the cabinet first came to the V&A the date in the marquetry read '1617'. It is likely that the transposal of figures was the work of a nineteenth-century dealer, which allowed him to sell the cabinet with a romantic association with Prince Maurice of Nassau (d.1625). Museum conservators have now reversed this transposal. S.M.

1. H. Kreisel, *Die Kunst des Deutschen Möbels* (Munich: Verlag C.H. Beck, 1970), vol.II, pp.90–91.

2. P. Thornton, 'A Cabinet for a Würzburg Patron', *Apollo*, vol.LXXXIX (1969), pp.448–53.

3. Ibid.

Fig.2. Detail of the main panels showing the arms of von Hohlach, inlaid with pewter and mother-of-pearl

Fig.3. The Shell *by Charles Robert Leslie, showing the cabinet in the background (Private collection)*

Chest

British (London): 1720

Attributed to James Moore the elder (d.1726). Made for Sir William Bateman, later 1st Viscount Bateman and Baron Culmore (d.1744) of Shobdon Court, Herefordshire. Carved oak, pine and gilt gesso

H: 78.8 cm; W: 144.8 cm; D: 67.3 cm
Museum No. w.33-1948
Purchased from the Spanish Art Gallery Ltd, London

Fig.2. Design by Jean Bérain (from 100 Planches Principales de Jean Bérain, *Paris, 1882)*

The form of this chest is based on sixteenth-century Italian *cassoni* (p.28) which Sir William Bateman saw on the Grand Tour in Italy. In 1718, Sir William inherited a fortune from his father who, as sub-governor of the South Sea Company and Lord Mayor of London in 1717, established a reputation for splendour. In contrast, 'William Bateman had all the advantages of education and when abroad on his travels made a better figure than some of the foreign princes…and collected…everything curious in painting and statuary'.[1] On his return to England he became engaged to Lady Anne Spencer, a granddaughter of the 1st Duke of Marlborough, who was then living with her mother at Blenheim Palace in Oxfordshire. By that date, the cabinet-maker James Moore was in charge of the building, having succeeded John Vanbrugh as architect. Sarah, Duchess of Marlborough, referred to Moore as her 'Oracle', and it is likely that the chest was commissioned from him to celebrate this marriage in 1720.

Italian *cassoni* were often intended to hold the bride's trousseau. The interior of the Bateman chest retains its original pink silk quilting suggesting that it was intended for this purpose. The survival of the lining indicates that its subsequent function was as a purely decorative enhancement of the patron's status. The top of the chest bears the cipher 'WB' for William Bateman and is surmounted by the Bateman family crest flanked by acanthus scrollwork in raised carved gesso (fig.1).

The sarcophagus form of the design was inspired by late seventeenth-century engravings of commodes by Jean Bérain and André-Charles Boulle (fig.2) and is an interesting example of the Baroque forms of furniture intended for grand Palladian interiors. Shobdon, the country house of the Bateman family, was built by Sir James Bateman about 1705 and was illustrated in the second volume of Colen Campbell's *Vitruvius Brittanicus* (1717). The chest appears in the Hall in an early photograph before the house was demolished in 1933, but its original location is not recorded.

Fig.1. Detail of top of Bateman chest

The art of gilded gesso decoration originated in Italy (p.28). The design was carved in the wood which was then coated with layers of gesso (powdered chalk and animal glue). When these had hardened the gesso was re-carved and the surface was gilded. In France and England gilt gesso furniture became fashionable from the last quarter of the seventeenth century. The technique was developed in England from 1689 by the Huguenot refugee Jean Pelletier and his two sons Thomas and René who worked at Hampton Court, Kensington Palace and Montagu House, Bloomsbury.

In contrast to the work of the Pelletier family, the decoration on the Bateman chest is bolder and more sculptural. The feathered and bearded American Indian masks are linked vertically by pendant husks to massive ringed lion's-paw feet which are found on a chest of similar curved outline made for Stowe House in Buckinghamshire.[2] A restrained chest with stand on lion's-paw feet at Boughton House, Northamptonshire, is associated with another chest from the Marlborough collections.[3] The forms of decoration on the Bateman chest anticipate gilded furniture made to William Kent's designs by James Moore senior and his former apprentice Benjamin Goodison.[4] T.M.

1. John Lodge, *The Peerage of Ireland* (London, 1789), p.249.

2. Ian Caldwell, 'James Moore & the Bateman Chest', *Antique Collector*, vol.LIX, no.2 (February 1988), pp.74–79, fig.2, p.75.

3. See J. Hardy in T. Murdoch (ed), *Boughton House: The English Versailles*, 1992, p.134, fig.132 and G. Beard, 'Three eighteenth-century cabinet-makers: Moore, Goodison and Vile', *Burlington Magazine*, vol.CXIX (July 1977), pp.479–84, pl.13.

4. Ian Caldwell, 'John Gumley, James Moore and King George I', *Antique Collector*, vol.LVIII, no.4 (April 1987), pp.65–71.

Console Table

British: circa *1730*

Designed by William Kent (1685–1748) and probably made by John Boson (active 1720–43) for Richard Boyle, 3rd Earl of Burlington (1694–1753) for the Sculpture Gallery at Chiswick House. Gilt pinewood supporting a Siena marble slab

H: 88 cm; w (of marble): 69.5 cm; D: 4.5 cm
Museum No. W.14-1971
Purchased from Sotheby & Co., London

This is an early example of furniture designed by an architect for a newly created Palladian setting. The designer, William Kent, was a close friend and protégé of the patron, the amateur architect Richard Boyle, 3rd Earl of Burlington. They met on the Grand Tour in Italy, where Burlington made a particular study of the work of Andrea Palladio (1508–80).

On his return from Italy, Lord Burlington created a villa at Chiswick between 1724 and 1727 which was in part inspired by Palladio's Villa Rotunda at Vicenza. The interior was decorated and furnished from 1726 under Lord Burlington's supervision to the designs of William Kent by a team of craftsmen including the cabinet-maker Benjamin Goodison (*c*.1700–67) and the carver and gilder John Boson. Much of the original furniture from Chiswick, including the pair to this console table, survives today in the Devonshire Collections at Chatsworth, Derbyshire.[1]

The pair of tables were probably intended for the Sculpture Gallery (fig.1) and would have been placed either side of the central Venetian window.[2] The Gallery is part of an intercommunicating series of rooms, planned as a circle, a rectangle with apses and an octagon, following the plan of the Baths of Diocletian. The Classical order in the Gallery is Corinthian. In the Round and Octagon Rooms the walls are ornamented with festoons of flowers issuing from woven baskets supported on female heads. They illustrate the story told in the first century AD by the Roman architect Vitruvius of the origin of the Corinthian capital: that a basket, placed on an acanthus plant, broke into leaf. The table's pedestal design is thus a play on the origin of the Corinthian capital.[3] Vitruvius also described the Corinthian Order as having feminine qualities. Dominated by a central female mask flanked by acanthus scrolls and husk festoons, the pierced carving conveys a lightness in contrast to the weight-bearing function of the carved giltwood support. The central Greek key motif recurs at the bases of the four niches for sculpture in the apses at either end of the Gallery which, by 1731, housed statues of Venus, Diana, a Muse and Mercury.[4] The design is original in its adaptation of architectural elements to create a new form of furniture.

Fig.1. The Sculpture Gallery from the Octagon Room, Chiswick House (English Heritage)

John Boson specialized in architectural carving and the production of marble chimneypieces. He is known to have carved stonework at Chiswick and to have supplied furniture.[5] A pair of stands from Chiswick attributed to Boson (fig.2) were acquired by the V&A in 1962.[6] Boson also worked to Kent's designs for furniture for the Gallery and Drawing Room at Kew Palace for Frederick, Prince of Wales. The carved giltwood mirror now in the V&A (fig.3) is almost certainly the 'Rich Tabernacle' which hung as a pier glass in the Drawing Room at Kew.[7] The style of the acanthus leaf carving is close to that on the Chiswick console table.

Much furniture of this period is attributed to William Kent and this is a rare documented example. Kent's wide-ranging designs for furniture, silver and sculpture were published by John Vardy in *Some Designs of Mr. Inigo Jones and Mr. Wm. Kent* (London, 1744) and included the design for this 'Table at Lord Burlington's at Chiswick' (pl.40). T.M.

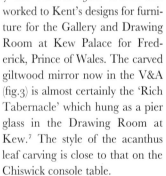

Fig.2. Pedestal, giltwood, one of a pair, from Chiswick House, c.1730 (V&A Museum No. W.47-1962)

Fig.3. Mirror, giltwood, from Kew Palace, 1734 (V&A Museum No. W.86-1911)

1. Lord Burlington's heiress married the Marquess of Hartington, later 4th Duke of Devonshire.

2. T. Rosoman, 'The Decoration and use of the Principal Apartments of Chiswick House, 1727–1770', *Burlington Magazine*, vol. CXXV, no.991 (October, 1985), pp.663–77.

3. Also the subject of the ceiling painting by William Kent in the Blue Velvet Room at Chiswick.

4. J. Harris, *The Palladian Revival: Lord Burlington, His Villa and Garden at Chiswick* (New Haven/London: Yale University Press, 1994), pls 90–91, p.125; fig.52, p.151.

5. R.T. Spence, 'Chiswick House and its gardens, 1726–1732', *Burlington Magazine*, vol.CXXXV, no.1085 (August 1993), pp.526, 529. Rosoman op.cit., note 2.

6. G. Beard and C. Gilbert, *Dictionary of English Furniture Makers* (Leeds, W.S. Maney & Son/Furniture History Society, 1986), p.89.

7. Vol.IV, 1733–4, p.238. The Duchy of Cornwall Archives.

Bookcase

British (London): 1740. One of a pair

Made by John Channon (1711–79) for Sir William Courtenay of Powderham Castle, Devon, where the pair remains *in situ*.
Veneered in padouk with marquetry in brass and carved giltwood; carcase of oak and pine
H: 383.5 cm; W: 250 cm; D: 104 cm
Museum No. W.I&A-1987
Purchased from Lord Courtenay with the assistance of the National Heritage Memorial Fund

Fig.2. Water, from a series of the Four Elements, engraved by Jean Bérain, c.1700

Fig.3. One of the bookcases as normally shown at Powderham, with its nineteenth-century base

Seldom does British furniture of the first half of the eighteenth century venture to compete with the strong designs and exotic materials of grand European pieces of the period. This bookcase (and its pair), dated 1740 and bearing the engraved brass plate (fig.1) of the cabinet-maker John Channon, are ambitious British essays in the Baroque.[1]

Bookcases, as a furniture form, had only developed in the last quarter of the seventeenth century.[2] Sir William Courtenay's care for his books may have reflected his concern for them as indicators of his status as a scholarly gentleman. Certainly in his will he declared that 'my Library, Globes and other things in my library…shall be deemed as heirlooms'.[3]

The pillared form with broken pediment derives from Baroque architectural designs for doorways or funerary monuments, particularly those by James Gibbs (1682–1754).[4] Such forms were very different from most case furniture produced in London in the 1730s and 1740s, and the closest parallels are to be found amongst German bookcases.[5]

However, the design of the brass inlay is taken from quite another source, the engraved plates of ornament by Jean Bérain (1674–1726) published in France in about 1700 and later in England. Such engraved sheets of designs were used by craftsmen in many materials who copied details or whole designs from them as they chose. The panels on the front and sides of the main plinths and the small motifs used as lockplates are all taken from a single plate of designs representing the element Water (fig.2)

and centring on a depiction of Venus on her shell. The engraving on the brass inlay, which is lively but not of the first quality, would have been undertaken in a specialist workshop in London. The use of brass for this decoration relates to the seventeenth-century French technique of boulle marquetry (pp.74,78), and research has shown that there were also connections between London craftsmen and visiting German cabinet-makers.[6]

The brass is inlaid into a veneer of padouk, a tropical hardwood similar in grain to rosewood. For many years these bookcases were thought to be of rosewood but scientific analysis has recently identified the rarer timber. Analysis of several other samples from brass-inlaid furniture has suggested that this timber was often used in conjunction with brass inlay.[7]

In about 1830 the appearance of both bookcases was altered when they were moved downstairs from the Library at Powderham. They were given deep plinths with giltwood dolphin 'mounts' as feet (fig.3).[8] It was only when the bookcases were moved in 1993 (the first time for many years) that it was discovered that these were an addition, masking and embellishing an originally shallow plinth. An old repair to one of the dolphins trapped a fragment of newspaper in a glue layer. This dates the repair to about 1863 and makes it clear that the dolphins themselves must have been provided some years before that.

The Powderham bookcases are not displayed at the V&A but remain at Powderham Castle in Devon; because of their unbroken history in the house (which is open to the public), it has been decided that they should not be moved. S.M.

1. C. Gilbert and T. Murdoch (eds), *John Channon and Brass-inlaid Furniture 1730–1760* (New Haven/London: Yale University Press, 1993), pp.106–13.

2. P. Macquoid and R. Edwards, *The Dictionary of English Furniture* (London: Country Life, revised edition, 1954), pp.78–84.

3. C. Gilbert and T. Murdoch, 'Channon Revisited', *Furniture History*, vol.XXX (1994), p.68.

4. James Gibbs, dedication page of J. Flamsteed, *Historiae Coelistis* (London, 1712), reproduced in T. Friedman, *James Gibbs* (New Haven/London: Yale University Press, 1984), pl. 74.

5. Gilbert and Murdoch, *John Channon*, op. cit., p.33.

6. Ibid., pp.24–36.

7. Ibid., pp.49–51.

8. Gilbert and Murdoch, 'Channon Revisited', op. cit., pp.63–8.

Fig.1. Engraved brass plaque with the maker's name and date

Side Table

British: circa 1740

Attributed to Benjamin Goodison (*c.*1700–67) and probably made for Sir Jacob Bouverie (1694–1761) for the new hall at Longford Castle, Wiltshire. Carved pinewood, painted white

H: 93.4 cm; W: 198 cm; D: 99 cm
Museum No. W.3-1953
Given by Mr E.E. Cook, Bath

Fig.1. Side table at Longford Castle, Wiltshire (Country Life)

This side table of architectural proportions has traditionally been associated with Coleshill House, Berkshire, where it was recorded in 1919 in a *Country Life* article. Coleshill was designed in the late 1640s for Sir George Pratt by his cousin, the gentleman-architect Sir Roger Pratt (1620–85), who had just returned from Italy with advanced architectural ideas. Coleshill consisted of a long, two-storey façade with interiors enriched with carved decoration and elaborate plaster ceilings.

By the mid-eighteenth century, the new owner, Sir Mark Pleydell, had discovered that Inigo Jones (1573–1652) had come with Roger Pratt to Coleshill and 'was also consulted abt ye Cielings'. The association with Inigo Jones attracted considerable interest from Richard Boyle, 3rd Earl of Burlington (1694–1753), who visited Coleshill and was so struck by the ceilings that he employed Isaac Ware to make 'very correct drawings' of them.[1] Inigo Jones had been the first to introduce to Britain the architectural designs of the sixteenth-century Italian architect Andrea Palladio (1508–80), and thus became the hero of Burlington's circle with their promotion of Palladianism.

Because of Sir Mark Pleydell's association with Lord Burlington and the link between Coleshill and Inigo Jones (whose work inspired Lord Burlington's architectural designs), it has been suggested that this table may have been designed by Lord Burlington's protégé William Kent (p.88).[2] The architectural form of the table combined with the sculptural quality of the Diana mask and supporting foxes are characteristic of furniture associated with Kent.

A similar side table supported by wolves with an identical mask of Diana is at Longford Castle, Wiltshire (fig.1).[3] This table is curved to fit the shape of the circular dining room (fig.2) and was probably commissioned by Sir Jacob Bouverie, who succeeded his father in 1736. It may have been supplied by the cabinet-maker Benjamin Goodison who was paid over £400 in 1740 for furniture for Longford including three gilt side tables with marble tops for the Picture Gallery.[4] As Benjamin Goodison is known to have worked to the designs of William Kent, it would appear that the association with the designer came through the craftsman rather than the patron in this instance.[5]

As Sir Mark Pleydell's heiress Harriet married the Hon. William Bouverie who inherited Longford Castle in 1765, the connection between the two families may suggest that the table was made for Longford Castle and only subsequently transferred to Coleshill. The similarity of the two painted side tables certainly suggests that both were supplied for the same patron. Both are painted white rather than gilded; they are of identical length with the same architectural mouldings, scroll supports, oak leaf garlands, Diana masks and scallop shells. The curved table still at Longford supports a slab of *verde antico* marble, whereas the V&A's slab is of grey-veined white marble, indicating that the tables may have been intended for different locations in Longford Castle. The straight-sided table may have been commissioned for the Palladian two-storeyed hall created on the north-west Entrance Front by Sir Jacob Bouverie in *c.*1740, but which was destroyed by Anthony Salvin's alterations in 1870.[6]   T.M.

Fig.2. Former dining room at Longford Castle, Wiltshire (Country Life)

1. H. Avray Tipping, 'Coleshill House, Berkshire', II, *Country Life*, vol.XLVI, no.1178 (2 August 1919), pp.138–46.

2. H. Avray Tipping, *English Homes*, Period IV, vol.I, *Late Stuart*, p.21, fig.9; H. Colvin, *Biographical Dictionary of British Architects 1600–1840* (London: John Murray, 1978), p.131.

3. R. Edwards, *Dictionary of English Furniture* (London: Country Life Ltd, revised edition, 1954), vol.III, p.284, fig.33.

4. C. Hussey, 'Furniture at Longford Castle', *Country Life* vol.LXX, no.1821 (12 December 1931), pp.679–82. See also notes taken from the Account Books of Sir Jacob Bouverie, Information Section, Department of Furniture and Woodwork, V&A).

5. G. Beard, 'William Kent's Furniture Designs and the Furniture Makers', *Antiques*, vol.CXXIX (June 1986), pp.1278–89.

6. C. Hussey, 'Longford Castle, Wiltshire', III, *Country Life*, vol.LXX, no.1823 (26 December 1931), pp.724–30.

Ornamental Casket

Italian (Turin): circa *1745*

Designed and made by Pietro Piffetti (1700–77). Mother-of-pearl veneer, gilt-bronze and gilt-copper mounts, kingwood and spindle wood veneered base, with engraved and painted ivory; carcase of poplar

H: 142.3 cm; W: 68.5 cm; D: 57 cm
Museum No. W.34-1946
Purchased from Christie, Manson & Woods Ltd, London

This casket on stand is an outstanding example of the work of Pietro Piffetti (1700–77), perhaps the greatest Italian cabinet-maker of the eighteenth century.[1] In July 1731 he was appointed royal cabinet-maker by Carlo Emanuele III, King of Sardinia (reigned 1730–73). In the preceding year, Piffetti was reported to be working in Rome,[2] where he may well have learnt his techniques from Pierre Daneau, a French cabinet-maker who specialized in making inlaid *trompe l'oeil* marquetry.[3] With the exception of a possible further visit to Rome in 1747, Piffetti seems to have spent the rest of his life in Turin, producing furniture and fittings mostly for the Palazzo Reale and the Palazzina di Stupinigi. These pieces were lavishly veneered with mother-of-pearl, tropical woods and engraved ivory, with gilt-bronze mounts supplied by François Ladatte (1706–87) and Giovanni Paolo Venasca (active 1730–50).

This stand, or its pair, was included in a lottery of 30 November 1779, organized by the Ospizio de' Catecumeni in Turin. The fourteenth item, valued at 5000 lire, was described as:

> an oval table…all veneered with small pieces of mother of pearl…with four legs linked with a cross-piece…on top of the said table is an urn with a lid, supported by four Sirens carried on four sea-animals…at the top is a Statue of Mars in gilt-bronze and the feet are in the form of four heads, which rest on a base inlaid with India and Brazil walnut, mother-of-pearl, ivory engraved to nature with flowers and leaves.[4]

The lottery description refers to 'Sirens' – half women half birds – on sea animals (*bestie marittime*) supporting the casket, which is surmounted by Mars. The equivalent supports on the V&A pieces are tritons, and the figure on the finial is definitely Minerva. Unless a clerical error was made, it is very likely that the V&A's piece originally formed a pair with the stand listed in the lottery.

The mother-of-pearl stand and casket are decorated with an abundance of gilt-bronze mounts and ornaments, such as tritons on turtles, and surmounted with a statuette of Minerva. On the lid of the casket the veneer is laid in ribs, giving a subtle undulating effect. The inside of the casket was re-lined with crimson leather, probably during the 1930s. The legs terminate in gilt-bronze moor's heads, in a manner very similar to a set of stools in the Palazzo Reale (fig.1), made by Piffetti with mounts by Ladatte.[5] The base is veneered with kingwood and spindle wood, with engraved ivory swags of flowers. Traces of red pigment on one of the flowers suggest that they were originally all coloured 'to nature'. A number of flowers and leaves were repainted grey at a later date to harmonize with the mother-of-pearl veneer.

Piffetti was pre-eminent among Italian cabinet-makers of the eighteenth century. His pieces, ranging from massive prie-dieux to spinning-wheels, were mostly executed for the royal family of the Kingdom of Sardinia. All were elaborately decorated in the costliest tropical woods, mother-of-pearl and gilt-bronze, and their sheer lavishness and virtuosity of execution outshone even the most extravagant pieces made in other workshops in Italy during the eighteenth century. Before the V&A acquired it, this stand belonged to Mr Lionel de Rothschild of Exbury House, Hampshire. It is not surprising that a piece of this nature would have appealed to the Rothschilds, with their love of the best French and continental furniture of the eighteenth century. J.Y.

1. G. Ferraris, *Pietro Piffetti e gli ebanisti a Torino (1670–1838)* (Turin: Umberto Allemandi & C., 1992), passim.

2. Ibid., pp.13, 197.

3. A. González-Palacios, *Fasto Romano: dipinti, sculture, arredi dai Palazzi di Roma* (Verona: Leonardo-De Luca, 1991), pp.161–2.

4. Ferraris, op. cit., p.218. Turin, Archivo di Stato, Controllo generale di Finanza, *Patenti e biglietti*, vol.57 (1779), p.139.

5. Ferraris, op. cit., p.22.

Fig.1. Stool from Palazzo Reale, 1731–3 (Palazzo Reale, Turin)

Hanging Cabinet

British: 1743

Designed by Horace Walpole (1717–97) probably
in collaboration with William Kent (1685–1748).
Veneered with padouk and ivory on a pine
carcase with oak drawer linings

H: 152.4 cm; W: 91.5 cm; D: 21.6 cm
Museum No. W.52-1925
Purchased from Mr Thomas Sutton, London, with
funds from the Murray Bequest

*Fig.1. Rosewood hanging
cabinet mounted with ivory
plaques, made for Thomas
Brand, about 1754 (Christie,
Manson & Woods Ltd)*

1. H. Walpole, *The Yale
Edition of Horace Walpole's
Correspondence*, ed. W.S. Lewis
(London/New Haven:
Oxford University Press/
Yale University Press,
1937–84), vol.XVIII, p.277.

2. H. Walpole, *The Works
of Horatio Walpole*, vol.III
(London: 1798), p.481.

3. W. King and M. Long-
hurst, 'A Relic of Horace
Walpole', *Burlington
Magazine*, vol.XLVIII,
no.276 (March, 1926),
pp.98–103.

4. H. Colvin, *A Biographical
Dictionary of British Architects
1600–1840* (London: John
Murray, 1978), p.493.

5. G. Beard and C. Gilbert,
*Dictionary of English Furniture
Makers, 1660–1840* (Leeds:
W.S. Maney & Son/
Furniture History Society,
1986), pp.387–9.

6. R. Edwards, 'Cabinets
made for Horace Walpole
and Thomas Brand',
Burlington Magazine,
vol.LXXIV, no.432
(March 1939), pp.128–9.
The cabinet was sold at
Christie's, 20 October 1938,
lot 72 and again on
27 November 1980, lot 24.

7. Ibid.

8. H. Walpole, *A Description
of the Villa of Mr Horace
Walpole...with an inventory
of the Furniture, Pictures,
Curiosities...*(London, 1784),
pp.56–61.

In July 1743, Horace Walpole wrote to his friend Sir
Horace Mann, 'I have a new cabinet for my enamels and
miniatures just come home, which I am sure you would
like'.[1] This unusual cabinet is like a memorial tablet in its
architectural design, and it supports ivory figures of three
of Walpole's artistic heroes: the Flemish sculptor François
Duquesnoy (1594–1644) and architects Andrea Palladio
(1508–80) and Inigo Jones (1573–1652). These figures were
copied from originals by Michael Rysbrack by James
Francis Verskovis 'an excellent carver in ivory' who was
also responsible for Walpole's arms on the pediment and
the eagle heads at the base.[2] The cabinet forms a Classical
Temple of Worthies to house Walpole's collection of
miniature portraits and was originally intended for his
London house in Arlington Street, Piccadilly. The exterior
is appropriately embellished with ivory reliefs of Classical
subjects, some probably by the Roman sculptor Andrea
Pozzo (active 1755–84) which were apparently acquired by
Walpole during his Grand Tour in Italy in 1740. These
include the central rectangular reliefs of *Judith and Holofernes* and *Perseus and Andromeda* (the latter is based on a
marble relief in the Capitol, Rome); the medallion heads
of Medusa and Minerva; and the oval relief of *Diomedes
with the Palladium*, based on famous antique gems. Some of
the medallion portraits at the corners of the doors are
apparently imaginary.[3]

Horace, the son of Sir Robert Walpole, England's first
Prime Minister, greatly admired his father's Palladian
house at Houghton, Norfolk, with its interiors by William
Kent. When Walpole returned from Italy in 1741, full of
enthusiasm for the Classical world, it is probable that he
conceived the form of this cabinet in consultation with
Kent who was then designing a neighbouring house in
Arlington Street for Henry Pelham.[4] The triangular pediment closely resembles some of the door cases at Houghton, Norfolk. The identity of the cabinet-maker is not
known, but William Hallett (*c.*1707–81) has been suggested
as he later worked for Horace Walpole at Strawberry Hill
(p.108). Hallett also supplied furniture for a number of
houses with which Kent was associated as a designer, including Badminton, Ditchley, Holkham and Rousham.[5]

A similar cabinet, but without the ivory figures on
the pedestal, was made for Thomas Brand of the Hoo,
Bedfordshire (fig.1), 'a very intimate friend' of Walpole.[6]
It incorporates similar ivory reliefs of Classical subjects.
Although Brand's cabinet was evidently a replica of
Walpole's, examination of both in 1938 suggested that
they came from the same workshop.[7]

Walpole's cabinet was eventually housed in the Tribune at Strawberry Hill (fig.2), where it was described as
'designed by Mr. Walpole' and the ivory relief of *Judith and
Holofernes* was mistakenly ascribed to Grinling Gibbons, a
carver whom Walpole much admired.[8]   T.M.

*Fig.2. The Walpole cabinet
in the Tribune at Strawberry
Hill from Horace Walpole,*
A Description of the
Villa...at Strawberry
Hill near Twickenham
Middlesex *(London, 1784)*

Writing Cabinet

German (Dresden): 1750–55, made for Augustus III,
King of Poland and Elector of Saxony (1696–1763)

Attributed to Michael Kimmel or Kümmel
(1715–94). Kingwood marquetry with mother-of-
pearl, ivory and brass; carcase of pine and
stained birch(?); carved giltwood mounts within,
incorporating the cipher of Augustus III; gilt-
bronze mounts. Some mounts stamped '7'

H: 250 cm; W: 136 cm; D: 75.5 cm
Museum No. w.63-1977
Purchased by H.M. Government from the estate of
the 6th Earl of Rosebery and allocated to the Victoria
& Albert Museum

The appeal of this cabinet is direct. Without knowledge of
its date or country of origin it is possible to enjoy and
admire the carefully controlled movement of the design
which makes this such a celebrated example of the German Rococo. The sophistication of the choice of materials
and of workmanship produces great delicacy of decoration
on what is, in form, a massive cabinet.

It represents the cosmopolitanism which characterized
fine court furniture of the eighteenth century throughout
Europe. The interior (fig.1) is crowned by a giltwood
carving with the cipher of Frederick Augustus, son of
Augustus the Strong, who succeeded as Elector of Saxony
in 1733 and was elected King of Poland in 1734. As a
young man he had travelled extensively and he was a
noted collector. His court at Dresden looked to Paris for
models of furnishings and interior decoration. His daughter, Marie-Josèphe, was married in 1747 to the Dauphin of
France, and this naturally brought the two courts closer.
Commodes with the stamp of the Parisian cabinet-maker
Bernard II Vanrisamburgh were made about 1750 for
Schloss Moritzburg, amongst other items supplied from
Paris.[1]

The maker of this cabinet is not known. Clearly it was
the product of one of the most ambitious workshops in
Dresden, possibly that of Michael Kimmel or Kümmel,
the court cabinet-maker. Little is known of his productions
but the description of him in 1749 as a 'young man highly-
skilled in working bronze and exotic woods and experienced in the decorative French and English designs',
would certainly support a possible attribution.[2] The closest
known parallels are four commodes (fig.2) also attributed
to Kümmel and associated with Augustus III, but these
equally lack any early documented provenance.[3] Their
construction is not of the same high quality as the V&A's
cabinet.

The form is based on the bureau cabinet popular in
Britain throughout the eighteenth century and copied
particularly in the German states.[4] In Dresden from 1734

Fig.1. Detail of the inside of the upper tier

it became one of the recognized forms for an apprentice
to offer as a masterpiece.[5] The date of the piece has been
much debated. It is unlikely to have been made during the
Seven Years War (1756–63) when Augustus III would
scarcely have been in Dresden. Although it is possible
that it was made after 1763, the existence of a cabinet by
C.F. Lehmann (active 1755–79), the German-born cabinet-
maker to the court of Copenhagen, which appears from its
design to derive from 1755, is a strong argument for its
dating closer to 1750.[6]

The cabinet was bought by Baron Mayer de Rothschild in 1835 when he was 17 years old for the large sum of
£1,000 and remained at Mentmore Towers, Buckinghamshire, until 1977. S.M.

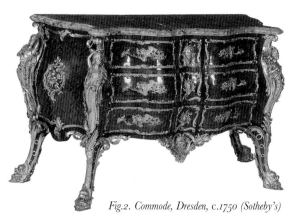

Fig.2. Commode, Dresden, c.1750 (Sotheby's)

1. A. Pradère, *French Furniture Makers. The Art of the Ebéniste from Louis XIV to the Revolution* (London: Sotheby's Publications, 1989), p.189.

2. G. Haase, *Dresdener Möbel des 18. Jahrhunderts* (Leipzig: VEB E.A. Seemann, 1983), pp.369–70.

3. Two sold Sotheby's, London, 12 December 1986, lot 237, and 16 June 1995, lot 75.

4. H. Hayward and S. Medlam, 'The Continental Context: Germany', in C. Gilbert and T. Murdoch (eds), *John Channon and Brass-inlaid Furniture 1730–1760* (New Haven/London: Yale University Press, 1993), pp.29–32.

5. H. Kreisel, *Die Kunst des Deutschen Möbels*, vol.II (Munich: C.H. Beck, 1970), p.258.

6. Ibid., pp.267–8, fig.836. Gilbert and Murdoch, op.cit., pl.26.

Table

French: 1750–60

Made by Adrien Dubois (master 1741).
Veneered with tortoiseshell and engraved brass
on a carcase of oak; mounts of gilt-bronze.
Stamped: 'A.DUBOIS' and 'JME'

H: 79.5 cm; W: 132 cm; D: 52 cm
Museum No. 1021-1882
Bequeathed by Mr John Jones, London

Though the pursuit of the newest style in furnishings was
important to the courtiers and other wealthy inhabitants
of Paris in the eighteenth century, the work of André-
Charles Boulle (1642–1732), who was cabinet-maker to
Louis XIV and his successors from 1672, never went out of
fashion. His sumptuous marquetry of tortoiseshell and
engraved brass (pp.74,78) remained desirable to connoisseurs throughout the eighteenth century and was
distinguished in sale catalogues of famous collections by
the mention of his name.

Not only were boulle pieces re-sold, they were also
adapted and re-used, though instances of re-use are more
common from the end of the eighteenth century. This table
top was made some time in the first two decades of the
eighteenth century. In the 1750s it was incorporated into
a fashionable, new framework by a cabinet-maker called
Adrien Dubois. From the mid-century members of the
cabinet-makers' guild in France were required to stamp
with their name pieces which they made or adapted. The
second stamp, 'JME' indicates that the piece had been
approved for quality of workmanship by the 'Juré'
(inspecting committee) of the guild.

This table top almost certainly started its life as the top
of a six-legged table, a design which can be attributed to
Boulle or to an employee in his workshop (fig.1).[1] The

Fig.2. Detail of the top

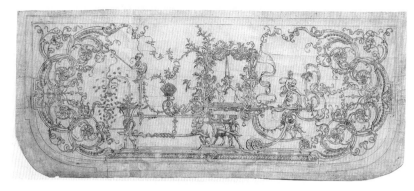

Fig.3. Engraved template for the design (Museum of Fine Arts, Boston)

engraving was part of a repertoire of designs for clocks
and furniture after models by the Boulle workshop, published by the Parisian print dealer, Mariette, in 1724.

Such tables were often supplied as pairs, with a second
table executed in *contre partie* (p.78) to the same design or
with a top of a different design. Surviving examples of the
six-legged table, which retain their original tops, show
either the 'Triumphal Car' which decorates this one (fig.2),
or a 'Circus Wagon'.[2] Both images derive from engravings
of the 1550s by Cornelis Bos (d.1556), evidence that the
Boulle workshop was not above incorporating into its
work a lively design which was already 150 years old,
dressing it out with more modern decorative details
derived from designs by Jean Bérain I (1640–1711).[3] Full-
size printed designs for both table tops survive in the
Museum of Fine Arts in Boston (fig.3).[4] Versions of these
may have been used for transferring the design to sheets of
tortoiseshell and brass before it was cut.

Dubois adapted the design of the legs to the sinuous
lines of the Rococo fashion of his own period, eliminating
the straight legs and stretcher of the original design and
accentuating the curve on each side of the frieze. The fact
that there are no marks on the frame to indicate that two
legs have been removed, proves that the frame was newly
made by Dubois, to receive the much-admired marquetry.
The mounts are of models known to have been used on
tables of the original form, and the quality of their casting,
chasing and gilding suggests that they, like the marquetry,
were made for an early-eighteenth century table, though
the key escutcheon may have been added by Dubois and
the *sabots* (foot mounts) on the back feet may be a yet later
replacement.   C.S.

Fig.1. Design for a table from Nouveaux Desseins de Meuble et
Ouvrages de Bronze et de Marqueterie, *Paris, 1724 (Musée des
Arts Décoratifs, Paris)*

1. The earliest documentary
evidence relating to this
model of table may be
the account for furniture
supplied to the Ménagerie at
Versailles in 1701, though it
is not possible to be certain
that the description of the
tables matches exactly the
six-legged design. Quoted
A. Pradère, *French Furniture
Makers. The Art of the Ebéniste
from Louis XIV to the Revolution*
(London: Sotheby's Publi-
cations, 1989), p.100.

2. F. Watson, *Wallace
Collection Catalogues. Furniture*
(London: HMSO, 1956),
no.F 425.

3. S. Schele, 'Cornelis Bos,
a study of the origins of the
Netherland Grotesque', *Acta
Universitatis Stockholmiensis.
Stockholm Studies in the History
of Art*, vol.X (1965).

4. R.H. Randall, 'Templates
of Boulle Singerie', *Burlington
Magazine*, vol.CXI (September 1969), pp.549–53.

Commode

French (Paris): 1750–60

Made by Bernard II Vanrisamburgh (after 1696–1766/7). Veneered with panels of Japanese lacquer, the borders japanned; carcase of oak; mounts of gilt-bronze; slab of *griotte d'Italie* marble. Stamped: 'BVRB' and 'JME' (mark of the Parisian cabinet-makers' guild)
H: 84 cm; W: 115.5 cm; D: 53.2 cm
Museum No. 1094-1882
Bequeathed by Mr John Jones, London

Fig.2. Back of commode (Museum No. 1105-1882) attributed to BVRB by reason of the fine, panelled construction

This commode combines the best Parisian cabinet-work of the eighteenth century with panels of fine oriental lacquer of an earlier date. Twentieth-century collecting has developed a deep concern with authenticity and absence of alteration or restoration which is very different from the French attitude in the eighteenth century. At that time connoisseurs and craftsmen sought to celebrate and enhance luxury materials and fine workmanship by presenting them in new forms with the best modern embellishments.

Oriental lacquer was much prized, particularly that from Japan.[1] Like oriental porcelain and textiles, it was imported into Europe by the East India Companies. In late seventeenth-century Paris, oriental lacquer made for the export market was imported and collected in its own right and in its original form as cabinets or coffers; by the middle decades of the eighteenth century it was likely to be stripped from its original carcase and veneered onto a modern, French form of furniture, and further embellished with lavish gilt-bronze mounts.

Such lacquer was supplied to the workshops of the French cabinet-makers by the *marchands merciers* (merchants of luxury goods) who are known to have bought lacquer in Amsterdam. The *marchands merciers* both supplied lacquer and, as specialist retailers, provided outlets for the furniture veneered with it.

The stamp 'BVRB' identifies the maker of this commode as Bernard II Vanrisamburgh, son of a German immigrant and the second of an important three-generation dynasty of that name (p.74). He worked in Paris between 1730 and 1766 or 1767 and is known to have worked for the *marchands merciers*.[2] Furniture by him is amongst the most luxurious produced in Paris at that time. For example, he supplied the merchant Thomas Joachim Hébert with a lacquer commode, veneered with Chinese lacquer, which was delivered to Fontainebleau by Hébert in 1737 for the apartments of the French Queen, Marie Leszczynska.[3] Some of the mounts on the Queen's commode are identical to those on the V&A commode, indicating that the same design for mounts might be used over a long period (fig.1).

The careful disposition of the mounts allows the landscape design of the large panel to be fully appreciated. The drawers are arranged *sans traverse*, without the bronze framing to each drawer which had been common earlier. The bronzes act as a frame to the decorative lacquer. Handles are either disguised or dispensed with: the top drawer is opened by the use of the key, while the handles for the lower drawer are incorporated into the lower framing mount. The areas outside the main frame are finished with a type of varnish (*vernis martin*) developed in France in the 1730s to imitate lacquer.[4] This is applied over thin, hardwood veneers, evidence of Vanrisamburgh's attention to detail in such a piece.

At a time when much French furniture showed relatively crude construction, this commode illustrates BVRB's concern for quality even in the carcase-work of his pieces. He used bevelled panels for the top, bottom, back, dust boards and sides, a technique which allowed for the inevitable movement of the wood. Such careful carcase-work was typical of his attention, so much so that the similar bevelled panel construction found on one of the other lacquer commodes in the V&A's collection (Museum No. 1105-1882, see fig.2) has served to support the argument that BVRB made that commode also. The swelling, bombé lines of the piece presented difficulties in veneering the 2 mm thick panels of lacquer: their survival in good condition is largely due to the care with which the carcase was constructed. c.s.

1. F. Watson, 'Beckford, Mme de Pompadour, the duc de Bouillon and the taste for Japanese lacquer in eighteenth century France', *Gazette des Beaux-Arts* vol.LXI (February 1963), pp.101–27. O. Impey and J. Whitehead 'From Japanese Box to French Royal Furniture', *Apollo* vol.CXXXII, no.343 (September 1990), pp.159–65.

2. A. Pradère, *French Furniture Makers. The Art of the Ebéniste from Louis XIV to the Revolution* (London: Sotheby's Publications, 1989), pp.183–99.

3. Ibid., pl.187.

4. J. Whitehead, *The French Interior in the Eighteenth Century* (London: Laurence King, 1992), pp.190–92.

Fig.1. Detail, front right corner mount

Bed

British (London): circa *1754*

Designed and supplied by William (*c.*1703–63) and John (1729–96) Linnell for the Chinese Bedroom at Badminton House, Gloucestershire. Japanned beechwood; the hangings not original.

H: 381 cm; D: 259 cm; W: 241.5 cm
Museum No. w.143-1921
Purchased from M. Harris & Sons, London

From the beginning of the seventeenth century, Europeans had been fascinated by objects imported from China. The exotic patterns of Chinese export porcelain, silks and lacquer inspired European designers and craftsmen to imitate and create their own fanciful vision of the East (p.72). By the mid-eighteenth century, the taste for Chinese furnishings was particularly characteristic in Britain of ladies' bedrooms and dressing rooms.

This spectacular chinoiserie bed was commissioned by the 4th Duke and Duchess of Beaufort from the Linnell firm of cabinet-makers in London for the Chinese Bedroom at Badminton House, Gloucestershire (fig.1).[1] The bed was accompanied by a set of eight armchairs (fig.2). The original design for the chairs (fig.3) demonstrates that their decoration consisted of red, blue and yellow japanning to match the original colours which survive on the bedstead. Their seats would have been upholstered *en suite* with the bed hangings, although the bed's present hangings of yellow silk are modern replacements. The chairs were probably redecorated in the mid-nineteenth century in black and gold, when the original upholstery was replaced.[2]

It seems likely that the Duchess of Beaufort was responsible for selecting the Chinese style of this commission, although it was the Duke who instructed his bankers, Messrs Hoare in Fleet Street, to pay the Linnells £800 between 1752 and 1754. However, some of the individual payments to the Linnells are itemized in 'The Duchess of Beaufort's Book of Disbursements on the Duke of Beaufort's Accounts', which suggests that it was the Duchess rather than the Duke who actually discussed the commission with the craftsmen.[3] In addition the Linnells supplied for the same bedroom two pairs of standing shelves and a commode.[4] This chinoiserie furniture was in place by 1754 when Dr Pococke visited Badminton and noted the 'Bedchamber finished and furnished very elegantly in the Chinese manner'.[5]

The earliest recorded English commission for household furniture in the Chinese manner came from Mrs Montagu, of blue-stocking fame, and was supplied by William Linnell for the Chinese room in her London house in Hill Street, Mayfair, in 1752. The japanned writing table and cabinet on stand from Mrs Montagu's Chinese room which survive at Came House, Dorset, both have applied lattice-work decoration similar to the japanned commode from Badminton.[6] The Chinese style was particularly fashionable for garden buildings and their furnishings. In 1750 William Halfpenny published designs for Chinese garden chairs in his *New Designs for Chinese Temples*. In an article on 'Taste' in *The World* (March 1753) the poet William Whitehead noted 'a few years ago everything was Gothic…according to the present prevailing whim everything is Chinese'. T.M.

1. H. Hayward, 'Chinoiserie at Badminton: the furniture of John and William Linnell', *Apollo*, vol.XC (August 1969), pp.134–9.

2. Bed and chairs sold at Christie's 30 June 1921: Now owned by the Bristol Museum and Art Gallery, the V&A, a private collection and with Malletts. The present upholstery dates from after the 1921 sale

3. H. Hayward and P. Kirkham, *William and John Linnell* (London: Studio Vista/ Christie's, 1980), pp.107–08.

4. The shelves are now in the Lady Lever Art Gallery, Port Sunlight, and the Irwin Untermeyer Collection at the Metropolitan Museum, New York; the commode is now in the V&A (Museum No. w.55-1952).

5. J.J. Cartwright (ed.), 'The Travels through England of Dr. Pococke', *Camden Society* 1888/9, vl.II, p.31.

6. H. Hayward, 'The Chinese Influence on English Furniture', *The Westward Influence of the Chinese Arts*, (London School of Oriental and African Studies, 1972) pp.60–62.

Fig.1. The Chinese Bedroom, Badminton House, showing the Linnell bed and three of the armchairs, 1908 (Country Life)

Fig.2. Armchair, one of eight, from the Chinese Bedroom, Badminton House (V&A Museum No. W.33-1990)

Fig.3. Design drawing for the set of eight armchairs for the Badminton Chinese Bedroom by John Linnell (V&A Museum No. E.71-1929)

Ornamental Stand and Urn

German (Brunswick): 1755–72

Made in the factory of Johann Michael van
Selow, Brunswick. Glass beads set in
composition, on a core of wood, with plaques
of glass, enamel and mother-of-pearl.
Unmarked

H: 169 cm; W: 47 cm; D: 49 cm
Museum No. W.45-1936
Given by Lt Col. J.N. Horlick, OBE, MC

*Fig.1. Table top in beadwork
(Städtischen Museum, Brunswick)*

*Fig.3. Tea caddy (Städtischen
Museum, Brunswick)*

This colourful but impractical object is a rare survivor
of a factory which worked for less than twenty years in
the middle of the eighteenth century in Braunschweig
(Brunswick), producing furniture and small decorative
objects entirely covered with glass beads set in composition.[1] The commonest survivors are oval table tops set
with formal garden scenes including topiary and fountains
(fig.1). Three-dimensional pieces are much rarer and only
one other urn on stand is known, in the collection of the
Lady Lever Art Gallery, Port Sunlight.[2] The Bowes
Museum, Barnard Castle, has a pelmet with imitation
drapery carried out entirely in this technique (fig.2).

In the Romanesque period beaded decoration had
been used for reliquaries and similar items of religious
significance, but there was no more recent history of its
use in the German states at the time of the founding of
this factory.[3] The first record of the factory's existence is in
a list of craftsmen resident in Brunswick in 1755 which
includes 'N.N. [sic] van Selow – a shell worker'. He was
soon to come under the protection of Duke Carl I of
Brunswick, who continued to underwrite and encourage
the factory, much as other rulers encouraged local porcelain factories.[4] In July of the following year the city
council received instructions to lend the manufacturer
Johann Michael van Selow 400 Reichstaler at the usual
interest, his goods to be used as collateral. In February
1756, at the time of the city fair, an advertisement in the
Braunschweiger Auseiger described the several sorts of large
and small tables in *corallen* (lit. 'coral' but probably meaning beadwork) which were for sale. They were described
as 'a new discovery' and said to be as hard as stone.[5]

Nothing is known of the origins of van Selow though
he may have come from Holland.[6] Despite the support of
the Duke the factory did not flourish. Of its employees we
know only that van Selow used 'free masters' for the
making of the wooden bases. These were mostly soldiers
discharged from the Seven Years War who, to prevent
their becoming a charge on the state, were allowed certain
rights to work, although they had not served formal
apprenticeships. This use of non-guild labour caused
difficulties, not least in ensuring the quality of the work.
Problems continued throughout the 1760s and the Duke

(in order to protect the trade) ordered van Selow to teach
his craft to the native artist Conrad Ludolph Pfeiffer, who
may have produced many of the designs.[7] In 1765 a lottery
failed to help the finances and in 1767 the direction of the
factory was taken over by Thiele Heinrich Eggeling, one
of the 'free masters', but this change did not prevent final
closure in 1772.

Though the beadwork was also applied to articles in
tinplate and pottery (fig.3), most pieces were made by
covering a wooden core with linen. Composition was then
applied, coloured as for the final pattern. The beads were
strung on linen thread and laid out on pasteboard patterns
before the strings were cut to size and laid onto the body
of the piece. Larger pieces of glass imitating various hardstones such as agate or porphyry were used, as were small
enamel plaques which were also embedded into the composition with mother-of-pearl and other materials.

Cracking and movement of the wooden frames make
these pieces quite fragile, which may be one reason for
their rarity; but the brilliant colours of the unfading glass
beads is a strong reminder of the vivid and cheerful
colours of the Rococo. S.M.

1. B. Bilzer, *Führer durch die
Schausammlung Perlmosaiken von
J.M. van Selow* (Brunswick:
Städtischen Museum, 1969).

2. Inventory number LL
4267.

3. G.E. Pazaurek, *Glasperlen
und Perlen-Arbeiten in Alter und
Neun Zeit* (Darmstadt:
Verlags Anstalt Alexander
Koch, 1911), pls 2 and 4.

4. F. Furse, 'Braunschweiger
Tische', *Der Cicerone*, 13
(1909), pp.409–15.

5. Bilzer, op. cit., p.4.

6. Ibid.

7. Ibid.

Fig.2. Pelmet, with imitation drapery worked in beads (The Bowes Museum, Barnard Castle)

Chair

British (London): 1754–5

Designed by Horace Walpole (1717–97) and
Richard Bentley (1708–82) and made by
William Hallett (*c*.1707–81) for Strawberry Hill,
Twickenham. Beech, stained black to simulate
ebony; leaf finial missing from top of back; the
rush seat not original

H: 126 cm; W: 61 cm; D: 52 cm
Museum No. w.29-1979
Purchased from Simon Redburn Fine Arts Ltd,
London, with a contribution from the Brigadier
Clark Bequest through the National Art Collections
Fund

*Fig.1. Watercolour of the interior of the Great Parlour at Strawberry Hill, by John Carter, 1788
(Lewis-Walpole Library, Farmington, Connecticut)*

This chair was one of the original furnishings of Straw-berry Hill, Twickenham, the country house of Horace Walpole (p.96). Walpole, the antiquarian, collector and novelist, and the son of Sir Robert Walpole, the first Prime Minister, devoted much attention to modifying and enlarging Strawberry Hill in the Gothic Revival style from 1748 onwards. He furnished the house with his collections and welcomed curious visitors. Such was the fame of Strawberry Hill that in 1774 a ticket system had to be introduced to regulate the flow of visitors wishing to view the house and its contents.[1] With an eye to posterity he left detailed descriptions of his work at Strawberry Hill in the form of accounts, letters and even a published guide.[2] As he no doubt intended, this careful and unusually full documentation has ensured Strawberry Hill a prominent place in the history of the Gothic Revival in the eighteenth century.

In order to advise him on the transformation of the house, Walpole convened what he termed a 'Committee on Taste' comprising himself, the designer Richard Bentley, and the amateur architect and owner of the Vyne, Hampshire, John Chute, whom Walpole had met on his Grand Tour. Chute, described by Walpole as '…my oracle in taste…the genius that presided over poor Straw-berry!',[3] was responsible for the exterior of the building, while Bentley produced designs for interior fittings based on engravings of ecclesiastical details which appeared in topographical books in Walpole's own library. Illustrations were freely adapted to suit the domestic interior: for example, a chimneypiece designed by Bentley was based on the tomb of the Bishop of Durham in Westminster Abbey.[4]

Bentley probably produced the design for this chair, which is one of a set of eight made for the Great Parlour.[5] The chairs can be seen in a contemporary watercolour of the room (fig.1). Walpole suggested that the backs of the chairs to be made for the Great Parlour should be based on the outline and tracery of a Gothic window. He wrote to Bentley on 27 July 1754: 'My idea is, a black back, higher, but not much higher than common chairs, and extremely light, with matted bottoms…I have been trying to make out something like windows…I would have only a sort of black sticks, pierced through…'.[6] Walpole ordered the chairs from William Hallett, a fashionable cabinet-maker in St Martin's Lane, London, noting the details in his account book: '1755 Sept. 20 pd Hallett for 8 black Gothic chairs at 3-15-0, 30-00-0'.[7]

In choosing to take his inspiration for his house and furnishings from the Gothic features found in medieval churches, Walpole was subscribing to a popular contemporary fashion. He was unusual however in that he re-modelled the entire house in the Gothic Revival style, and that he looked directly at published engravings of medieval architecture as source material, rather than relying on contemporary pattern books. He became one of the best-known exponents of the style in the eighteenth century. C.S.H.

1. Twickenham, Orleans House Gallery, *Horace Walpole and Strawberry Hill* (London: London Borough of Richmond upon Thames Libraries Department, 1980), p.26.

2. P. Toynbee (ed.), *Strawberry Hill Accounts* (Oxford: Claren-don Press, 1927); W.S. Lewis (ed.), *The Yale Edition of Horace Walpole's Correspondence* (London/New Haven: Oxford University Press/ Yale University Press, 48 vols, 1937–83); H. Walpole, *A Description of the Villa of Horace Walpole, youngest son of Sir Robert Walpole, Earl of Orford, at Strawberry Hill, near Twickenham* (Strawberry Hill: privately printed by T. Kirkgate, 1774, second edition illustrated and enlarged, 1784).

3. Quoted in W.S. Lewis, 'The Genesis of Strawberry Hill', *Metropolitan Museum Studies*, vol.V, part one (June 1934), p.63.

4. Ibid., p.60.

5. Strawberry Hill sale, 1842; four of the chairs are in the Lewis-Walpole Library in Farmington, Connecticut.

6. Quoted Lewis (1937–83) op. cit., vol.35, 1973, pp.181–2.

7. Toynbee, op.cit., p.6.

Candlestand

British (London): 1756–60

The design attributed to Thomas Johnson (1714–*c*.1778), and supplied to George, 1st Lord Lyttelton, for Hagley Hall, Worcestershire. Carved and painted pine, iron candle-branches with gilt-brown nozzles

H: 157.5 cm; w (of base): 58 cm;
span of branches: 98 cm
Museum No. w.9-1950
Purchased from Sotheby and Co., London

Fig.2. Thomas Chippendale, design for a candlestand, detail of plate CXLV, The Gentleman and Cabinet Maker's Director, 1762

When George, 1st Lord Lyttelton (1709–73), built Hagley Hall, Worcestershire, between 1754 and 1760, the severely restrained Palladian exterior bore little relation to the interiors, which were decorated with Rococo plasterwork and fashionably furnished in a variety of styles. The Gallery, with its views across the recently landscaped park, was supplied with candlestands, girandoles and pier glasses elaborately carved with natural and rustic imagery. The adjoining Drawing Room was furnished in the more sophisticated French style with floral tapestries and white and gilt chairs.

This candlestand is one of a set of four which were supplied to flank the pier tables in the Gallery.[1] With the lightness and delicacy of its outline, its asymmetry and naturalistic motifs, the stand represents the English Rococo style of the mid-eighteenth century at its most exuberant. The original painted surface consists of dark brown (representing mahogany) and a contrasting stone colour. Much of the imagery is aquatic, from the stalactites dripping from the top, to the scaly dolphins entwined around the central columnar support and the fountain playing in the grotto enclosed by scrolling supports. The candle-branches, shaped to represent gnarled oak twigs, are entirely irregular.

The overall form of the stand relates so closely to a design by Thomas Johnson (fig.1) that it can be safely attributed to his workshop, at 'The Golden

Fig.1. Thomas Johnson, design for candlestand. Detail of plate 13 in a book of designs without a title page, 1758 (V&A Museum No. E.3731-1903)

Boy', in Grafton Street, Soho, London.[2] Johnson, described in Mortimer's *Universal Director* (1763) as a 'Carver, Teacher of Drawing and Modelling and Author of a Book of Designs for Chimney-pieces and other ornaments and several other pieces', evidently supplemented his income as a carver both by teaching drawing and by publishing his skilful and fluent designs.[3] This was common practice at the time, when craftsmen published their designs both to solicit orders of furniture and for others to use. Johnson drew freely on the work of other designers for his motifs: the dolphins may derive from an engraving of a candle-stand by François Cuvilliés (1695–1768).[4] In turn, Thomas Chippendale (1718–79) appears to have adapted Johnson's design in the third edition of *The Gentleman and Cabinet Maker's Director*, 1762 (pl. CXLV) (fig.2).

Several pieces of furniture have been identified as following Johnson's designs, and indeed the size of his workshop indicates that he must have produced a quantity of carved work.[5] However, owing to the lack of documentary evidence no objects can be firmly attributed to him. Johnson's name does not appear in any known household accounts; as a carver he may have supplied his goods through an upholsterer or cabinet-maker. Evidence suggests that furniture for Corsham Court, Wiltshire, and Blair Castle, Scotland, which follow closely designs by Johnson, was supplied by the upholsterer George Cole, who had an establishment in Golden Square, London, between 1747 and 1774.[6]   C.S.H.

1. One at Temple Newsam House, Leeds, Yorkshire; two in the Philadelphia Museum of Art.

2. P. Macquoid and R. Edwards in *The Dictionary of English Furniture* (London/New York: Country Life, 1927), vol.III, p.145. The design, issued 1756–7, and re-published in a collected edition, 1758. A further edition, *One Hundred and Fifty New Designs*, was published in 1761.

3. G. Beard and C. Gilbert (eds), *Dictionary of English Furniture Makers 1660–1840*, (Leeds: W.S. Maney & Son/Furniture History Society, 1986), pp.491–2.

4. Cuvilliés published furniture designs between 1745 and 1755 in Munich and Paris. H. Hayward, *Thomas Johnson and English Rococo* (London: Alec Tiranti, 1964), p.18. P. Ward-Jackson, *English Furniture Designs of the Eighteenth Century* (London: HMSO, 1958), pl. 357.

5. H. Hayward, op.cit., pp.36–40.

6. Ibid., p.36.

Medal Cabinet

British (London): 1760–61, one section of 'His Majesty's Grand Medal Case' made for George III, perhaps as Prince of Wales

Attributed to the partnership of William Vile and John Cobb (active 1751–64). Mahogany with carved decoration.

H: 200.5 cm; W: 66 cm; D: 43 cm
Museum No. W.11-1963
Bequeathed by Mr Claude Rotch, London

In the late eighteenth century the collector's cabinet held the position of cabinets on stands in the late seventeenth century. They were indicators of erudition and connoisseurship in the library of an educated and travelled gentleman, containing natural history specimens, cameos or coins.

This cabinet, together with its companion (fig.1), now in the Metropolitan Museum, New York, was originally part of a large medal cabinet, made for George III, probably in 1760, the year of his accession. In 1761 the bills of the royal household from the firm of William Vile and John Cobb (appointed royal cabinet-makers in that year) record work on the Grand Medal Case to provide doors and drawers between the legs of the open stand, presumably to increase its capacity in line with the King's growing collection.[1]

The firm was noted for finely carved decoration set against plain panels (fig.2). Their workshop was in St Martin's Lane, then the heart of the cabinet-making district.[2] They were neighbours and trade rivals of Thomas Chippendale (1718–79), whose workshop was also noted for excellent carving. Though Vile and Cobb lost their royal warrant at the end of 1763, they supplied in that short time some important pieces of furniture. In particular, the bookcase made for Queen Charlotte in 1762 (fig.3) shares similarities with the medal cabinets. Though accounts do not survive, it is thus assumed that the Grand Medal Case was made as well as altered in their workshops.

Such bookcases and cabinets provided for the personal interests of the King. When George III succeeded to the throne in 1760 he felt the oppressive weight of court ceremony at St James's Palace and began to seek a house in which he could have respite from public life. Buckingham House was purchased, ostensibly for the Queen, and became at once his centre of interest.[3] In particular the house was enlarged and adapted to cater for the King's enormous and growing library. In the early 1760s there was large expenditure on bookcases and presses for medals, maps and drawings.[4]

In 1823 George III's medal collection was transferred to the British Museum together with his library but it seems

Fig.2. Detail of the upper door of the V&A cabinet

Fig.1. Pair to the cabinet (Metropolitan Museum of Art, New York)

that the case was not part of the deal. Given George IV's habit of altering and transforming furniture it is possible that he created the new cabinets, recognizing the quality of the earlier piece, but no record exists.[5]

Each cabinet bears evidence of an original carved motif in the pediment, possibly the Prince of Wales's feathers. Such an emblem might well have been removed when the cabinets left the royal collection. By the mid-nineteenth century they were reputedly owned by the Duke of Wellington at Stratfield Saye. The remaining emblem of the Order of the Garter would, of course, have been quite suitable for the hero of Waterloo.   S.M.

1. D. Shrub, 'The Vile Problem', *Victoria & Albert Museum Bulletin*, 4 (October 1965), pp.26–35.

2. G. Beard and C. Gilbert (eds), *English Furniture Makers 1660–1840* (Leeds: W.S. Maney & Son/Furniture History Society, 1986), pp.923–8.

3. H. Clifford Smith, *Buckingham Palace* (London: Country Life Ltd, 1931), pp.30–33.

4. Ibid., p.73. The King's mentor, Lord Bute, perhaps led this taste. His own pair of medal cabinets were of similar form: sold Christie's 3 July 1996, lot 32. Many noblemen and gentlemen followed the King's lead in commissioning such cabinets.

5. H. Roberts, 'Metamorphoses in Wood', *Apollo*, CXXXI (1990), pp.382–90.

Fig.3. Bookcase, supplied to Queen Charlotte in 1762 by Vile and Cobb, for Buckingham House, London (The Royal Collection, copyright Her Majesty the Queen)

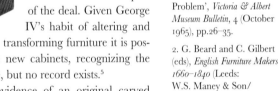

Armchair

British (London): 1759–65
From a set of four settees and six armchairs

Designed by James Stuart (1713–88) for the Painted Room in Spencer House, London, for Earl Spencer (1734–83), and now on loan to Spencer House. Probably carved by Thomas Vardy (active 1751–88).[1] Carved and gilded lime-wood, the upholstery of silk damask not original

H: 94 cm; W: 65 cm; D: 65 cm
Museum No. W.1-10-1977
Purchased from the Earl Spencer, Althorp, with a contribution from the Brigadier Clark Fund through the National Art Collections Fund

Fig.2. Detail of the frieze of the Choragic Monument of Lysicrates, Athens, from the Antiquities of Athens

These chairs and settees, amongst the earliest designed in Britain in the Neo-Classical taste, are breathtaking in their boldness. The strongly sculptural supports in the form of winged lions are carved with such verve that they seem to be about to walk away with their seats. Not only are they superb examples of the inventiveness of one of the leading architect-designers of the period, they also provide the clearest possible illustration of the close relationship between interior decoration and the design of furniture which developed in the second half of the eighteenth century. Two of the settees were made with curved backs to fit particular spaces in the apsidal end of the Painted Room and each of the other pieces had a determined position in this tightly designed interior. Not only their surface decoration but their very form contributed to the sophisticated iconographic decoration of the room (fig.1).

Spencer House, overlooking Green Park, is a celebrated and luxurious house built between 1756–65 for John, 1st Earl Spencer, who succeeded to a large fortune in 1755 and married in the following year.[2] It became a centre for the political and artistic world in London and its elegance and opulence were widely praised. In 1772 Arthur Young described Spencer House as 'astonishingly beautiful' and superior in 'richness, elegance and taste' to anything that he had ever seen.[3] He wrote further, 'I do not apprehend there is a house in Europe of its size, better worth the view of the curious in architecture, and the fitting up and furnishing of great houses'.

Lord Spencer's first architect was John Vardy (d.1765), the follower of William Kent.[4] However, from the autumn of 1758 the task of completing the interiors was given to James Stuart, often known as 'Athenian' Stuart by reason of his championship of Grecian antiquities as the proper source for the design of buildings and their decoration. During the 1750s a number of publications of engravings had directed educated taste towards the arts of Greece, and from 1762 Stuart was himself to publish the best known series of these illustrated volumes, *The Antiquities of Athens*, based on his travels in 1751.

Stuart's first design for the Painted Room was made in 1759. The iconographic programme is a celebration of marriage, with one of the painted roundels depicting an Classical Greek wedding. At that date the painted decoration of the walls, based on what Stuart had seen in Pompeii and Herculaneum in 1748 or in Rome, was a fresh fashion indeed.

For the forms of seat furniture he looked to Classical thrones in stone and marble where mythic beasts frequently formed supporters.[5] Winged lions on a similarly heroic scale to those Stuart had already recorded from an Athenian frieze (fig.2) were to be seen on a throne which formed part of the Arundel Collection of marbles. This had been given to the University of Oxford in 1755 and would have certainly been known to Earl Spencer.[6] S.M.

1. Thomas Vardy was the brother of the architect John Vardy, and a carver of high repute; though no record exists of his involvement with this furniture he did provide ornamental woodwork for the house. J. Friedman, *Spencer House, Chronicle of a Great London Mansion* (London: Zwemmer, 1993), pp.74–5. G. Beard and C. Gilbert (eds), *The Dictionary of English Furniture Makers 1660–1840* (Leeds: W.S. Maney & Son/Furniture History Society, 1986), p.919.

2. J. Friedman, op.cit.

3. A. Young, *A Six Weeks Tour through the Southern Counties of England and Wales*, 2nd edition (London: Printed for W. Strachan, 1769), p.361.

4. Designs for tables in the Neo-Classical taste for the Ante Room and the Dining Room were supplied by Vardy in 1758, as shown in Friedman, op. cit., pls 60 and 78; pl.77 shows one of the pair of surviving tables for the Dining Room (V&A Museum No. W.7-1974), which are supported on winged leopards.

5. D. Udy, 'The Classical Sources of English Neo-Classical Furniture', *Arte Illustrata*, no.52 (February 1973), pp.96–104.

6. D.[E.]L. Haynes, *The Arundel Marbles* (Oxford: Ashmolean Museum, 1975), pl.21.

Fig.1. The Painted Room, Spencer House, London (R.I.T. Capital Partners, photo: Mikes Fiennes)

Cabinet

*British (London): 1767, adapted
from a clothes press of 1764*

Designed by Robert Adam (1728–92)
for Croome Court, Worcestershire.
Made and adapted by the partnership
of William Vile and John Cobb
(active 1751–64), the carving by
Sefferin Alken (active 1744–83).
Mahogany; carcase of pine and oak

H: 264 cm; W: 176 cm; D: 74 cm
Museum No. w.20-1978
Purchased from Mr Neil Sellin,
New York

Though in most cases the discovery that a
piece of furniture has been altered is a signal
for an apologetic label in any museum,
there are occasions when the alterations
themselves are an important part of the
history of the furniture. This cabinet is one
of a pair which started life as parts of a
single, four-doored clothes press, designed
in 1764 by Robert Adam for the 6th Earl of
Coventry (1722–1809) for his country house,
Croome Court in Worcestershire.

In 1764 Adam charged 7 guineas for a
'Design of clothes press for My Lady's Bedchamber richly
ornamented' (fig.1).[1] It was made by the London firm of
Vile and Cobb and the decoration was the work of the
specialist carver, Sefferin Alken.[2] John Cobb (who completed the commission after William Vile's retirement in
1764) charged £129 for the press on 26 February 1766.[3]
The account itemizes 'fixing on all the Carv'd Ornaments
on the pannell' (clearly these were supplied separately by
Sefferin Alken), the lining of the shelves with baize and, on
2 April, a separate charge, made after the piece had been
assembled at Croome, for £5 for 'Varnishing the Large
Wardrobe in the Roome'.

The design was for a press of distinctly architectural
scale and presence. Its utility was subservient to its appearance, which was derived directly from conventions of wall
decoration, with a dado below, the main panels articulated by pilasters and surmounted by a frieze. Adam had
studied and recorded arabesque decoration similar to that
on the doors during his travels in Italy in the late 1750s. A
drawing by him of decoration at the Villa Pamphili illustrates the sort of source material he had brought back
(fig.2). At Croome Court Adam had in 1763 designed
bookcases for the Library in strictly architectural form, the
pilasters decorated with Neo-Classical scrolls of acanthus.
These are now also in the V&A (Museum No. w.76-1975).
In France such arabesques for wall decoration (more often

Fig.1. Robert Adam's design for the original clothes press (Sir John Soane's Museum, London)

executed in paint or in low relief on painted panelling)
were also just coming into fashion in the 1760s in schemes
such as those proposed for the Hôtel d'Uzes.[4] The Earl
of Coventry would have been very conscious of current
decorating styles in France, anxious to emulate the taste of
the city which led fashion and eager to accept Adam's
most modern designs. The Earl and Countess were often
in Paris during the 1760s. They bought furniture and
bronzes and ordered for Croome Court a whole room
of tapestry hangings, now in the Metropolitan Museum,
New York.[5]

In 1767 the Earl decided to have the press altered. It
was returned to John Cobb who divided the piece and
reduced the height. He charged £96 for the alterations.[6]
The design for the new base is close to an Adam design
for an organ for Lord Bute, dated 1763, but we know
nothing of the architect's involvement at this stage.[7] One
of the cupboards was fitted with the sliding trays which
were standard for a clothes press (at this time clothes were
stored flat); the cabinet now in the V&A was fitted with
two banks of plain, small drawers. S.M.

*Fig.2. Detail of drawing by Adam of the rotunda at the
Villa Pamphili (V&A Museum No. D.362-1885)*

1. Adam Drawings,
vol.XVII, no.215. Sir John
Soane's Museum, London.

2. G. Beard and C. Gilbert,
*Dictionary of English Furniture
Makers* (Leeds: W.S. Maney
& Son/Furniture History
Society, 1986), pp.8, 181–4,
923–8).

3. Croome Court Archive.

4. S. Eriksen, *Early Neo-
Classicism in France* (London:
Faber & Faber, 1974), pl.64.

5. G. Beard, 'Decorators
and Furniture Makers at
Croome Court', *Furniture
History*, XXIX (1993),
pp.95–6; aspects of the
Tapestry Room were
discussed in the *Bulletin of the
Metropolitan Museum of Art*,
XVIII, No.3 (1959),
pp.77–93.

6. The bill was dated 23 July
1767 and detailed the work
in 'Making the Top part in
to two'. It was paid 2 July
1768 (Croome Court
Archive). The other press is
now in the collections of
Bolling Hall Museum,
Bradford (inv. no.D8/1978).

7. Adam Drawings,
vol.XXV, no.4, Sir John
Soane's Museum,
reproduced in P. Ward-
Jackson, *English Furniture
Designs of the Eighteenth Century*
(London: HMSO, 1958),
pl.204.

Armchair

British (London): 1764–5

Designed by Robert Adam (1728–92), for Sir Lawrence Dundas (c.1710–81) for 19 Arlington Street, London. Made by Thomas Chippendale (1718–79). Gilded beechwood and walnut, the upholstery of silk damask not original. Marked with a chisel under the front rail: 'VII'

H: 106 cm; W: 77 cm; D: 77 cm
Museum No. w.1-1937
Purchased from M. Harris & Sons, London

This armchair unites two of the best-known personalities in the history of interiors and furniture in Britain, the architect Robert Adam and the cabinet-maker Thomas Chippendale. It is part of the only known set of furniture made by Chippendale to Adam's design. It formed part of a set of eight armchairs and four sofas made in 1765 for the Great Room at 19 Arlington Street, the London house of the successful entrepreneur Sir Lawrence Dundas. The watercolour design supplied the year before, and almost exactly conforming to the sofas as executed, is in Sir John Soane's Museum (fig.1).[1] A bill for the seat furniture, dated 9 July 1765, records that each of the armchairs cost £20, a very high price at that time. They are described as 'carved in the Antick manner & gilt in oil Gold stuffed and coverd with your own damask and strong castors on the feet'.[2]

The eight chairs and the four sofas were clearly of great importance to the client for they were supplied with two sets of protective covers, one of leather lined with flannel (presumably for use when the house was shut up and costing 1 guinea each for the armchairs) and another of 'check' (presumably checked linen, for use at all other times except when important visitors were expected, and costing 15 shillings each). Though none of the protective covers for this set survives it is pleasing that the 'strong castors' specified are still in place.

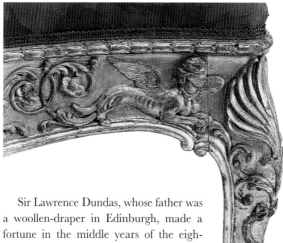

Fig.2. Detail of the carving on the seat rail

Sir Lawrence Dundas, whose father was a woollen-draper in Edinburgh, made a fortune in the middle years of the eighteenth century as a merchant contractor, supplying goods to the army in Germany. By the 1760s he was eager to establish his family in both Scotland and England, and the marriage of his son in 1764 to Lady Charlotte Fitzwilliam spurred on his ambition. The decoration and furnishing of houses became an important tool in the advancement of the family's status. At Moor Park in Hertfordshire and at their London house at 19 Arlington Street, Dundas called on Robert Adam to undertake schemes of re-decoration and the most eminent cabinet-makers were commissioned to provide for these rooms. Different firms were engaged for different types of work and Chippendale's pre-eminence as a supplier of carved mahogany carcase pieces and carved giltwood seat furniture is reflected in his commissions. Two opulent sets of seat furniture were supplied for adjacent rooms at Arlington Street.

By 1762, as is evident in a few of the engraved designs in the third edition of his *Gentleman and Cabinet Maker's Director*, Chippendale was already experimenting with Neo-Classical motifs. In these chairs, with the firm encouragement of Adam's strong championship of the new style and the confident design drawing which he supplied, Chippendale's workmen carved the fashionable motifs boldly (fig 2). Yet the chairs were still firmly in the Rococo tradition in form and scale, with broad, low backs and strongly curving outlines. A comparison with chairs from another set at Arlington Street, supplied by Chippendale to Dundas the following year (fig.3), shows how innovative the Adam design was. For precedents in furniture we should look to the chairs made in 1759–65 to designs by James Stuart (1713–88) for Dundas's close neighbour at Spencer House (p.114). s.m.

1. In 1764 Adam charged Sir Lawrence £5 for a 'Design of Sopha chairs for the Salon'; Adam Drawings, vol.xvii, no.74, Sir John Soane's Museum, London.

2. C. Gilbert, *The Life and Work of Thomas Chippendale* (London: Studio Vista/ Christie's, 1978), pp.154–8. Sir Lawrence must have considered this suite carefully, for he could have received designs from his supplier, Chippendale, at no extra charge.

Fig.3. Armchair, from the seat furniture supplied by Chippendale, for the Long Drawing Room, 19 Arlington Street, 1766 (Photo courtesy the Earl of Rosse)

Fig.1. Design for a sofa for the Great Room, 19 Arlington Street, by Robert Adam, 1764 (Sir John Soane's Museum, London)

Cabinet Bedstead

British (London): 1768–70

Supplied by Thomas Chippendale (1718–79) to David Garrick (1717–79) for his villa at Hampton, Surrey. Carved and painted pine with brass handles

H: 249 cm; W: 165 cm; D: 69 cm
Museum No. W.21-1917
Given by Mr H.E. Trevor, with the co-operation of some admirers of David Garrick

In 1754 David Garrick , actor and manager of the Drury Lane Theatre, acquired as country retreat a villa on the banks of the River Thames at Hampton, about fourteen miles outside London. He and his wife employed their friend Robert Adam (1728–92) to make the necessary architectural improvements and one of the largest cabinet-making and furnishing firms, that of Thomas Chippendale, to supply the furniture. In keeping with the rural and informal atmosphere of the villa much of the furniture was japanned, or painted, rather than veneered or gilded. When Mrs Delany, celebrated artist and correspondent, visited in 1770 she wrote: 'The house is singular…and seems to owe its prettiness and elegance to her [Mrs Garrick's] good taste…on the whole it has the air of belonging to a genius.'[1]

This cabinet bedstead formed part of a suite of furniture supplied by Chippendale for the 'best bedroom' at the front of the house overlooking the Thames, in 1768.[2] The bed would have folded up inside the cabinet so that the room could be used as an extra reception room during the day. The other furnishings included armchairs, a sofa, a dressing-table and a wardrobe, all painted blue and white to match, with upholstery of blue silk damask, and matching curtains.[3]

Cabinet bedsteads, also known as 'press beds' (in the form of a clothes press), were common in the eighteenth and nineteenth centuries when the relatively small size of even fashionable houses in London created a market for such convertible furniture. Chippendale had also supplied several for the lesser bedrooms at Garrick's London house in the Adelphi. They were usually made to look like pieces of cabinet furniture including low cupboards and bureaux, but this bed seems to have been intended to look like a bookcase. It was referred to as a 'bookcase bedstead' both in a later Chippendale account for a minor repair, and a 1796 account from a different firm for refurbishing the bed-clothes.[4] Bookcases of similar outward appearance were supplied by Chippendale to Brocket Hall, Hertfordshire.[5]

During the nineteenth century the bed was repainted green and white and converted into a wardrobe. It was acquired as such by the V&A in 1917, and it was not until 1970 when the inventory of the villa taken after Garrick's

Fig.1. Bed from the Chinese bedroom at Garrick's villa (V&A Museum No. W.70-1916)

death in 1779 came to light that its true function was realized; the overpainting was later removed to reveal the original surface treatment.[6]

The bed is decorated with the attenuated Classical motifs characteristic of Robert Adam's later work, unlike the furniture from Garrick's own bedroom which is painted white with light-hearted chinoiserie motifs in green (figs 1–2).[7] Some motifs, such as the guilloche moulding above the drawers and the indented corners to the panels, are found on both suites. Painted decoration rivalled marquetry as a fashionable finish for furniture in the latter half of the eighteenth century, though, as it is relatively easily damaged, many painted pieces must have been discarded. It is fortunate that owing to the fame of its original owner this group and its associated documentation have survived. C.S.H.

Fig.2. Wardrobe from the Chinese bedroom at Garrick's villa (V&A Museum No. W.22-1917)

1. Lady Llanover (ed.), *The Autobiography and Correspondence of Mary Granville, Mrs. Delany*, (London: Richard Bentley, 1861–2), second series, vol.I, p.284, quoted in C. Gilbert, *The Life and Work of Thomas Chippendale* (London: Studio Vista, 1978), p.237.

2. Bill from Chippendale to Garrick, 21 May – 23 September 1768, Gilbert, op. cit., p.243. Although the bed is not specified in the bill it is clearly part of this suite.

3. L. Galbraith, 'Garrick's Furniture at Hampton', *Apollo*, vol.XCVI, no.125 (July 1972), pp.46–55.

4. Gilbert, op. cit., p.248. A bill to Mrs Garrick from Clarkson, Knight and Pratt, Linen and Woollen Drapers, 4 July 1796, itemizes work (V&A Museum No. L.4631a-1970).

5. Gilbert, op. cit., pl.80.

6. In the 1779 inventory the description began 'A blue & white japanned Cabinet Bedstead' (V&A Museum No. L.4631a-1970).

7. The furniture in the V&A from the Chinese bedroom includes the bed, two wardrobes (Museum Nos W.22 & 23-1917), a corner cupboard (Museum No. W.24-1917) and a dwarf bookcase (Museum No, W.14-1994).

Table

British (London): 1769

Designed by Sir William Chambers (1723–96).
Made by Georg Haupt (1741–84).
Satinwood, inlaid with ebony, the top inlaid with specimen marbles; carcase of pine and oak.
Inscribed under the top in ink: 'Cette Table à Eté Commandé & Dessiné/por Monsr. Chambers Premier Architect/de Sa Majesté Brittanique/& Executé par Son/Très Humble Serviteur/George [sic] Haupt/Suédois/Londres le 4 février/1769'.
(This table was commissioned and designed by Mr Chambers, chief architect to His Britannic Majesty and executed by his most humble servant Georg Haupt, Swede, London 4 February 1769)
H: 75 cm; W: 43 cm; D: 43 cm
Museum No. w.38-1977
Purchased from Phillips & Harris, London, with the assistance of the Brigadier Clark Fund through the National Art Collections Fund

Furniture designed for personal use is often amongst the most innovative (p.138). Sir William Chambers, the Swedish-born son of a Scottish merchant, became architect to King George III and one of the most influential architects in Britain in the second half of the eighteenth century.[1] This small table is one of the very few pieces of furniture known to have been designed by Chambers and illustrates his constant awareness of new ideas in architecture and design.

Chambers was truly a European. After an early career with the Swedish East India Company and three voyages to China he moved to England. Study in Paris under the architect Jean-François Blondel (1705–74) was followed by two long visits to Rome, before he returned to London in 1755 where he became architectural tutor to the Prince of Wales. Styles were languages to him, and he translated himself easily from the Chinese buildings with which he embellished Kew to the Rococo decoration of the State Coach. But in architecture his major work was all Neo-Classical, culminating in the great project for public offices at Somerset House (1776–96). In 1759 his work with the Prince resulted in the publication of *A Treatise on Civil Architecture*. In 1761 he was appointed as Architect of the King's Works and by 1782 was Surveyor General.

Designs for furniture by him are not uncommon, but few pieces are known. Those that do exist show great variety, a keen exploration of the possible forms and decoration for furniture in the Classical taste. The small scale of this table indicates that it was a most personal piece, used perhaps in a study. The elegantly attenuated legs are stronger statements of Chambers' personal style.

Fig.1. Commode by Georg Haupt, 1779 (V&A Museum No. 1108-1882)

For these he was looking back to illustrations of seats or stands on Greek urns or stands surviving from Classical times, to create a form of small table which prefigures French *Directoire* furniture of the 1790s. The setting of tables with specimen marbles was in high fashion in the 1760s and 1770s, reflecting both the table slabs frequently brought back by Grand Tour travellers for mounting in Britain and the increasing interest in marbles and hardstones deriving from fashionable study of natural history. Originally the contrast between the pale wood and the marquetry would have been much stronger, and with the marbles, would have made this a very colourful piece. The swags of marquetry laurel were to become common motifs on Neo-Classical furniture, as can be seen in a commode made by the same cabinet-maker a decade later (fig.1).

The inscription (fig.2) identifies the maker of the table as a fellow-Swede, Georg Haupt, who lived in London from about 1767 to 1769 before returning to Sweden to become cabinet-maker to the King.[2] After an apprenticeship in Sweden he had worked in Germany and France before joining the small community of Swedish craftsmen who were so influential in the London cabinet-making trade in the 1760s and 1770s.[3] He may well have worked with the cabinet-maker John Linnell (1729–96), perhaps indeed through the influence of Chambers.[4] s.m.

1. J. Harris, *Sir William Chambers, Knight of the Polar Star* (London: Zwemmer, 1970).

2. G. Beard and C. Gilbert (eds), *Dictionary of English Furniture Makers 1660–1840* (Leeds: W.S. Maney & Son/Furniture History Society, 1986), pp.410–11.

3. J. Hayward, 'Christopher Fürhlohg, an Anglo-Swedish Cabinet-Maker', *Burlington Magazine*, vol.CXI (November 1969), pp.648–55.

4. H. Hayward and P. Kirkham, *William and John Linnell* (London: Studio Vista/Christie's, 1980), pp.63–5.

Fig.2. Inscription on the underside of the table

Mirror

British (London): 1770–72

Designed by Robert Adam (1728–92) and made by Sefferin Alken (active 1744–83) for the London house of George William, 6th Earl of Coventry (1722–1809) in Piccadilly.
Carved giltwood frame, mirror glass

H: 340 cm; w: 190 cm
Museum No. w.6-1991
Purchased from the Pelham Galleries, London, with assistance from the National Art Collections Fund, the National Heritage Memorial Fund, the Brigadier Clark Fund and the Jones Fund

The design of this mirror represents Robert Adam's mature style of interior decoration and reflects both his formative years in Italy and the confidence which his patron, the Earl of Coventry, placed in him. The mirror incorporates Adam's characteristic motif of draped female figures. They flank the oval glass which they appear to hold up by clasping the ropes from which the glass is suspended (fig.1). The ropes are attached above to a medallion embellished with a lion's mask and extend beyond the figures and medallion in decorative bows with suspended tassels. This conceit was probably inspired by Adam's knowledge of Italian Baroque art. The mirror is close to Robert Adam's designs for the giltwood girandoles supplied for the Long Gallery at Osterley Park, Middlesex, in 1770 (fig.2).

Lord Coventry succeeded his father in 1751 and enjoyed an income of £10,000 a year from the family estates in Worcestershire. He became Lord Lieutenant of the County and commissioned Capability Brown to remodel his Jacobean country house, Croome Court. When Robert Adam returned from Italy in 1758, Lord Coventry was one of the first to recognize his talent, and between 1760 and 1781 Adam provided a series of designs for the interiors at Croome (p.116).

On the accession of George III, Lord Coventry was appointed Gentleman of the Bedchamber to the King and set about acquiring and furnishing a suitable London house. Coventry House, Piccadilly, was situated close to the Court of George III at Buckingham House and St James's Palace. The house had been built for Sir Hugh Hunlock in 1761; the original architect is not known. From 1765 Robert Adam provided designs for the interiors, several of which survive in the Sir John Soane Museum, London, including an elaborate design for the painted ceiling of the first floor Dining Room, which is still *in situ*.[1] The mirror is based on a design by Robert Adam inscribed 'Glass frame for Lord Coventry' (fig.3).[2] Bills preserved in the Coventry family archives at Croome confirm Robert Adam's charges for mirror designs for Coventry House from 1769 to 1771.[3] In February 1772, the Danish carver Sefferin Alken charged Lord Coventry 80 pounds for 'two carved Oval Gilt Glass Frames'.[4]

Much of the eighteenth-century interior decoration still survives at Coventry House. Careful observation and analysis of the original bills suggests that the mirror was one of a pair which adorned the side walls of the Eating Room. This was the front room on the ground floor, which still retains its earlier Palladian cornice and overdoors. When, earlier this century, great London houses were abandoned in favour of the country house, the contents were often disbanded.[5] The Coventry House mirror is thus a rare example of well-documented furniture commissioned for an aristocratic London house. T.M.

1. Adam Drawings, vol.XI, no.40, Sir John Soane's Museum, London, Coventry House, now no.106 Piccadilly.

2. Adam Drawings, vol.XX, no.68, Sir John Soane's Museum, London.

3. Coventry Papers, F.62/61, Croome Estate Office. Two designs for mirrors for the Eating Room were presented in 1769 and 1770, one for mirrors for the Dining Room in 1771. See also T. Murdoch, 'A Mirror designed by Robert Adam', *National Art Collections Fund Review* (1992), pp.45–7.

4. Coventry Papers, F.62/55, see G. Beard, 'Decorators and Furniture Makers at Croome Court', *Furniture History*, vol.XXIX (1993), appendix C, p.102, no.55.

5. Although the Coventry family ceased to live there in 1848, it is not known when the original furnishings left the house. The mirror was in Benjamin Sonnenberg's collection, New York, and sold Sotheby Parke-Bernet, 5–9 June 1979, lot 1628, and again at Doyle's Auction Room, New York, 25 October 1989.

Fig.1. Detail of mirror

Fig.2. Giltwood girandole from the Long Gallery at Osterley supplied in 1770 (V&A Museum No. O.P.H. 102-1949)

Fig.3. Design for a 'Glass frame for Lord Coventry', by Robert Adam (Sir John Soane's Museum, London)

Commode

French (Paris): 1774

Supplied by Gilles Joubert (1689–1775) for the bedroom of Madame Adelaïde (1732–1800) at the Château de Marly. Marquetry of tulipwood, kingwood and other woods on a carcase of oak; gilt-bronze mounts; marble slab. Painted on back: '2767' and 'M.N.122'; printed label inside top drawer 'ÉBÉNISTE MARQUETEUR'

H: 84 cm; W: 129 cm; D: 66 cm
Museum No. 464-1895
Bequeathed by Mrs Lyne Stephens, Paris

Fig.2. Detail showing infant triton corner mount

Fig.3. Secretaire, 1774, supplied by Joubert for use in the French royal residences (V&A Museum No. W.17-1970)

While the fascination with the *ancien régime* has led to many pieces of French furniture acquiring spurious royal associations, occasionally a piece can be matched with documentary evidence and a royal provenance proved. The Garde-Meuble, the administrative body in charge of furnishing French royal residences, kept extensive records of their activities, an indication of the importance attached to such furnishings. Painted on the back of this commode are two inventory numbers (fig.1) allocated by the Garde-Meuble, representing two generations of numbering systems. The earlier number, 2767, can be traced in the Journal de la Garde-Meuble de la Couronne, a register recording the delivery of new furnishings. It gives a detailed description of the commode and also states that the piece was delivered by the royal cabinet-maker, Jean-Henri Riesener (1734–1806), on 22 June 1774 for use in the bedroom of Madame Adelaïde, one of the daughters of Louis XV, at Marly, near Versailles.[1]

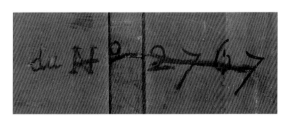

Fig.1. Detail of back of commode showing inventory numbers

The commode, combining both the serpentine lines of the Rococo and the geometrical severity of Neo-Classicism (the style which superseded it), can be described as being 'transitional' in form. It has a curvilinear, Rococo plan and cabriole legs, but the front and side elevations, composed of essentially rectangular frames enclosing the geometric marquetry, belong to the rectilinearity of Neo-Classicism. Although the production of fully-fledged Neo-Classical furniture had become well established in Paris in the 1760s, it is not unusual to find commodes in the transitional style dating, as does this piece, from the first half of the 1770s.[2]

The record of the delivery of the commode is misleading, suggesting that it came from Riesener's workshop, but it is now thought to have been made by his predecessor Gilles Joubert.[3] Riesener had replaced Joubert as 'ébéniste du roi' (chief cabinet-maker to the King) in June 1774, the very month in which the commode was delivered. It is therefore quite possible that Riesener was delivering a piece for which Joubert had organized the production.[4] The trellis-pattern marquetry of this commode, studded with gilt-bronze rosettes, and the finely sculpted and chased infant triton corner mounts (fig.2) appear on a number of other pieces recorded as being delivered to the royal household by Joubert, including a secretaire also in the V&A's collection (fig.3).[5] The precise extent of Joubert's involvement in these pieces is difficult to determine. They were delivered mainly between 1769 and 1774, when Joubert was over 80 years old. Some of these pieces bear the stamp of other cabinet-makers and clearly Joubert sub-contracted work extensively. During the period 1748 to 1774 when he was supplying the Crown, he delivered nearly 4,000 pieces of furniture, a demand which far exceeded the capacity of his workshop.[6] However, because the furniture which Joubert supplied to the Crown can be very similar, sharing the same or similar forms, mounts and marquetry, even when pieces are stamped by different cabinet-makers, it seems likely that Joubert retained considerable control over the design of the work he subcontracted.[7] E.J.

1. P. Verlet, *French Royal Furniture* (London: Barrie and Rockliff, 1963), p.120.

2. S. Eriksen, *Early Neo-Classicism in France* (London: Faber & Faber, 1974), p.78.

3. Verlet, op. cit., p.120. Verlet had earlier discussed the commode as by Riesener in P. Verlet, 'A Commode by Riesener in the Victoria and Albert Museum', *Burlington Magazine*, vol.LXX (1937), pp.188–91.

4. Ibid., p.121.

5. The pieces are listed in A. Pradère, *French Furniture Makers: The Art of the Ebéniste from Louis XIV to the Revolution* (London: Sotheby's Publications, 1993), pp.213–15.

6. Ibid., p.209.

7. Eriksen, op. cit., p.320; Pradère, op. cit., p.212; H. Roberts, 'Gilles Joubert as Subcontractor: Some Recent Discoveries', *Furniture History*, vol.XXI (1985), pp.33–4.

Commode

Germany (Neuwied): 1776–9

Made in the workshop of David Roentgen (1743–1807); marquetry panels almost certainly after Januarius Zick (1733–97); lockwork possibly by Peter Kinzing (1745–1816).
Walnut, box and sycamore, with marquetry of several woods, on a carcase of oak; drawer linings in beech (some veneered in burr walnut or mahogany); mounts of gilt-bronze; steel and brass locks; slab of *bleu turquin* marble.
Graffiti on the carcase; paper label (early twentieth century) of H.J. Hatfield and Sons Ltd; paper label inscribed: 'Wermar/R Tallof/21'
H: 88.5 cm; W: 155.2 cm; D: 67.2 cm
Museum No. w.51-1948
Bequeathed by Sir Bernard Eckstein Bt

David Roentgen, whose workshop created this commode, was celebrated throughout Europe in the late eighteenth century, both for the excellence of his marquetry and cabinet-making and for the intriguing complexity of his locks and mechanical devices.

He was the son of another famous cabinet-maker, Abraham Roentgen (1711–93), who had moved his workshops to Neuwied, near Koblenz on the Rhine in 1751. David was an innovative entrepreneur, who directed a large workshop and sought out markets from Paris to St Petersburg.[1] He directed what was, in effect, a furniture factory. He made speculative selling expeditions to Russia in the 1780s and in 1779 justified his membership of the Paris furniture makers' guild and the venture of maintaining an agent in Paris by being appointed Ebéniste mécanicien du Roi et de la Reine. The Neuwied workshops continued in production until 1792, when French Revolutionary troops arrived in the Rhineland.

The panels with scenes from the *commedia dell'Arte* (fig.1) are almost certainly designed by Januarius Zick, Court Painter of the Elector of Trier, who regularly collaborated with Roentgen. The marquetry shows Roentgen's departure from the established practice of indicating three-dimensional modelling by scorching the edges of individual pieces of wood in hot sand to suggest shading. Instead, he used separate pieces of differently coloured veneer to create shadows and modelling. The V&A owns other pieces by Roentgen in the same technique, which was much admired at the time and allowed Roentgen to depict scenes with great detail and realism.[2]

All the doors and drawers of this commode are opened by a variety of actions of the single key working in a single keyhole which, when not in use, is disguised by a mount. Such sophisticated devices as the hinged inner drawers

Fig.1. Detail of one panel with scenes of the commedia dell'Arte

(fig.2) were typical of the workshop's technical supremacy, as were features such as the detachable feet of this commode, which made packing and transport easier. For the most important pieces, like those sent to the imperial court in St Petersburg, very startling gadgetry was invented: reading stands, secret drawers and other marvels appearing at the touch of a key or spring, sometimes to musical accompaniment.[3]

Roentgen frequently repeated forms of furniture or decoration, altering details to ensure variety and individuality.[4] A commode in the Bayerisches Nationalmuseum, Munich, is almost identical to this piece.[5] Another, in the Metropolitan Museum, New York, shares the shape and the central marquetry panel, though the flanking panels differ and the mounts are closer to French models. The New York commode bears the brand mark for the Château de Versailles, indicating royal ownership before the Revolution.[6]   s.m.

1. H. Huth, *Roentgen Furniture. Abraham and David Roentgen: European Cabinet Makers* (London/New York: Sotheby Parke-Bernet, 1974); J.M. Greber, *Möbel für Europa* (Starnberg: Josef Keller Verlag, 1980); D. Fabian, *Roentgenmöbel aus Neuwied* (Bad Neustadt: Internationale Akademie für Kunstwissenschaften, 1986), the commode illustrated pp.147–9.

2. Including a small table (Museum No. 1060-1882). Another table (Museum No. 1076-1882) was made up in the nineteenth century using Roentgen panels.

3. In his fairy story *Melusine* (1816), the poet Goethe compared 'a trick writing desk made by Roentgen' to a 'palace [unfolding] before our eyes'. Cited in Huth, op. cit., p.16.

4. Framed panels of marquetry with similar subjects are in the Musée des Arts Décoratifs, Paris, possibly from a dismantled commode. A table with the same central panel is illustrated in H. Huth, *Abraham und David Roentgen und Ihre Neuwieder Möbel Werkstatte* (Berlin: Deutscher Verein für Kunstwissenschaft, 1928), pl. 90.

5. Inv. no.90/307. G. Himmelheber, 'Roentgenmöbel in Münchner Museen', *Weltkunst* LXI (1991), pp.3012–15; O. von Falke, 'Eine Roentgen-Kommode', *Pantheon* XV (1935), pp.105–08.

6. *Metropolitan Museum of Art. Jack and Belle Linsky Collection* (New York: Metropolitan Museum of Art, 1984), pp.223–5.

Fig.2. Commode open, with hinged drawers evident

Combined Music-stand and Writing-table

French (Paris): table circa 1777–85,
Sèvres plaque dated 1777

Made in the workshop of Martin Carlin (*c.*1730–85). Veneered with tulipwood, sycamore and other woods on a carcase of oak; gilt-bronze mounts; Sèvres porcelain plaque. Stamped 'M CARLIN JME' twice and 'J PAFRAT' twice; hand written label 'Sevre China Table/the Gift of/ Queen Marie Antoinette/to my mother – afterwards/Lady Auckland/in 1786/Emily Eden/ 1852'; fragment of label from the South Kensington Special Loan Exhibition of 1862. Sèvres plaque painted in blue with interlaced 'L's enclosing date letter 'z'; 'B' (for Jean-Pierre Boulanger (1722–85), probably for the gilding); Sèvres factory price ticket inscribed '216' [*livres*] in black ink; later inscriptions

H: 78 cm; W: 41 cm; D: 34 cm
Museum No. 1057-1882
Bequeathed by Mr John Jones, London

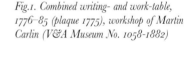

Fig.1. Combined writing- and work-table, 1776–85 (plaque 1775), workshop of Martin Carlin (V&A Museum No. 1058-1882)

Fig.2. Combined music-stand and writing-table, c.1775, workshop of Martin Carlin, shown closed (Waddesdon Manor, Buckinghamshire, National Trust)

The practice in Paris of decorating furniture with porcelain plaques was developed chiefly by the *marchand mercier* (merchant in luxury goods) Simon-Philippe Poirier from the late 1750s, and later by his partner Dominique Daguerre (active 1772–96). They had a virtual monopoly on the purchase of these plaques and controlled the production of such furniture.[1] The encyclopaedist Denis Diderot described the *marchands merciers* as 'marchand[s] de tout et faiseur[s] de rien' (dealers in everything and makers of nothing), but their creative influence should not be under estimated.[2] They took a leading role in importing, adapting and commissioning innovative luxury goods (p.102).[3] For such a piece as this, it is probable that Poirier or Daguerre would have bought the porcelain plaque and commissioned the production of the table.

The main market for furniture set with porcelain plaques was amongst rich and fashionable women. This table and its companion (fig.1) were probably given by Queen Marie Antoinette to Eleanor Eden in 1786 while she was accompanying her husband, William Eden, to Paris for the important trade negotiations which led to the Eden Treaty. The tables bear manuscript inscriptions recording the gift, and while such evidence should be treated with care, the special attention Marie Antionette paid to Eleanor Eden, as noted in William Eden's correspondence, supports this provenance.[4] Furthermore, the unusual presence on both tables of the stamps of two

cabinet-makers, Martin Carlin and Jean-Jacques Pafrat (d.1793), suggests that the pieces have a closely related history. As Carlin specialized in such small tables it is likely that the pieces were only finished in Pafrat's workshop or possibly acquired by John Jones, directly from Lady Eden or her family.

Given the costs of designing and producing such furniture it is not surprising to find that forms were repeated over a small number of pieces with minor variations of detail or material. A table at Waddesdon Manor, Buckinghamshire (fig.2), differs only in the decoration of its porcelain plaque, while one in the Wrightsman Collection (Metropolitan Museum, New York) is mounted with Japanese lacquer. The plaques of the tables from the V&A and Metropolitan Museum bear original Sèvres price tickets of 216 and 150 *livres* respectively.[5] Price depended on size and decoration: trophies tended to be more expensive than flowers, while painted figures were the most expensive. The price of 216 *livres* indicates a fairly expensive plaque. The painting is extremely fine and, appropriately for a music-stand produced during a period captivated by fantasies of rustic life, it is decorated with a trophy combining images of musical instruments and emblems of pastoral love. A shepherdess's staff is depicted with Cupid's bow and quiver and a music book is open at a comic pastoral love song. The fine detail of the painting has even allowed the song to be identified.[6]   E.J.

1. R. Savill, *The Wallace Collection Catalogue of Sèvres Porcelain* (London: Trustees of the Wallace Collection, 1988), vol.3, p.838.

2. *Encyclopédie, ou dictionnaire raisonné des sciences, des arts et des métiers...* (Neufchastel: Samuel Fauche & Cie., 1765), vol.10, p.369.

3. C. Sargentson, *Merchants and Luxury Markets: the Marchands Merciers in Eighteenth Century Paris* (London/Malibu: Victoria & Albert Museum/J. Paul Getty Museum, 1996).

4. The relevant letter is quoted in A. Dawson, 'The Eden Service: Another Diplomatic Gift', *Apollo*, vol.CXI, no.218 (April 1980), p.295.

5. By way of comparison, at this time, the lowest paid servants earned about 200 *livres* a year, while the annual income of 'a person of quality' was about 10,000 *livres*. A. Pradère, *French Furniture Makers* (London: Sotheby's Publications, 1989), pp.26–7.

6. From Jean-Joseph Rodolphe's *L'Aveugle de Palmyre*, an operatic pastoral comedy performed in 1767.

Chair

British: 1780–85 (one of two, from a set)

Designed for Woodhall Park, Hertfordshire, for
Sir Thomas Rumbold (1736–91). Beechwood,
carved and painted; seats caned; squab cushions
not original

H: 98 cm; W: 61 cm; D: 52 cm
Museum No. W.18-1931
Purchased from M. Harris & Sons, London

Painted furniture, which was highly fashionable in the
last two decades of the eighteenth century, has rarely survived subsequent gilding or stripping. The concern of Neo-
Classical architects in both France and Britain to decorate
wall surfaces with flat patterns and with painted panels
called into play the talents of decorative painters. For
such interiors, furniture was often decorated in the same
technique.

Classical myth or history were used as sources for form
and decoration as much as Classical architecture or
sculpture. In this chair Music is clearly the theme, with
lyre and flutes forming the very structure of the back. The
arms, carved as dolphins, remind the onlooker of the story
of the Grecian poet Arion, who was carried to safety by a
dolphin (attracted by his music) when he was thrown
overboard by jealous shipmates. The ribbons decorating
the back and the legs were Classical symbols indicating
revelry, often combined with swags or garlands of leaves
and flowers.

The chairs were almost certainly part of a larger set
and were supplied to Sir Thomas Rumbold, who made
his money in the East India Company. In the late 1770s
he bought the estate of Woodhall, Hertfordshire, but

returned to India as Governor of Madras from 1778–86.
However, before he left England, he must have commissioned the architect Thomas Leverton (1736–91) to build
him a new house at Woodhall.[1] Work clearly continued
while he was absent because a design for his 'Engravings
Room' (fig.1), by the print dealer R. Parker, is dated 1782.[2]

Other interiors at Woodhall were decorated with
shallow relief plaster work or with painted decoration in
advanced 'Etruscan' taste, the walls elegantly and sparsely
painted with pilasters, arabesques, formal foliage and
Classical female figures holding garlands. The furniture
throughout the house was as fashionable as the decorations. Several carved and painted pieces are recorded,
though the chairs are the only items with quite such an
idiosyncratic design.[3] At one time it was suggested that
they were Italian. They show certain similarities with designs for furniture published in *The Builder's Magazine* by
John Carter (1748–1817), which do, indeed, owe much to
the designs of Giovanni Battista Piranesi (1720–78).[4]
Sadly, no maker has been identified for any of the furniture from
Woodhall, though it is likely that more than one workshop
was involved.

It was at one time thought that the chairs had been
made for the 'Engravings Room' because they matched its
walls. However, in 1995 a pair of clearly related console
tables and a mirror appeared on the market (figs 2 and 3).[5]
They were also painted and the legs of the tables wound
round with 'ribbons' in an identical fashion. The table
tops were decorated with 'filigree' or rolled paper work, a
rare survival of a fashionable decorative technique of the
1780s and 1790s. The tables and mirror were too small to
have been made for the 'Engravings Room' and it is now
thought that they and the chairs may have been made for
the dressing room. In 1799, sale particulars of the house
described this also as 'ornamented with prints'. s.m.

1. H. Avray Tipping,
'Woodhall Park', *Country
Life*, LVII (1925), pp.164–71,
198–205.

2. The design is illustrated
in F. Russell, 'Microcosm
of 18th-Century Taste',
Country Life, CLXII (1977),
pp.924–6.

3. M. Jourdain, 'Furniture at
Woodhall Park', *Country Life*,
LXVII (1930), pp.611–13.
One cabinet with roundels
after Angelika Kauffmann
(now in the Philadelphia
Museum of Art) is illustrated
in M. Forbes Adam and M.
Mauchline, '*Ut pictura poesis*,
Angelika Kauffmann's
literary sources', *Apollo*,
vol.CXXXVI (1992),
pp.345–9.

4. P. Ward-Jackson,
*English Furniture Designs of the
Eighteenth Century* (London:
HMSO, 1958), pls 269–73.

5. Christie's, 6 April 1995,
lots 213 and 214, with com-
mentary by John Hardy.

*Fig.3. One of a pair of
tables with tops of rolled
paper work, from the same
suite of furniture (Christie,
Manson & Woods)*

Fig.1. The 'Engravings Room' at Woodhall (Country Life)

*Fig.2. Mirror, from the same suite of
furniture (Christie, Manson & Woods)*

Harpsichord

French (Paris): 1786

Made by Pascal-Joseph Taskin I, Paris (1723–93)
Japanned case, giltwood stand. Inscribed on the
nameboard: 'FAIT PAR PASCAL TASKIN A PARIS
1786'. Inscribed round the rosette: 'PASCAL TASKIN
1786'. Inscribed on the inside of the nameboard:
'Refait par Charles Fleury facteur de pianos à
Paris an 1856 fleury'

H: 73.5 cm; L: 181.5 cm; W: 73.5 cm
Museum No. 1121-1869
Purchased from Monsieur Baur, Paris

The Taskin harpsichord is probably the only instrument
of this type to be fitted with miniature keys.[1] It could have
been built for the child of rich parents, possibly even for
Queen Marie Antoinette's eight-year-old daughter, Marie-
Thérèse. It has also been suggested that it could have
been owned by Louise-Honorine, Duchesse de Choiseul
(d.1801). She was an accomplished clavichord player of
diminutive stature who is known to have had small furniture specially made for her.[2] Following the death of her
husband in 1785, she entered a convent in the rue du Bac,
in Paris. She may possibly have ordered this instrument
for solace in her cloistered surroundings.[3]

The instrument is contained in a japanned case, the
decoration of which is far closer to Far Eastern lacquer
than that of the 'Vaudry harpsichord' (p.72). Indeed the
figures are depicted in oriental poses (fig.1) playing oriental
instruments. Owing to the strict guild regulations in
France, such cases were usually built by *menuisiers* (makers
of carved furniture) and decorated by specialist painters
from different workshops. In choosing this style, the decorator, possibly M. Doublet *fils* (active 1783–9), no doubt had
in mind the contemporary fashion for incorporating old
Japanese lacquer panels into French furniture (p.102).[4]
The soundboard, nameboard and lid-prop are lavishly
decorated with garlands and sprigs of flowers (fig.2), and
are thought to be the work of M. Doublet *père* (active
1770–83). M. Doublet *fils* published his advertisement in
the *Almanach Musical* (1783), claiming to have taken over
from his father in the art of painting and decorating
harpsichords). The instrument is set on a gilt frame (fig.3)
with a scrolled frieze and fluted Neo-Classical legs, very
much in the style of furniture of the period, and the
carving and gilding of this would have been the work of a
third workshop. The rosette (the decorated soundboard
hole), takes the form of a gilt-metal Maltese Cross; it is
unlike any other surviving example by Taskin and is
thought to be a later replacement.

Pascal-Joseph Taskin came from Verviers in Flanders,
and worked in Paris under the celebrated François-
Étienne Blanchet the younger (c.1691–1761), marrying his

Fig.1. Detail

Fig.2. Detail of rose with maker's name

widow in 1766.[5] In 1774 he became Court Instrument
Maker and Keeper of the King's Instruments to Louis
XVI. Not wishing to leave Paris for Versailles, he man-
aged to delegate much of his royal work to his nephew,
Pascal-Joseph II. In addition to harpsichords and spinets,
Taskin's work included pianos.

In 1856 Charles Fleury restored the harpsichord: he
added an extra course of strings at the treble end and
shifted the keyboard a semi-tone to the right, to allow the
strings to be tuned at a higher pitch than was normal in
Taskin's time. These alterations were reversed in 1971, and
the instrument has been restored as near to its original
condition as possible. By about
1800 the piano had supplanted
the harpsichord as the most
popular keyboard instrument
and old instruments were
discarded.[6] Thus Fleury's
work is an early example
of restoration of harpsi-
chords in the spirit of the
Early Music Revival. J.Y.

*Fig.3. Detail of stand
and nameboard with
maker's inscription*

1. C. Engel, *A Descriptive
Catalogue of the Musical Instru-
ments in the South Kensington
Museum* (London: G.E. Eyre
and W. Spottiswoode 1874)
pp.278–9; R. Russell, *Victoria
& Albert Museum, Catalogue of
Musical Instruments*, vol.I,
Keyboard Instruments (London:
HMSO, 1968), pp.47–8; and
H. Schott, *Victoria & Albert
Museum, Catalogue of Musical
Instruments*, vol.I, *Keyboard
Instruments* (London: HMSO,
1985), pp.102–03.

2. Letter from Miss J. Clark
to P. Thornton, 10 July
1984, *Furniture & Woodwork
Departmental Catalogue – Keyboard Instruments*, vol.I, np.

3. B. Scott, 'The duc de
Choiseul – A Minister in
the Grand Manner', *Apollo*,
vol.XCVII (January, 1973),
pp.42–53.

4. S. German, 'Monsieur
Doublet and his confrères –
The harpsichord decorators
of Paris, parts 1 and 2', *Early
Music* (October 1980, April
1981), pp.435–53, 192–207.

5. D.H. Boalch, *Makers of
the Harpsichord and Clavichord,
1440–1840*, 2nd edition
(Oxford: Oxford University
Press, 1974), pp.176–7.

6. J.B. Weckerlin, *Nouveau
musicana* (Paris, 1890), p.94,
quoted in F. Hubbard, *Three
Centuries of Harpsichord Making*
(Cambridge, Mass: Harvard
University Press, 1972).

Piano

Spanish: circa *1800*

Made by Francisco Flórez (d.1824).
Mahogany case with gilt-bronze
mounts and medallions of cut horn
against a blue paper background.
Marked in ink: 'Flórez' on the side,
'Madrid' on the bottom of the
lowest key, and 'Flórez' on the side
of the top key

H: 29.1 cm (90.9 cm above floor);
W: 71.4 cm; D: 59.5 cm
Museum No. 48-1876
Purchased from Señor Juan Riaño, Madrid

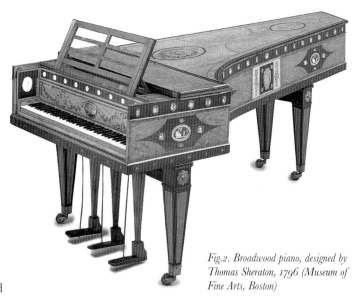

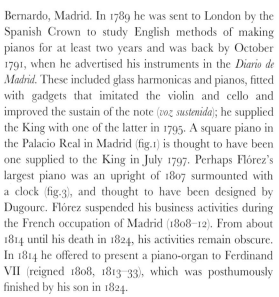

*Fig.2. Broadwood piano, designed by
Thomas Sheraton, 1796 (Museum of
Fine Arts, Boston)*

*Fig.3. Upright piano by Flórez,
1807 (Palacio Real, Madrid)*

This fine example of Spanish Neo-Classical casework
closely resembles an unsigned instrument in the Palacio
Real in Madrid (fig.1).[1] It may well have been made for
someone at the court of Carlos IV (reigned 1788–1808) as
Francisco Flórez is known to have supplied instruments
to the King and the Condesa-Duquesa de Benavente.
Although no records of his workshop survive, Flórez must
either have employed both cabinet-makers and gilt-bronze
specialists to produce this elaborately decorated piano or
have had access to such skills from specialist workshops.

Spanish Neo-Classical furniture tends to be more
exuberant than its French or English counterparts. The
abundance of gilt-bronze, medallions and geometrical
plaques on the carcase, and the elaborate decoration on
the legs are characteristics of Spanish royal furniture of the
period, often based on designs by the French designer
Jean-Démosthène Dugourc (1749–1825), and made in the
Real Taller (Royal Workshop) in Madrid. This establishment included French, German and Italian, as well as
Spanish specialists in cabinet-making, gilding, and the
making of gilt-bronze and *pietre dure* (hardstone).[2] Between
1784 and 1790 Dugourc had worked extensively for the
French royal family and one of his earliest designs for the
King of Spain was for a ceremonial coach in 1790.

French tastes prevailed at the court but English goods
were also much sought after, including pianos: in 1796,
Don Manuel de Godoy, the King's chief minister and
favourite of Queen María Luisa, was awarded the title of
'Prince of Peace', and in return presented her with a
piano, commissioned from John Broadwood of London
and designed by Thomas Sheraton (fig.2). The decoration
of that piano with plaques by Wedgwood and Tassie was
to be copied by Flórez, who used carved horn against a
blue background to imitate ceramics.[3]

Francisco Flórez was Spain's foremost piano maker
during this period. He is known to have been making
instruments from 1784. From November 1784 he advertised in the *Gaceta de Madrid* as working at the calle San

Bernardo, Madrid. In 1789 he was sent to London by the
Spanish Crown to study English methods of making
pianos for at least two years and was back by October
1791, when he advertised his instruments in the *Diario de
Madrid*. These included glass harmonicas and pianos, fitted
with gadgets that imitated the violin and cello and
improved the sustain of the note (*voz sustenida*); he supplied
the King with one of the latter in 1795. A square piano in
the Palacio Real in Madrid (fig.1) is thought to have been
one supplied to the King in July 1797. Perhaps Flórez's
largest piano was an upright of 1807 surmounted with
a clock (fig.3), and thought to have been designed by
Dugourc. Flórez suspended his business activities during
the French occupation of Madrid (1808–12). From about
1814 until his death in 1824, his activities remain obscure.
In 1814 he offered to present a piano-organ to Ferdinand
VII (reigned 1808, 1813–33), which was posthumously
finished by his son in 1824.

This square piano has a range of five and a half octaves,
FF–c4. The highest notes are mounted on an extra frame
under the soundboard, and their hammers emerge through
a slot at the edge to strike the strings.[4]   J.Y.

1. C. Ibáñez, 'Dos
Constructores de Pianos en
Madrid: Francisco Flórez y
Francisco Fernández',
Revista de Musicología, vol.XI,
no.3 (September–December
1988), pp.807–26.

2. J.J. Junquera, *La decoración
y el mobilario de los palacios de
Carlos IV* (Madrid:
Organización Sala Editorial,
1979), pp.43–59.

3. D. Wainwright, *Broadwood
by Appointment. A History*
(London: Quiller Press,
1982), pp.85–8.

4. H. Schott, *Victoria & Albert
Museum. Catalogue of Musical
Instruments*, vol.I, *Keyboard
Instruments* (London: HMSO,
1985), pp.109–10.

Fig.1. Square piano by Flórez, about 1797 (Palacio Real, Madrid)

Pier Table

British (London): circa *1800*

Designed by Thomas Hope (1769–1831) for his house in Duchess Street, London. Possibly made in London by French craftsmen. Giltwood with marble top, mirror back and bronze mounts

H: 90 cm; W: 152 cm; D: 52 cm
Museum No. W.19-1976
Purchased from Mrs Ceila Blairman with a donation from Mrs George J. Levy in memory of her father, the late Mr Philip Blairman

Fig.1. The Aurora or Star Room, from Hope's Household Furniture *(London, 1807)*

This table, from the collection of the wealthy connoisseur and patron Thomas Hope, was one of a suite forming part of the furnishings of the Aurora or Star Room in his London house in Duchess Street (fig.1).[1] Hope's intention in decorating and furnishing the house, which he acquired in 1799, was to influence and educate patrons, designers and craftsmen in the use of symbolic ornament in interior decoration (particularly that derived from Classical sources). To achieve this ambition he opened the rooms on the first floor containing his collection of Classical antiquities and vases, contemporary art, and furniture, to selected members of the public from 1804. He published his theories with views of the interiors and furnishings in *Household Furniture and Interior Decoration executed from Designs by Thomas Hope* (London, 1807).

The principal feature of the Aurora Room was John Flaxman's statue of Aurora and Cephalus, commissioned by Hope in 1790 when staying in Rome during his Grand Tour of 1787–95. Hope's scheme, symbolizing this theme of Night and Day, included blue, black and orange hangings, a black marble chimneypiece ornamented with owls and stars, and on the table a clock carried by Isis representing the moon, all described and illustrated in *Household Furniture*. The black marble slab of the table, and presumably those on the flanking side tables (fig.2), corresponded with that of the chimneypiece. The caryatids, according to Hope, represent the four *horae* or parts of the day and the medallions on the frieze represent the gods of Night and Sleep. Hope commented that the furniture was mainly of giltwood in order to contrast with the colourful scheme for the interior decoration.

There is a similarity between the design of the table, resting on double supports, and English sideboard tables with pairs of legs, of the late eighteenth and early nineteenth centuries. However the uncompromising Classical severity of the form, with the caryatids on individual plinths apparently supporting a shelf, is closer to French console tables, particularly those supplied for Napoleon's palaces by the firm of Jacob-Desmalter (active 1803–25) after designs by Charles Percier (1764–1838) and P.-F.-L. Fontaine (1762–1853).

Hope's favourable reference to Percier and Fontaine's work in the introduction to his book indicated his knowledge of their designs, published in outline engravings in their *Recueil de Décorations intérieures*, beginning in 1801. His preference for French fashions, mentioned and illustrated in *Household Furniture*, was echoed by his need to employ foreign craftsmen to execute his designs, since he considered no English artisans to be sufficiently skilled. Although he gives no details of the maker of this table it is quite possible that it was one of the many *emigré* craftsmen then resident in London.[2]

The immediate influence of Hope's Greek Revival designs, as epitomized in this table, can be seen in George Smith's *Collection of Designs for Household Furniture and Interior Decoration*, published in 1808, although some plates are dated 1804 and 1805. The Greek Revival, as promoted and defined by Hope, became the dominant style for Regency furniture and remained popular in a simpler form well into the mid-nineteenth century. F.C.

1. For a full account of Hope's collections and influence, see D. Watkin, *Thomas Hope (1769–1831) and the Neo-Classical Idea* (London: John Murray, 1968).

2. For further discussion of Hope's French furniture see P. Thornton and D. Watkin, 'New Light on the Hope Mansion in Duchess Street', *Apollo*, vol.CXXVI, no.307 (September 1987), pp.162–77.

Fig.2. Pier table from Duchess Street (Henry E. Huntington Museum, San Marino, photo. H. Blairman & Sons)

Side Table

British: circa 1805

Probably designed by Sir John Soane (1753–1837)
for the Gothic Library, Stowe, Buckinghamshire.
Ebonized mahogany and ivory

H: 92 cm; W: 141.5 cm; D: 44 cm
Museum No. W.32-1972
Purchased from the family of Mr and
Mrs Charles Handley-Read, Beaconsfield

*Fig.1. Octagonal table, from the Gothic Library at Stowe
(Brighton Museum and Art Gallery)*

*Fig.2. Ebony chair, Indo-Portuguese, mid-seventeenth century, from the collect.
William Beckford, Fonthill (V&A Museum No. 413-1882)*

This severe and monumental table is an
unusual example of Regency Gothic. Such
furniture was generally lighter and more
decorative. It was probably designed by
the architect Sir John Soane as part of his
work on the Gothic Library at Stowe from
1805 to 1807 for the Marquess of Bucking-
ham. The table is one of a pair, *en suite* with an octagonal
table (fig.1), which were sold at the great sale of the contents of Stowe in 1848.[1] The suite, found by an important
collector of nineteenth-century furniture, Charles Handley-
Read, in the Portobello Road street market in London,
remained together until the dispersal of the Handley-Read
Collection in 1972.

Soane is better known for his Classically inspired furniture than for Gothic pieces and very little Gothic furniture
by him has been identified. All his designs for furniture are
distinguished by the same restraint and skill in adapting
architectural forms and details. The tomb of Henry VII
in Westminster Abbey, used by him as a model for the
interior of the Library, may also have provided sources for
the Gothic detailing and tracery on this table.

As well as the three tables, the Library contained some
seventeenth-century Indo-Portuguese ebony chairs (fig.2)
and furniture of black wood with ivory Gothic decoration.
Ebony furniture had been particularly associated with the
Gothic Revival from the mid-eighteenth century. Horace
Walpole (1717–97) had furnished his library and other
rooms at Strawberry Hill from 1759 with a mixture of old
ebony pieces and ebonized Gothic chairs specially designed for the house (p.108).[2] Ebony and ivory furniture
was also supplied in 1806 for the Gothic Library at
Carlton House, home of the Prince of Wales, though the
rest of the house was predominately Neo-Classical in style.

One of these ebonized mahogany and ivory tables was
in the Library at Stowe by 1809, as recorded in a watercolour (fig.3). This also shows two Indo-Portuguese ebony
chairs with low backs and cane seats, from the set of
twelve listed in the 1848 sale catalogue.[3]

The surviving correspondence between Lord Buckingham and Soane shows that Buckingham had very clear
ideas about the design of the Library's interior. He wrote
to Soane in February 1805, 'I think you have departed a

little too much from Hy 7ths [Henry VII's] Screen which I
wish to take as the bookcase round the room'.[4] Such an
exacting patron almost certainly commissioned the rest
of the furniture from Soane in order to complete his
intended effect.

It is not clear why Buckingham chose Gothic for his
new Library which was created on the ground floor by
Soane, below the existing large library. The Gothic
Library, originally known as the Saxon Room, was
intended to house the collection of Saxon manuscripts
bequeathed to Buckingham in 1803 by Thomas Astle,
formerly Keeper of Records at the Tower of London.
Buckingham subsequently acquired a collection of early
Irish manuscripts and the room's name was changed to
reflect its distinctive interior.   F.C.

1. Messrs Christie and
Manson, *Catalogue of the
Contents of Stowe House*, on the
premises, thirty-third day's
sale, 28 September 1848, lots
2509 (pair of pier tables) and
2510 (octagonal table),
bought by Philip Box of
Radclive, near Buckingham.

2. Wainwright, *The Romantic
Interior* (New Haven/London:
Yale University Press, 1989),
pp.90–92.

3. *Catalogue*, op. cit.

4. Private Correspondence,
XIII.C.2.(8). Sir John
Soane's Museum, London.

Fig.3. Drawing of the Gothic Library, 1809 (Stowe School, photo: Courtauld Institute of Art)

Cabinet

British (London): circa 1817

Designed by George Bullock (1782 or 1783–1818). Made in the workshop of George Bullock. Maple and ebony veneer with marquetry of maple on ebony ground; carcase of mahogany, pine and oak

H: 111.8 cm; W: 171.5 cm; D: 56.5 cm
Museum No. W.32-1979
Purchased from Phillips and Harris, London

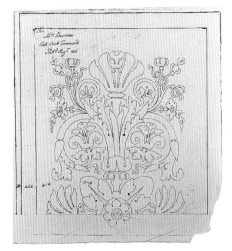

Fig.1. *Marquetry design from the Wilkinson Tracings, 1820 (Birmingham Museum and Art Gallery, unbound no.240)*

Fig.3. *Chair, oak with gilding and red paint, from Battle Abbey, Sussex, c.1816 (V&A Museum No. W.53-1980)*

For this handsome cabinet, George Bullock used maple and ebony veneers, a very unusual combination of woods for Regency furniture. The dramatic contrast of dark inlay on a lighter ground is typical of his idiosyncratic work, as is the architectural form of the cabinet. This cabinet is one of a number of surviving examples of this form. The cabinet is in the Greek Revival style, the most fashionable for Regency furniture, as shown both by its overall design and by the use of anthemia (honeysuckle) and other Classical motifs.

One of Bullock's innovations was the use of flat pattern, particularly inlay and marquetry, instead of the three-dimensional gilt-bronze or giltwood mounts favoured by his contemporaries. This did not necessarily represent an economic decision to avoid costly mounts, as might be thought, but instead can be attributed to Bullock's desire to experiment with marquetry, which had fallen out of fashion in the last decade of the eighteenth century. The subtle effects he developed can be seen in the decoration of the frieze, doors and plinth of this cabinet. He repeated the marquetry design for the doors on other cabinets, notably a grand version in ebony on a brass ground (Fitzwilliam Museum, Cambridge) and a smaller cabinet in maple and oak with ebony inlay (private collection).[1] The design for the marquetry is among a collection of tracings, originally bound in a scrapbook inscribed 'Tracings by Thomas Wilkinson, from the designs of the late Mr. George Bullock 1820' (fig 1).[2]

Although not immediately apparent from the striking exterior the three cupboards inside the cabinet are fitted with shallow drawers (fig.2), designed for collections of coins, medals or natural history specimens. The central raised section on the top was presumably intended for a piece of sculpture or other decorative object, which would complete the effect of the whole.

Bullock, a highly original and creative designer, established his furniture workshop in London at 4 Tenterden Street, Hanover Square, in 1814 after a successful career as a modeller, sculptor and furniture designer in Liver-

pool. Rapidly acquiring a range of fashionable clients, his most famous commission was the furnishings ordered by the British government for the exiled Emperor Napoleon on St Helena in 1815.[3]

Unlike contemporary cabinet-makers Bullock showed an unusual interest in native woods, using oak, holly, yew, larch and laburnum for his furniture although he continued to acknowledge the fashion for exotic woods such as rosewood, maple and ebony. Similarly his designs for inlay and marquetry included such native flora as hops, as well as the standard Classical motifs of *thyrsi* (staves wound with garlands) or anthemia. As his contemporary Richard Brown wrote, Bullock showed that 'we need not roam to foreign climes for beautiful ornaments, but that we have abundance of plants and flowers equal to the Grecian, which if adopted, would be found as pleasing as the antique.'[4]

In addition to Greek Revival furniture, Bullock's workshop also produced pieces in other fashionable styles for various clients. A commission for Sir Godfrey Vassall Webster at Battle Abbey, Sussex (1816–17), included some Elizabethan Revival chairs (fig.3).   F.C.

1. *George Bullock Cabinet Maker* (London: John Murray in association with H. Blairman & Sons, 1988).

2. The inscription on the design, 'For Mrs Barrons [Barrows?]/Oak Book Commode/Pubd Augt 1816', suggests that this may have been available through a printed source.

3. Bullock, op. cit. The St Helena commission will be published by M. Levy in *Furniture History*, vol.XXXIV (1998).

4. R. Brown, *The Rudiments of Drawing Cabinet and Upholstery Furniture* (London: J. Taylor, 1822), p.55.

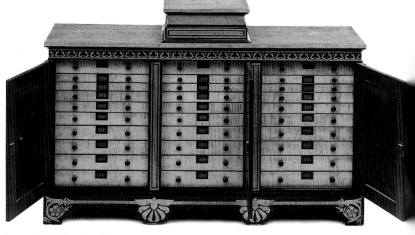

Fig.2. *Detail of interior of cabinet*

Wardrobe

British: 1820–30

Probably designed by Thomas Hopper
(1776–1856). Carved oak
H: 224.5 cm; W: 166.5 cm; D: 80.5 cm
Museum No.: w.35-1980
Purchased from Mount Street Galleries, London

This somewhat overwhelming example of the Norman Revival looks more like a door removed from a twelfth-century church than a wardrobe. It combines an essential and practical function with one of the less familiar historical revivals of the early nineteenth century. Regency enthusiasm for historicism included not only Gothic and Elizabethan revivals but also the more esoteric Norman or Saxon style. The difficulty for those wishing to design and make Neo-Norman furniture was the lack of original examples, unlike Gothic or Elizabethan furniture of which a certain number of domestic or ecclesiastical examples survived. Indeed, Norman forms and motifs had to be taken from stone rather than wooden models, and this may explain why Norman Revival furniture never achieved the popularity of Gothic or Elizabethan Revival pieces.

Norman Revival details derived from architectural sources cover the exterior of the wardrobe. Most familiar is the use of rounded arches and of variations on zig-zag carving, combined with figurative carving, incised columns and roll-mouldings. The overhanging cornice, deep pediment and use of rustication (carving which imitates deeply cut stonework) have less certain origins in Norman architecture. The heavily decorated front of the wardrobe is formed of two doors which open to reveal a conventional interior, similar to those in eighteenth-century clothes presses (p.116). The upper section of the interior is fitted for sliding trays, which no longer survive, and a later hanging rail has been inserted. Underneath are two short and two long drawers.

George Smith (active 1801–28), who popularized many contemporary furniture styles, clearly anticipated early interest when he illustrated Norman Revival designs for chairs in his influential publication, *A Collection of Designs for Household Furniture and Interior Decoration* (London, 1808) (fig.1). The discovery of the famous chessmen (now in the British Museum, London) on the Isle of Lewis, off the north-west coast of Scotland, in 1831, stimulated further engagement with this style nearly a generation later. The chairs of the kings, queens and bishops from this chess set encouraged *The Architectural Magazine* to publish suggestions for Neo-Norman furnished interiors.[1]

The architect Thomas Hopper is particularly associated with Norman Revival interiors and furniture. He established his medieval credentials with the Gothic Conservatory he added, 1807–09, at Carlton House, London,

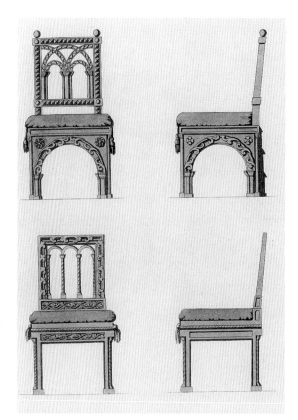

Fig.1. Parlour chairs, fronts and profiles, from George Smith, A Collection of Designs for Household Furniture, *pl.38*

for the Prince Regent. Although he had an extensive practice as a country house architect, working in a variety of styles, perhaps his most interesting works were the two Norman Revival castles he designed. Gosford Castle, Co. Armagh, Northern Ireland, which was built 1819–20 for the 2nd Earl of Gosford (1776–1849), was the first Norman Revival castle in the British Isles. Penrhyn Castle, Bangor, North Wales, constructed between 1821 and 1841, was commissioned by George Dawkins Pennant (1764–1840) who made his fortune from slate quarries. The contents of Gosford were dispersed early this century but Penrhyn survives, with much of its original furniture and other furnishings intact (fig.2). Recent research suggests that this wardrobe, originally thought to have been designed by Hopper for Penrhyn, differs stylistically from examples of furniture from that commission and therefore may be a rare survival of the furniture designed for Gosford.[2]   F.C.

1. E.B. Lamb,'Design for a Villa in the Norman Style of Architecture', *The Architectural Magazine*, vol.I (1834), pp.333–46.

2. J. Marsden, "'Far from elegant, yet exceedingly curious" Neo-Norman furnishings at Penrhyn Castle', *Apollo*, vol.CXXXVII, no.374 (April 1993), pp.263–70.

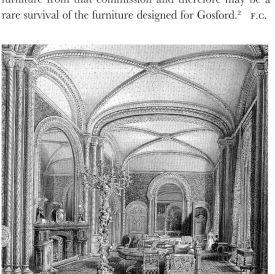

Fig.2. The Drawing Room at Penrhyn Castle, lithograph by G. Hawkins, 1846 (National Trust, Penrhyn Castle)

Chair

Italian (Turin): 1838–40

Designed by Filippo Pelagio Palagi (1775–1860) for the Castello di Racconigi, Turin. Made by Gabrielle Cappello, Turin (1806–76). Veneered in maple and mahogany on a carcase of mahogany. Chisel-marked on front seat rail: 'IIII'

H: 99 cm; W: 53.5 cm; D: 48.8 cm
Museum No. w.3-1988
Purchased from Old Master Ltd, London

Fig.1. Armchair, originally designed by Pelagio Palagi for the gabinetto etrusco, *Castello di Racconigi, and manufactured by J.-P.-F. Jeanselme (d.1860), Paris, c.1851 (V&A Museum No. W.28-1969)*

This chair formed part of a suite of furniture for the royal Drawing Room and adjacent Bedchamber of the Castello di Racconigi, the Gothic Revival hunting lodge to the south of Turin belonging to King Carlo Alberto I of Sardinia (reigned 1831–48). It was designed by Filippo Pelagio Palagi[1] – 'the famous Bolognese painter Palagi', as Stendhal referred to him in *The Charterhouse of Parma* (1839).[2] Summoned to Turin in 1832 by King Carlo Alberto I to direct the Scuola di Ornato of the newly founded Accademia Albertina di Belle Arti, Palagi undertook the redecoration of the State Apartments of both the Palazzo Reale in Turin and the Castello di Racconigi, between about 1835 and 1845. Carlo Alberto's defeat by the Austrians at the Battle of Novara (1849) and subsequent abdication and death in exile meant that his enjoyment of Palagi's Neo-Classical schemes was short-lived.

The chair is designed in the rich, Italian version of the Empire style. A veneer of mahogany and bird's-eye maple motifs covers a carcase mainly of mahogany. The original surviving fragments of the upholstery on a chair from the same set (Metropolitan Museum, New York) are blue and silver silk brocade, decorated with Apollo's harp and rosette motifs. The scholarly use of ornament on this furniture was largely the result of Palagi's passionate interest in archaeology and his possession of a enormous collection of antiquities, which he bequeathed to the city of Bologna. The decoration of these chairs was influenced to a large extent by Etruscan bronzes (the crest of the chair rail) and Greek vases (the inlaid anthemion or flower head and tendril motifs in the frame). The latter motif recurs in many of Palagi's works, such as the furniture of the *gabinetto etrusco* (Etruscan cabinet) at Racconigi (fig.1).

Initially trained as a artist, Palagi undertook all aspects of interior decoration from painting murals and ceilings to designing curtain rails. He enjoyed the use of a fine team of craftsmen, which included the carver Giovanni Battista Ferrero, the upholsterer Giuseppe Bogliani and the firm of Colla-Odetti, which specialized in bronze mounts. The bulk of the furniture was supplied by Gabrielle Cappello (1806–76) known as 'il Moncalvo'. While much thought is clearly given to the appearance of the furniture, il Moncalvo was also experimenting with a new technique of construction: though it is not immediately apparent because of the veneered surface which covers all the joints, the legs of this chair are attached to the seat frame by metal bolts or rods. Il Moncalvo's particular technique of inlay consisted of taking two sheets of wood of different colours, cutting out the motif on the upper one, and hollowing out the lower one to receive it.[3] By such methods, he could rapidly produce extremely smooth pieces of marquetry, which played on the contrasts between light and dark woods and were well suited to the linear nature of Palagi's designs. Such marquetry decoration became a characteristic of furniture executed for Carlo Alberto. Indeed his *gabinetto etrusco* furniture was hailed as 'deserving of a place in the palace of any sovereign'[4] and won him a medal at the Great Exhibition of 1851.[5] J.Y.

1. Bologna, Museo Civico, *Pelagio Palagi artista e collezionista* (Bologna: Grafis Bologna, 1976), passim.

2. Stendhal, *The Charterhouse of Parma*, transl. by M.R.B. Shaw (London: Penguin, 1958), p.395.

3. L. Bandera Gregori, 'Filippo Pelagio Palagi, an artist between Neo-classicism and Romanticism', *Apollo*, vol.XCVII, no.135 (May 1973), pp.500–09, and D.C. Finocchietti, *Della scultura e tarsie in legno* (Florence: G. Barbèra, 1873), p.215.

4. *The Crystal Palace Exhibition Illustrated Catalogue* (New York: Dover Publications, 1970, reprint of 1851 edition), p.323.

5. *Great Exhibition of the Works of Industry of all Nations, 1851. Official Descriptive and Illustrated Catalogue*, vol.III (London: HMSO, 1851), p.1304, no.64.

Chair

German (Boppard-am-Rhein): 1836–40

Designed and made by Michael Thonet (1796–1871), Boppard-am-Rhein, Prussia. Laminated walnut frame with walnut surface veneers, solid wood bracing blocks to back, cane seat; rear stretcher missing. Stencilled inscription (retailer's mark) on underside of chair rail (in two sections, the lower half repeated but blurred): 'Mö[bel] [Mag]azin/von Peter/Mündnich/Hof Tischler/COBLENZ'; handwritten signature in pencil on underside of chair rail: 'Mrs Maslen' (?)

H: 89 cm; W: 43 cm; D: 46 cm
Museum No. w.5-1976
Purchased from the firm of Peter Francis, London

On first glance this chair would appear to be an unexceptional and late example of Biedermeier furniture, the term indicating the Neo-Classical, late-Empire style which flourished in middle Europe and Scandinavia from 1815 until about 1835.[1] On closer inspection, however, the chair reveals its exceptional method of manufacture: it is made entirely from laminated rather than carved wood (fig.1), the shaping resulting from heating and bending. The chair is well documented as among the very earliest work of the man who founded one of the largest and most international furniture companies of the nineteenth century.[2]

The name of Thonet is synonymous with commercial bentwood furniture of a type used mainly in restaurants, cafés and hotels (fig.2) and with the ubiquitous form of the bentwood rocking chair.[3] However, Michael Thonet began his career as a cabinet-maker producing conventional Biedermeier furniture which was characterized by the use of flat surfaces decorated mainly with the rich grain of surface veneers. According to family tradition, in about 1830 he began searching for an alternative to

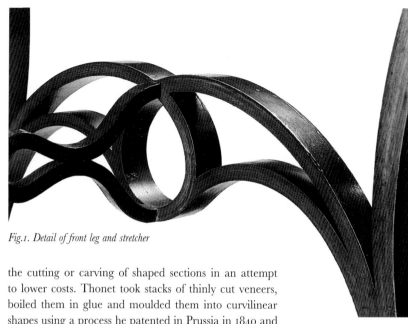

Fig.1. Detail of front leg and stretcher

the cutting or carving of shaped sections in an attempt to lower costs. Thonet took stacks of thinly cut veneers, boiled them in glue and moulded them into curvilinear shapes using a process he patented in Prussia in 1840 and later in France (1841) (fig.3) and Austro-Hungary (1842). These parts were then sanded and joined, veneers were applied to most surfaces to hide the exposed striations of the veneers (fig.1) and give the chair a uniform surface appearance; finally, the chair was varnished. The result was a remarkably lightweight chair – this example weighs a mere 2.1 kg – possessing great tensile strength. It was said to be relatively inexpensive. Thonet made such furniture in a successful workshop near Koblenz which by 1842 employed 20 to 25 journeymen.[4]

Thonet's technical innovation was part of the search for improved methods of manufacture spurred on by increased competition and made possible by the availability of woodworking machinery, including the circular saw. The 1820s saw not only the importation of many new technical methods and machines from England but the invention and patenting of scores of new woodworking machines.[5] Thonet himself was to spend the 1840s perfecting methods for bending laminated and solid wood, and by the 1850s he was massproducing 'bentwood' furniture made from solid wood in a modern factory using machinery designed and built by his own firm, Gebrüder Thonet (Thonet Brothers). C.W.

Fig.2. Bentwood chair (solid frame, laminated back inset), this version made by Gebrüder Thonet c.1866 (V&A Museum No. W.6-1969)

1. G. Himmelheber, *Biedermeier Furniture* (London: Faber & Faber, 1974).

2. Illustrated in *Michael Thonet, der Erfinder und Begrunder der Bugholzmobel-Industrie* (Brunn: np, nd [1926]), pl.I, which draws its text almost entirely from *Michael Thonet. Ein Gedenkblatt aus Anlass der hundertsten Wiederkehr seines Geburtstages* (Vienna: privately printed, 1896).

3. See C. Wilk, *Thonet: 150 Years of Furniture* (Woodbury, NY: Barron's, 1980) and D. Ostergard (ed.), *Bent Wood and Metal Furniture 1850–1946* (Seattle/New York: University of Washington Press/AFA, 1987).

4. *Michael Thonet*, op. cit., p.14.

5. Himmelheber, op. cit., p.93.

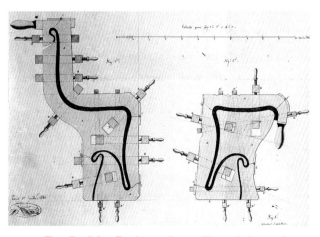

Fig.3. Detail from French patent (brevet d'invention), granted 16 November 1841 (Photo courtesy A. von Vegesack)

Armoire (Bookcase)

British (London): 1851

Designed by A.W.N. Pugin (1812–52).
Made by J.G. Crace (1809–89), London.
Oak, with carved decoration and painted
shields and brass panels and handles

H: 243 cm; W: 303 cm; D: 61 cm
Museum No. 25-1852
Purchased by the Board of Trade for the
Museum of Manufactures from the Great
Exhibition of 1851

Fig.1. The Medieval Court, lithograph by L. Haghe from Dickinson's Comprehensive Pictures of the Great
Exhibition *(London, 1854), vol.II, pl. XII*

This cabinet was the first piece of British furniture chosen for the Museum of Manufactures, the ancestor of the Victoria & Albert Museum.[1] It was designed in 1850 for the Medieval Court of the Great Exhibition by A.W.N. Pugin. He was a prolific architect and designer, and the most influential figure of the Gothic Revival.

Pugin took full advantage of the opportunity offered by the Exhibition to propagandize for Gothic as the only true Christian style and organized the display in the Medieval Court as well as designing all the contents (fig.1). He and the manufacturers of his designs, J.G. Crace, John Hardman (1812–67), Herbert Minton (1793–1858) and George Myers (1804–75), arranged a joint display of furniture, textiles, metalwork, ceramics, wood carvings and sculpture in the Gothic Revival style. The Medieval Court was most unusual in that it was not organized like the rest of the Exhibition, by type of manufacture or by country, but instead by style. It clearly influenced the Medieval Court in the International Exhibition held in London in 1862.

Pugin's successful achievement can be judged by the number of complimentary reviews not only of the Court but also of this particular cabinet, which was placed amongst a group of domestic furniture.[2] The cabinet did not receive a medal, probably because Crace, in whose name it was exhibited, was one of the jurors for Class XXVI (Furniture): his exhibits were therefore ineligible for judging. However it was recognized as 'one of the most important pieces of furniture in the Medieval Court'.[3]

Described by Pugin as an *armoire* and based on the most elaborate examples of medieval carved furniture, the cabinet commemorates his expert knowledge of Gothic form and detail. The sensitive placing of the carved panels within the structure and the design of the brasswork were significant factors in the choice of the cabinet for the Museum of Manufactures at Marlborough House in 1851. It was described in the catalogue as 'Remarkable as a piece of furniture in which the construction has been carefully considered, and the decoration confined to the

enrichment of the necessary spaces and framing in the true style of the old work...'.[4]

Pugin's long and fruitful association with Crace, whose firm made most of Pugin's furniture, is commemorated in the painted decoration of the shields. Pugin wrote to Crace:

> The shields on the bookcase refer to you. 1. The 2 with initials 2. The plummet which is an emblem of uprightness – the principle on which you conduct your business – the flourishing state of which is shown by the flowers. 3. The compass shows that you keep within estimates. The flourishing result of which is also exemplified by floriated work. We could not put any heraldry on them till we know who is the fortunate possessor & this will look very rich & well.[5]

By 1933 official appreciation of the Gothic Revival was at its lowest and Oliver Brackett, then Keeper of the Department of Woodwork, was considering the disposal of the cabinet from the V&A. Saved by use as an office bookcase at Bethnal Green Museum, the cabinet's importance was acknowledged by its inclusion in the exhibition of Victorian and Edwardian Decorative Arts, held at the V&A in 1952, and the first major public assessment of nineteenth-century decorative art. F.C.

1. The Purchase Committee, consisting of Pugin, Henry Cole, Owen Jones, Richard Redgrave and J.R. Herbert, spent £5,000 on 244 objects for the Museum (then in Marlborough House) which were listed in *Department of Practical Art: A Catalogue of the Articles of Ornamental Art selected from the Exhibition of the Works of Industry of all Nations in 1851 and Purchased by the Government* (London: Chapman and Hall, nd [1852?]). This cabinet cost £154.

2. A plan of the Medieval Court in *The Journal of Design*, vol.V (1851), p.37, indicates that the display was divided into Ecclesiastical Furniture on the east side and Domestic Furniture on the west.

3. *Art Journal Illustrated Catalogue of the 1851 Exhibition* (London: G.Vertue, 1851), p.318, illus.

4. *Department of Practical Art*, op. cit., p.48.

5. Letter from Pugin to J.G. Crace, April 1851, Crace MSS, PUG 8/27, RIBA, London.

Table

French (Paris): 1855

Made by the firm of Edouard Kreisser (active 1843–63), Paris. Marquetry of tulipwood and other woods on a carcase of oak; porcelain plaques; mounts in gilded and silvered bronze. The plaques carry the monogram 'VA' for Queen Victoria and Prince Albert and the royal arms. Signed in marquetry: 'E. Kreisser/à Paris. 52 Rue Basse du Rempart. Exposition Universelle/de Paris 1855.'

H: 83 cm; W: 119 cm; D: 61.2 cm
Museum No. W.9-1964
Presented by Mr George Farrow, Farnborough Park, Kent

Fig.1. Detail of the top

Fig.2. Detail of the signature in the marquetry

1. Philadelphia Museum of Art, *Art in France under Napoleon III* (Philadelphia: Philadelphia Museum of Art, 1978), p.75.

2. G. de Bellaigue, *The James A. de Rothschild Collection at Waddesdon Manor, Furniture, Clocks and Gilt Bronzes*, II (Freiburg: Office du Livre, 1974), no.106.

3. D. Ledoux-Lebas, *Les Ebénistes du XIXe Siècle, 1795–1889, Leurs Oeuvres et Leurs Marques* (Paris: Editions de l'Amateur, 1989), pp.395–6.

4. G. de Bellaigue, 'Queen Victoria Buys French in 1855', *Antique Collector* (April 1975), pp.37–41.

5. Ibid., fig.6.

The Exposition Universelle of 1855 in Paris was France's answer to the British success of the Great Exhibition in 1851. Naturally the French cabinet-makers wanted to show the extent of their skill and artistry. The fine workmanship shown in this table, and particularly in the marquetry of the top (fig.1), echoed the finest work produced under the guild-system which had prevailed before the Revolution, in style as much as in technique.

Just as Napoleon Bonaparte had used the Empire style as a way of affirming his political importance, so the restoration of the monarchy encouraged revival styles which celebrated the powerful role played by the Bourbon court in the artistic life of France in the eighteenth century. By the 1840s conventions had arisen whereby the furniture of certain periods was deemed suitable for certain rooms. Whereas the styles of Louis XIII and Louis XIV, in carved oak or boulle marquetry (pp.74, 78), were considered suitable for dining rooms or libraries, for the more feminine rooms of the house, the *salons*, bedrooms and boudoirs, the later styles of Louis XV or XVI were favoured.[1] Far from rejecting these royalist references, the Empress Eugénie cherished a particular sentimental idealization of Queen Marie Antoinette and the arts which had flourished about her court.

The Empress bought furniture which had belonged to Marie Antoinette herself but was also pleased to commission rooms and furniture in Revival style. The growing collectors' market of the mid-century would have supplied many models to stimulate invention. The ambition of the marquetry and of the two-coloured metal mounts on this table are reminiscent of the works of Adam Weisweiler (1744–1820, master from 1778) and Jean-Henri Riesener (1734–1806, master from 1768), both of whom supplied furniture for Marie Antoinette.[2]

Edouard Kreisser, maker of this table (fig.2), worked at various addresses in Paris between 1843 and 1863. During the reign of Louis-Philippe he had been cabinet-maker to the Queen and the Princes. His workshops produced decorated porcelain plaques and gilt-bronze, as well as cabinet-work (both manufactures and restoration). He also kept a shop which sold furniture, clocks and decorative furnishings, Sèvres and Meissen porcelain and oriental porcelain.[3] Despite an obviously flourishing trade, almost no pieces by him are known, except those made for the 1855 exhibition.

In that year Queen Victoria made a celebrated state visit to France to cement good relations with the new Emperor. She made three visits to the Exposition, but it was not until her return to London that she ordered this table and a cabinet by the same maker (fig.3).

The table was given by the Queen to Prince Albert as a Christmas present in 1855 and the cabinet on his birthday in August 1856.[4] Almost certainly these pieces are the ones paid for on a bill dated 19 June 1856 from Kreisser. The table cost 2,500 francs and the packing of it 30 francs. In the 1870s and 1880s the two pieces were used together in Osborne House, Isle of Wight, but it is not known when this table left the royal collections.[5] S.M.

Fig.3. Cabinet by Kreisser, also bought by Queen Victoria from the 1855 exhibition. Kensington Palace (The Royal Collection, copyright Her Majesty the Queen)

Cabinet

British (London): 1858

Designed by William Burges (1827–81).
Made by Harland and Fisher, London.
Painted by E.J. Poynter (1836–1919).
Commissioned by H.G. Yatman, possibly for his London house, 41 Welbeck Street. Pine and mahogany, painted, stencilled and gilded, with metal leaf, lock and hinges of iron.
Inscribed: 'HERBERT GEO. YATMAN CAUSED ME TO BE MADE/IN THE YEAR OF OUR LORD MDCCCLVIII'
H: 234 cm; W: 133 cm; D: 37 cm
Museum No. Circ. 217-1961
Given by Lt Col. P.H.W. Russell, Haslemere, Surrey

William Burges was one of the most distinguished architects of the nineteenth century, who designed not only furniture but also metalwork, stained glass and interior decoration.[1] A prominent enthusiast for the Middle Ages, he gained detailed knowledge of medieval forms, construction methods and decorative techniques which he then incorporated into his furniture.[2] This knowledge was acquired through his examination of surviving examples of English and continental furniture and woodwork, including the Coronation Chair of King Edward I in Westminster Abbey, and his study of medieval and contemporary publications.

This cabinet was commissioned, with two smaller side cabinets, by H.G. Yatman, an important patron for whom Burges designed other examples of painted furniture in 1858.[3] By 1862, when Burges helped to arrange the Medieval Court in the London International Exhibition, eighteen pieces of painted furniture were on display, including the 'Yatman Cabinet' and the 'St George's Cabinet', painted by William Morris (p.158). However the Burges pieces, unlike those by Morris, are worked out so that the painted decoration is carefully framed within the structure. Morris's early enthusiasm for medieval painted furniture did not survive after the 1860s; Burges, on the other hand, continued to design such pieces until his death.[4]

Reminiscent of a building with a steeply pitched roof, tall chimneys and dormer windows, the cabinet was inspired by the famous medieval painted cabinet then in Noyon Cathedral, France, which Burges had seen in 1853. The carcase is completely covered with painted decoration so that none of the timber is exposed, a method also originally used in medieval pieces, surviving examples of which have now been stripped. Another medieval technique found by Burges in the eleventh-century manuscript of the monk Theophilus, a layer of metal leaf covered with transparent paint, is used on the roof.

Furniture designed by Burges (fig.1) is distinguished by the careful iconographic painted decoration he devised as appropriate for the function of the piece.[5] Intended for use as a desk, the Yatman cabinet is fitted with a writing flap and pigeon holes and decorated with Classical and medieval scenes representing Literature, the Alphabet and Printing.[6] On either side the cupboard doors are painted with medallion heads of Pericles and his teacher, the philosopher Anaxagoras, on the outside and portrait heads of Burges himself (fig.2) and E.J. Poynter on the inside. F.C.

1. See J. Mordaunt Crook, *William Burges and the High Victorian Dream* (London: John Murray, 1981).

2. He published his theories, with particular mention of the decorative techniques, including painting and gilding, used for medieval furniture, in his book *Art Applied to Industry* (Oxford/London: John Henry and James Parker, 1865), pp.69–82.

3. These innovative examples of medieval painted furniture were exhibited at the Architectural Exhibition in 1859 and established Burges's reputation.

4. Burges's development as a furniture designer was discussed by his friend, E.W. Godwin, in his article, 'The Home of an English Architect', *The Art Journal*, vol.48 (1886), pp.301–05.

5. Including a sideboard depicting the Battle between the Wines and the Beers, acquired from the 1862 Exhibition by the South Kensington Museum (V&A, Museum No. 8042-1862).

6. The dormer windows contain calendars for the days of the week and days of the month. The painted decoration includes scenes representing the story of Cadmus, who introduced the alphabet to Greece.

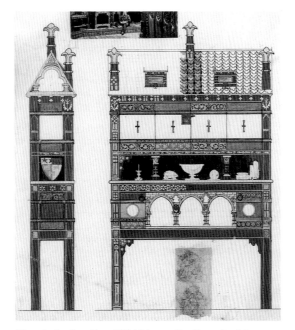

Fig.1. Design for cabinet (V&A Museum No. Circ.216-1961)

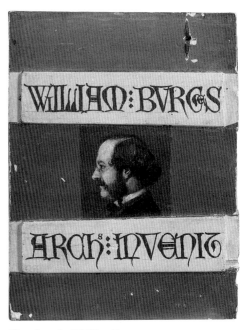

Fig.2. Portrait of William Burges

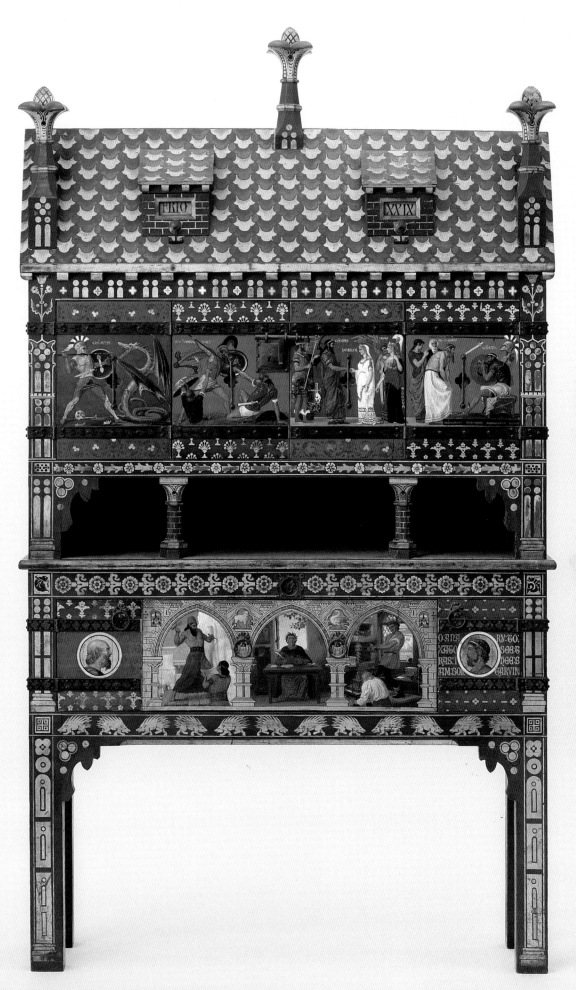

Sofa

American (New York): circa 1856

Designed by John Henry Belter (1804–63) and made by J.H. Belter and Company, New York. At one time part of the furnishings of New Hall, Sutton Coldfield, near Birmingham.
Laminated and carved rosewood, chestnut (?) or oak strengthening blocks, varnished; upholstery not original
H: 148.6 cm; W: 232.4 cm; D: 114.9 cm
Museum No. W.22-1983
Purchased from Richard and Eileen Dubrow Antiques, Bayside, New York

This robust and dynamic example of the American Rococo Revival style is exceptional not merely for the quality and profusion of its carving, but equally for the technological innovation that it represents. The very tall cresting of the sofa was made not from solid pieces of carved wood (in the traditional manner) but from seven large sheets of veneer which were glued together to form a curving plywood back, approximately 2 cm thick (fig.1). The cresting stops just below the upholstery line; below this the back is composed of solid uprights upholstered at the front and backed with fabric. The carved ornament of the cresting was, in part, cut (or 'pierced') through the plywood back; in addition, solid wood blocks were applied directly onto this (fig.2) and additional flowers, acanthus leaves, grapes and scrolls carved from the blocks to complete the designs. Although Belter's use of laminated wood was unusual, his methods for applying and carving solid wood, and for supporting the back, were typical of heavily ornamented furniture of the period. The seat rail, on which the back rests, and the feet which extend from it, are all carved from solid wood. It should be noted that Belter made chairs, the backs of which were made entirely of laminated wood.[1]

Belter's use of plywood must have been motivated by a desire to simplify the difficult process of making such large pieces of furniture from solid wood, to save money on the use of expensive rosewood (the wood that he favoured), and to manufacture stronger and lighter furniture than was possible with solid wood. It is unlikely, however, that he could ever have envisaged using the technique to make inexpensive furniture in the Rococo style. Despite the use of plywood, this sofa must have been very expensive and it was to the upper end of the market that Belter catered.

Although Belter was but one of a number of makers of extravagant Rococo Revival furniture, some of whom also eventually used plywood, a cabinet-maker in a competitor's firm later recalled that 'heavy, over-decorated parlour suits with round perforated backs [were] generally known as "Belter Furniture" from the original inventor…'.[2]

While some competitors made furniture which bore a closer resemblance to eighteenth-century French Rococo models, Belter's approach was freer; his was a less antiquarian, more inventive revivalism. He drew not only on contemporary French furniture – described at the time as 'stand[ing] much higher in general estimation in this country than any other'[3] – which he would have known from journals such as the *Le Garde-Meuble*, but also on furniture from his native Germany as published in magazines such as *Journal für Möbelschreiner und Tapeziner*.

Born Johann Heinrich Belter in Germany (the exact place is the subject of debate), Belter emigrated to the United States about 1833.[4] He was thus part of the wave of German emigration which swelled in the succeeding decades and which provided America with scores of its most distinguished furniture designers and makers including Gustav and Christian Herter, George Hunzinger (see p.170), Daniel Pabst and Anthony Kimbel. By convention Belter would probably have attained the status of master cabinet-maker before leaving Germany. He set up his own workshop in New York City by 1844 and in 1850 built an architect-designed factory for his firm. Between 1847 and 1860 he received four patents covering machinery and processes for making his furniture.   C.W.

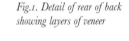

Fig.1. Detail of rear of back showing layers of veneer

Fig.2. Detail of top of back showing applied solid blocks of wood, carved in place, and de-laminating of veneer

1. See M.D. Schwartz, E.J. Stanek and D.K. True, *The Furniture of John Henry Belter and the Rococo Revival* (New York: E.P. Dutton, 1981).

2. Ernest Hagen quoted in E. Ingerman, 'Personal Experiences of an old New York cabinetmaker', *Antiques*, vol.84 (November 1963), p.578.

3. A.J. Downing, *The Architecture of Country Houses* (New York: Appleton, 1850), p.432, quoted in, Schwartz *et al.*, op. cit., p.30. Downing, p.410, also referred to the 'mania…for French furniture and decorations'.

4. Schwartz, op. cit., p.24, writes that he was born in Ulm and arrived in the United States in 1840; however, no documentation is offered. E. and R. Dubrow, *American Furniture of the 19th Century* (Exton, Pennsylvania: Schiffer, 1983), p.15, reproduce his passport, valid for a specific trip to America for one year, which is said to be dated 5 September 1833, and which states that he was born in Hitler, Iburg (Hannover).

Cabinet

British (London): 1861–2

Designed by Philip Webb (1831–1915). Painted by
William Morris (1834–96). Exhibited by Morris,
Marshall, Faulkner & Co. at the London International Exhibition, 1862. Mahogany, oak and
pine, painted and gilded, with copper handles

H: 95.9 cm; W: 177.77 cm; D: 43.2 cm
Museum No. 341-1906
Purchased from Christie, Manson and Woods, London

William Morris, one of the giants of the nineteenth century, designed very little furniture. This cabinet was actually designed by his lifelong friend and collaborator, Philip
Webb, and painted by Morris, whose drawings for the
panels, depicting the legend of St George and the Dragon,
survive (fig.1). The cabinet is a rare example of Morris's
painted work and typical of the large pieces of furniture,
medieval in form and crude in construction, associated
with Morris and his circle from 1858. It was exhibited at
the International Exhibition in London in 1862, priced
at £50, by the firm Morris established with friends and
which he subsequently owned.[1]

The theme of St George's cabinet, an act of heroism by
England's patron saint, epitomizes Morris's youthful enthusiasm for medieval romance and literature.[2] Family
and friends were used as models in the work of Morris and
his friends, Edward Burne-Jones and Dante Gabriel Rossetti – Morris's wife, Janey, was the model for the Princess
depicted here. Morris's travels in Northern France with
Burne-Jones in 1855–6 may have prompted the city background of the right-hand panel. May Morris, his daughter,
perfectly described such an effect: 'we are looking through
a peep-hole at a medieval town'.[3]

*Fig.1. St George and the
Princess, pen and ink drawing
by William Morris (V&A
Museum No. E.2789-1927)*

Both the cabinet and another early painted piece on
which Morris, Burne-Jones and Webb collaborated, 'The
Prioress's Wardrobe' (Ashmolean Museum, Oxford), illustrate the same lack of co-ordination between physical
structure and painted decoration. In this cabinet the five
scenes of the story of St George's rescue of the Princess
from the Dragon are divided unequally between three
doors. Contemporary criticism of the design concentrated
on this immature, idealistic view of medieval painted
furniture. *The Building News* commented that 'This studied
affectation of truthfulness, in placing ironwork in the
middle of a picture, is one of the many sins which have to
be purged from the Mediaevalists.'[4]

The decoration of the interior is, however, a startling
reminder of Morris's early interest in pattern design, a skill
he was to develop with great expertise in his wallpapers
and textiles. The decorative motifs (fig.2), particularly the
flowers, possibly daisies, and the abstract form of the
copper handles, derive from a variety of sources, possibly
a combination of oriental and medieval. The technique
Morris used, layers of tinted varnish on a ground of silver
leaf, was a medieval method revived by William Burges
and used on his 'Yatman Cabinet' of 1858 (p.154).

Philip Webb, who charged £1 10s for the design of the
cabinet, was responsible for the furniture produced by
Morris, Marshall, Faulkner & Co., and until his retirement
in 1890, by its successor, Morris & Co.[5] Morris, however,
retained overall control of all the firm's products. Webb's
stand incorporates columnar legs with castellated bases,
like a table he designed for Edward and Georgiana Burne-
Jones (V&A Museum No. w.45-1926), and similar stands
were still available in the Morris & Co. catalogue about
1910.[6] F.C.

Fig.2. Detail of the interior of the central cupboard

1. D.G. Rossetti, an
important early influence
on Morris and a partner in
the firm, enthused about the
cabinet in January 1862. See
O. Doughty and J.R. Wahl
(ed.), *Letters of D.G. Rossetti*
(Oxford: Clarendon Press,
1965), p.436.

2. J. Banham and J. Harris
(eds), *William Morris and the
Middle Ages* (Manchester:
Manchester University
Press, 1984).

3. M. Morris, *William Morris:
Artist Writer Socialist* (Oxford:
Basil Blackwell, 1936), p.33.

4. 9 August 1861, p.99.
Particular criticism was also
directed at the poor quality
of the drawings.

5. However the firm became
identified with ebonized
furniture, reflecting vernacular pieces of the seventeenth
and eighteenth centuries,
rather than the medieval
painted furniture of the
1860s.

6. The cabinet did not sell
in 1862. It was subsequently
owned by Lawrence Hodson
of Compton Hall, Wolver-
hampton, a client of Morris
& Co. in the 1890s.

Bookcase and Writing-table

British (London): 1861

Designed by Richard Norman Shaw (1831–1912).
Made by James Forsyth (1827–1910), London.
Metalwork by James Leaver, Maidenhead.
Oak, inlaid with satinwood, rosewood, walnut,
bird's-eye maple, and oak; partially painted; with
steel hinges

H: 280.8 cm; W: 142.0 cm; D: 78.7 cm
Museum No. Circ.96-1963
Purchased from Sotheby & Co., London

This stunning example of Gothic Revival woodwork was Shaw's earliest and most idiosyncratic example of furniture design. Intended for his own use, it was the climax of his architectural apprenticeship with G.E. Street (1814–81) and probably reflects the influence of that prominent and experienced architect who specialized in ecclesiastical commissions.[1] Made by Shaw's friend James Forsyth, an ecclesiastical sculptor and carver, and presumably intended for Shaw's architectural office, the bookcase was originally described as a bookcase and writing-table in the catalogue of the Architectural Exhibition in 1861. The piece incorporates bookshelves, cupboards with pigeon holes, and a writing surface which pulls out below the tier of drawers.

Shown by Forsyth at the Architectural Exhibition of 1861, it was selected for illustration by *The Builder* (fig.1). The journal praised the construction of the metalwork, particularly the lock (fig.2), and approvingly announced that Shaw was 'thoroughly embued with the Mediaeval spirit'.[2] However, the strongly architectural appearance of the bookcase, possibly influenced by the work of William Burges (1827–8) (a fellow exhibitor at the Architectural Exhibitions), did not receive universal approval; a highly critical letter in *The Builder* pointed out that the design was derived from medieval architecture in stone and therefore unsuitable for a piece of wooden furniture.[3]

The influence of Burges's 'Yatman Cabinet' (p.154), first exhibited at the Architectural Exhibition of 1859, is demonstrated by the use of the same decorative technique employed on the roof of Shaw's bookcase. This involved covering the wood with tin foil and then applying layers of tinted varnish.[4] Appropriately, Shaw's piece was also shown in the Medieval Court, arranged by Burges, at the London International Exhibition of 1862, where it was praised as a fine example of a thirteenth-century bookcase.[5]

Forsyth's experience of ecclesiastical woodwork and its construction was used to the full with the combination of exposed dowels, blind arches, gouged quatrefoils and other decorative details. The introduction of painted and

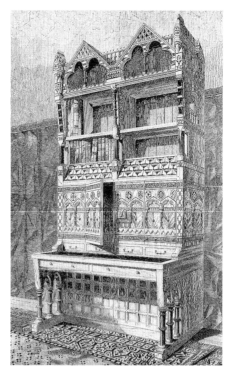

Fig.1. 'Writing-table and Bookcase' (The Builder)

Fig.3. Detail of side of the bookcase

inlaid woodwork instead of more conventional carving reflected contemporary interest among architects and designers in the revival of medieval techniques, promoted by Pugin and Burges, and their relationship with Japanese ornament, such as that used on the sloping sections below the shelves. Originally the woodwork was rubbed with oil, while the inlay of satinwood, rosewood, walnut, bird's-eye maple, and oak, was intended to be highly polished.

Shaw's bookcase, like other Gothic Revival furniture of the 1850s and 1860s designed by architects involved in church commissions, incorporates such features as stumpy columns and geometric inlay (fig.3) derived from ecclesiastical sources. This Reformed Gothic furniture, as it became known, was popularized by influential publications including Charles Eastlake's *Hints on Household Taste* (London 1868) and by successful commercial designers, such as B.J. Talbert (1838–81). Simplified versions of Reformed Gothic furniture were produced, in response to popular demand, in the 1860s and 1870s by fashionable cabinet-making firms, including Holland and Co. F.C.

1. Shaw eventually gave the object to his daughter's convent, the Sisters of Bethany, London, who, following discussions with the V&A, consigned it to Sothebys.

2. *The Builder* (20 April 1861), pp.267, 269.

3. Letter from Alphonse Warington, *The Builder* (27 April 1861), p.290.

4. Burges probably used R. Hendrie's translation of a medieval manuscript, *An Essay upon various arts,… by Theophilus…of the eleventh century* (London, 1847).

5. *Cassell's Illustrated Family Paper Exhibitor* (28 June 1862), p.44.

Fig.2. Detail of lock

Cabinet on Stand

French (Paris): 1861–7

Made by the firm of Henri-Auguste Fourdinois
(1830–1907) to designs by Hilaire and Pasti
(figures) and Néviller (arabesque ornaments) for
exhibition at the Exposition Universelle, Paris,
1867. Ebony, partly veneered on oak, with inlay
and carved decoration in box, lime, holly, pear,
walnut, mahogany and hardstones.
Inlaid inscription on lower tier: 'ANNO HENRI
FOURDINOIS 1867'

H: 249 cm; W: 155 cm; D: 52 cm
Museum No. 721-1869
Purchased from the firm of Fourdinois, Paris

When first exhibited at the Exposition Universelle in Paris
in 1867 this cabinet was hailed in several publications
as the masterpiece of the exhibition.[1] The manufacturer,
Henri-Auguste Fourdinois,[2] was granted the Grand Prix.
So impressed were the authorities of the South Kensington Museum (predecessor of the V&A) that they paid the
huge sum of £2,750 for it, far more than they would have
spent at the time on any piece of historic furniture.

What attracted them was its craftsmanship, the combined work of a thoroughly educated designer and of
skilled craftsmen. Henri-Auguste's father, Alexandre-
George, had built up a considerable cabinet-making
business from 1835, with both royal and imperial patrons
under different regimes. His son joined the firm in 1860
and took over its direction in 1867. He had studied with
Jacques-Félix Duban (1797–1870), architect of the restoration of the Louvre, and had also worked with the Parisian bronze manufacturer Victor Paillard; two years of his
training had been spent in London working for the French
goldsmith Jean-Valentin Morel.[3]

Historic revivals had fuelled design throughout Europe
from the 1820s. At the 1855 Paris Exposition the firm
showed a carved walnut cabinet, which was also acquired
by the South Kensington Museum (fig.1). In 1867 they
showed a second cabinet in the style of the sixteenth century, also in carved walnut. The Committee charged with
purchasing for the V&A actually preferred that cabinet
but purchased the ebony one 'on account of the profuse
and highly finished character of the ornamentation, which
would furnish innumerable details and motives of further
use to an art workman than the specimen of purer outline'.[4]

This ebony cabinet derives from late sixteenth-century
French forms, articulated by the columns and panels
which divide the façade according to architectural conventions, the forerunners of the cabinets on stands which
were to become the most elaborate form of parade furniture throughout seventeenth-century Europe (p.58).

*Fig.1. Carved walnut cabinet shown by Fourdinois at the 1855 Paris
Exposition (V&A Museum No. 2692-1856)*

As on many early cabinets the decoration of this
follows a comprehensive iconographic programme, with
Minerva, the goddess of Wisdom, presiding over Peace,
Painting, Architecture and the four quarters of the globe.
The figures were designed by Hilaire and Pasti and the
arabesques were designed by Néviller,[5] these artists so far
unidentified, though it is known that Néviller was a col-
league of Fourdinois in the London workshops of Morel.[6]

The Fourdinois firm was particularly known for its
technical sophistication and above all for fine carving.
Indeed, until 1848 Alexandre-Georges worked with the
specialist carver Jules-Auguste Fossey (1806–58).[7] The
craftsmen on which Henri-Auguste might call to execute
his designs were highly skilled, well able to experiment
with his new technique, *marqueterie en plein*. Instead of
applying fine carved detail to the surface of the piece, the
lighter-coloured woods were inlaid into the ebony ground
to a depth of about 9 mm and through the entire thickness
of certain sections. The technique held the inlay firmly
and prevented movement. Fourdinois created two
samples to illustrate the method, and these
have always remained with the cabinet, one (fig.2) showing half as
first inlaid (the effect
very block-like
and crude)
and half
with the inlay
as finished by the
carver. S.M.

1. In Britain the chief
accounts of the cabinet wer
in: *The Illustrated Catalogue
of the Universal Exhibition.
Published with the Art Journal*
(London, August 1868),
p.141, illus.; *Illustrated London
News*, vol.LI (1867), p.75; an
*Reports on the Paris Universal
Exhibition* (London, 1867),
vol.II, pp.286–7.

2. D. Ledoux-Lebas, *Les
Ebénistes du XIXe Siècle, 1795-
1889. Leurs Oeuvres et Leurs
Marques* (Paris: Editions de
l'Amateur, 1985), pp.203–08

3. *The Second Empire,
1852–1870. Art in France under
Napoleon III* (Philadelphia:
Philadelphia Museum of Ar
1978), p.104.

4. V&A Archive, Ed84/18.

5. J.H. Pollen, *Ancient and
Modern Furniture and Woodwor*
(London: Chapman and
Hall, 1874), pp.61–4.

6. *The Second Empire*, op. cit.
p.104.

7. Ledoux-Lebas, op. cit.,
p.201.

*Fig.2. Sample panel
showing the technique of*
marqueterie en plein
*(V&A Museum No.
721:2-1869)*

Cabinet

British (London): 1867

Designed by Mr Crosse. Made by Wright and Mansfield, London. Exhibited at the Exposition Universelle, Paris, 1867. Satinwood with marquetry in various woods, giltwood mounts, and Wedgwood plaques; carcase of satinwood

H: 337 cm; W: 235 cm; D: 61.5 cm
Museum No. 548-1868
Purchased from Wright and Mansfield, London

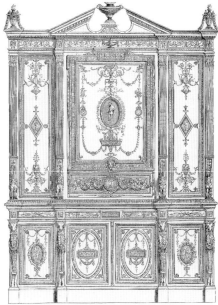

Fig.1. The cabinet as shown in 1867, The Art-Journal Illustrated Catalogue of the Paris Universal Exhibition *(London and New York: Vertue and Company, 1868), p.281*

Fig.2. Chair, painted satinwood, bought from Wright and Mansfield's sale in 1886 (V&A Museum No. 240-1887)

Reproductions and revivals in furniture have generally been poorly regarded in the twentieth century, regardless of the quality of the pieces. Nineteenth-century thinking was very different. Historical styles were widely copied and seen as inspiration for new designs. This cabinet, an elegant essay in the style of Robert Adam (1728–92), was designed by a Mr Crosse, about whom nothing is known, for display at the Paris Exposition Universelle of 1867 (fig.1). The makers, Wright and Mansfield, specialized in furniture based on English eighteenth-century designs, a fashionable revival in the 1870s and 1880s known as the 'Adams' style'.

Inspired by the furniture and interior decoration designed by Adam, this style combined Classical motifs like ram's heads, urns, and swags with marquetry and other eighteenth-century techniques and occasionally included the use of Wedgwood plaques. Wright and Mansfield's first public display of such furniture was at the International Exhibition held in London in 1862, but did not attract much comment in contemporary periodicals.

At the 1867 exhibition Wright and Mansfield's light satinwood cabinet caused a sensation among both British and foreign critics and visitors. As J.H. Pollen commented,

> The most fashionable material, as we see it this year, seems to be ebony. Marqueterie, though exhibited in the French, Italian, Spanish, Portuguese, Austrian, American, and other sections, is generally of a deeper tone – red, brown, or gray; that of Messrs. W. and M., together with one exhibited by Mr. Crace, is on a ground of satinwood, and rich and brilliant in consequence.[1]

The Englishness of the satinwood and Neo-Classical decoration was also acknowledged by Pollen, who mentioned Wright and Mansfield's declared intention to 'avoid the production or copy of any foreign period, and to illustrate English art in every respect'.[2] Wright and Mansfield won the only gold medal awarded for British furniture at the exhibition and the cabinet, originally valued at £1,400, was bought by the Museum at a reduced price of £800.[3]

Wright and Mansfield's success in promoting furniture in the 'Adams' style' included the display of a satinwood sideboard with marquetry decoration at the Philadelphia Centennial Exposition in 1876. Furniture incorporting such materials and techniques was obviously expensive and even their wealthy country house clients were shocked at their high prices.[4] Although it is not known why the firm closed in 1886 it may have been connected with difficulties over the cost of their work.

Comments on the sale of their stock in 1886 acknowledged that the firm

> must be accounted the leaders of that pleasing fashion which has happily bought back into our houses many of the charming shapes of the renowned eighteenth century cabinet makers. The best forms of Chippendale, Heppelwhite [sic], and particularly Sheraton, have been made to live again under the renovating influence of these able manufacturers.[5]

The Museum acquired several decorative panels and pieces of furniture at Wright and Mansfield's sale so that it could show its visitors the difference between eighteenth-century furniture and nineteenth-century reproduction pieces of the highest quality (fig.2). By 1897, when Frederick Litchfield illustrated the cabinet in order to encourage contemporary manufacturers 'to do good work on the lines of the best traditions of the past', the original shallow vase in the centre of the pediment had been replaced by a taller example.[6] F.C.

1. J.H. Pollen, *Reports on the Paris Universal Exhibition*, 1867 (London: Eyre and Spottiswood for HMSO, 1868), vol.II, 'Report on Fancy Furniture' (Class 14), p.290.

2. Pollen, op. cit., p.289.

3. Furniture with Wedgwood plaques was also shown by James Lamb and J.G. Crace at the 1867 exhibition and satinwood pieces with marquetry were exhibited by Crace and L.W. Collmann.

4. I. Gow, 'Victorian Splendour at Haddo House', *Heritage Scotland*, vol.9, no.1 (Spring 1992), p.13.

5. *The Cabinet Maker & Art Furnisher*, vol.VII (1 July 1886), p.23, illus. p.14.

6. F. Litchfield, 'Descriptions and Hints to Manufacturers XIII', *The Artist*, vol.XX (1897), pp.395–6. It was he who used the term 'Adams' style'.

Screen

British (London): 1867

Designed by W.E. Nesfield (1835–88). Made by
James Forsyth (1827–1910). Given by Forsyth to
Agnes and Richard Norman Shaw (1831–1912) in
1867 as a wedding present. Ebonized wood with
gilt and fretted decoration and panels of Japanese
paper. Painted inscription: 'Richard & Agnes
Shaw AD 1867 From James Forsyth'

H: 207 cm; w (overall): 252 cm; D: 2 cm
Museum No. w.37-1972
Purchased from the Fine Art Society Ltd, London

Fig.1. Detail of one ebonized and gilded panel

The Anglo-Japanism of the 1860s is usually associated
with the spare and symmetrical furniture designed by
E.W. Godwin (p.168) but this elegant and attractive screen
of 1867 shows that others were also exploring the new
style. Designed by the architect W.E. Nesfield and made
by James Forsyth, the ecclesiastical carver and sculptor, it
was given to the architect Richard Norman Shaw and his
wife, Agnes, by Forsyth in 1867 as a wedding present. It
represents not only the long personal and professional
association between Forsyth and Nesfield but also the
friendship and architectural partnership of Nesfield and
Shaw.

The screen contains twelve panels of paper, painted in
watercolour, six on each side, which are Japanese, of the
late eighteenth or early-nineteenth century. Although it is
not possible to identify a distinct theme for the panels,
they are complementary in their common use of birds
perched on floral sprays. Such panels could have been
easily obtained from one of the specialist shops in London
which offered imported Japanese papers, prints, fans,
screens, textiles and ceramics.

Whilst screens incorporating oriental panels were not
uncommon, this example is distinguished by Nesfield's
designs for the rest of the decoration. Above the paintings
are panels of gilded and carved motifs with a band of open
fretwork on top. Below the paintings are ebonized and
gilded panels, with larger sections of open fretwork below.
Both the carved and painted decorative panels incorporate patterns and motifs based on traditional Japanese
sources such as textiles (fig.1).[1]

The dedication, Shaw's monogram, and Agnes's name
are incorporated into the two centre carved panels on
both sides of the screen. On one side the inscriptions on
the outer panels are from the Old Testament: Proverbs 31:
30–31, and the Song of Solomon 8: 7, both celebrating
the value of a good woman. On the reverse of the screen
(fig.2) the inscriptions on the two outer panels are taken
from the first two verses of Henry Longfellow's poem,
'The Builders', an appropriate choice for an architect and
for a newly married couple.

A suitable gift for Shaw, who collected blue and white
porcelain, the screen also illustrates Nesfield's ability to
combine Japanese panels with his own Anglo-Japanese
designs. He too was a collector and decorated his office
with 'a very jolly collection of Persian, Indian, Greek, and
Japanese things.'[2] The screen is also a rare example of his
furniture, little of which apparently survives. Forsyth, who
worked as a carver in stone and in wood for both Nesfield
and Shaw, is still a relatively shadowy figure but this
screen and the Gothic bookcase he made for Shaw in 1861
(p.160) illustrate the range of his carving skills.

The eclectic nature of the screen with its combination
of delicate Japanese watercolours and vigorous gilded and
ebonized woodwork is a reminder of the more decorative
aspects of Anglo-Japanism in the 1860s. F.C.

1. Many of the Japanese
motifs are identified by M.
Komanecky and V. Fabbri
Butera, *The Folding Image:
Screens by Western Artists of
the Nineteenth and Twentieth
Centuries* (New Haven: Yale
University Art Gallery,
1984), pp.122–8.

2. Letter from Simeon
Solomon, probably
September 1869,
The Swinburne Letters ed.
C.Y. Lang (New Haven:
Yale University Press,
1959), vol.2, p.33.

Fig.2. Back of the screen

Sideboard

British (London): 1867–70

Designed by E.W. Godwin (1833–86). Probably made by William Watt & Co. (1857–85), London. Mahogany, ebonized, with silver plated handles and inset panels of embossed leather paper

H: 178 cm; W: (overall) 256 cm,
(with flaps down) 162 cm; D: 87 cm
Museum No. Circ.38-1953
Purchased from Mrs E.M. Hartree, Plymouth, Devon

Fig.1. Sideboard, ebonized mahogany, c.1867, with flaps down (Bristol Museum)

This sideboard is today one of the most famous pieces of nineteenth-century furniture. Its stark geometric form and plain ebonized surfaces have appealed greatly to Modernists throughout the twentieth century.[1] The original version was designed by the architect E.W. Godwin in 1867 for himself. It epitomized the influence of Japanese art and design on British decorative art in the 1860s and 1870s (p.166). Godwin also produced designs for furniture in a wide range of styles, including Anglo-Egyptian, Greek and Gothic and Jacobean Revival.

Godwin's interest in Japanese art and culture was reflected in his interior design, decoration and furniture for his own homes. A version of the sideboard was made for his dining room in ebonized deal with no additional decoration. 'Such effect as I wanted I endeavoured to gain, as in economical building, by the mere grouping of solid and void and by a more or less broken outline'.[2] Interestingly he found deal unsuccessful, probably because of its softness, and substituted mahogany with incised gilt decoration.

The success of his buffet, as he called it, is demonstrated by the number of examples which survive (at least six ebonized versions), all different with varying numbers of legs. One, from Ellen Terry's collection (Bristol Museum), may be the example Godwin designed about 1868 for their home in Hertfordshire (fig.1).

Although the sideboard was illustrated in William Watt's trade catalogue *Art Furniture* (London, 1877) (fig.2), Godwin had designed an ebonized deal buffet in 1867–8 for the Art Furniture Company, London. Unauthorized copies of Godwin's designs were available, as mentioned in his preface to *Art Furniture* (1877) and might explain the different versions of the sideboard. He also designed furniture for other firms including Collinson and Lock, London, who employed him from 1872 for about three years.

Contemporary interest in Anglo-Japanese furniture was fostered by the display of Japanese art at the International Exhibition held in London in 1862, and by the availability of Japanese goods in London shops.[3] Although there was very little Japanese furniture in the country, the influence of other pieces of decorative art and the plethora of prints and illustrations enabled designers, makers and

their clients to appreciate Japanese design more fully. The result was the development of Art Furniture in the 1860s and 1870s, with ebonized finishes and painted or inlaid decoration reflecting not only oriental but also Classical influences. However, the overall design and structure of most commercial 'Art Furniture' relied on eighteenth-century forms rather than on Japanese sources. F.C.

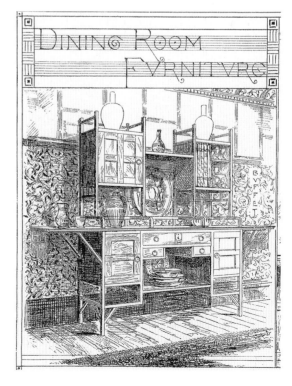

Fig.2. Dining Room Furniture, Art Furniture, 1877, plate no.6

1. Although praised for its proto-Modernism by H. Muthesius, *Das Englische Haus* (Berlin: Wasmuth, 1904–05), transl. as *The English House* (London: Crosby Lockwood Staples, 1979), p.157, the first serious assessment of Godwin's furniture was by N. Pevsner, 'Art furniture of the 1870s', *Architectural Review*, vol.CXI (1952), pp.43–50.

2. 'My chambers, and what I did to them. Chapter I. A.D. 1867', *The Architect*, vol.XVI, (1 July 1876), pp.4–5.

3. Farmer and Rogers, Oriental Warehouse, 179 Regent Street, acquired exhibits at the 1862 Exhibition dispersal sales as Godwin did himself. These sales included Japanese papers imitating leather, examples of which are incorporated into the V&A sideboard. See N.B. Wilkinson, *Edward William Godwin and Japonisme in England*, Ph.D. thesis, University of California, Los Angeles, 1987, pp.45–6, 53–4.

Chair

American (New York): circa 1876

Designed and made by George Hunzinger
(1835–98), New York. Turned and painted
maple, steel seat and back (each metal strip
covered with braided wool). Stamped on
back of rear, right leg: 'HUNZINGER/PAT
MARCH 30/1869 /N.Y./PAT APRIL 18 1876'
(lines stamped individually, first four upside
down)

H: 84.5 cm; W: 50.8 cm; D: 54 cm
Museum No. w.14-1985
Purchased from the firm of Catherine Kurland,
New York

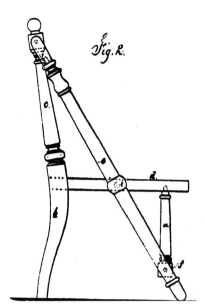
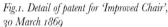
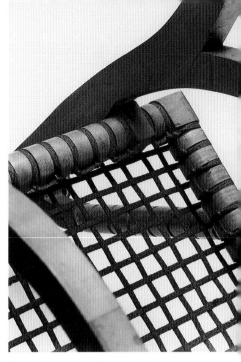

*Fig.1. Detail of patent for 'Improved Chair',
30 March 1869*

Fig.2. Detail of underside of chair

In nineteenth-century America patents were used not only
to protect original designs or the technical features of
products but, increasingly, as a selling device to signal
novelty and innovation. In 1867 George Hunzinger
advertised himself as 'Manufacturer of Patent Folding,
Reclining and Extension CHAIRS', and virtually all his
extant pieces are marked with details of his patents.[1] In
an expanding and increasingly competitive marketplace,
patents represented a way for Hunzinger and others to
distinguish their goods and to establish an identity.

This chair is covered by two patents: the first (fig.1) was
for the diagonal side braces designed to strengthen the connection of seat and back, which Hunzinger described as
the part of any chair most liable to loosening, 'particularly
the case with the more expensive character of chairs,
where there are not any side rails between the back and
front legs'.[2] Hunzinger also specifically mentioned the
tendency of men to tilt backwards while seated as a further
cause of damage to chairs.[3] The side brace, which he used
on numerous designs, performed its function admirably
and because of its length and prominence contributed
decisively to the unusual appearance of Hunzinger's chairs.

The second patent covered the use of 'wire' or flat
metal strips (fig.2) in place of cane for seats and backs,
'to insure great strength and beauty'.[4] The strips were
'covered with threads wound or braided…[and] might be
painted or varnished' so the sitter did not come into direct
contact with the metal. The patent covered the manner in
which the strips were laid into grooves cut into the seat
frame and the technique for securing the strips by means
of pins set into the underside of the frame. This ingenious
and unusual use of metal in domestic seating resulted in a
remarkably strong structure, evident from the condition of
such chairs, now more than a century old.

The unusual appearance of Hunzinger's chair derives
not only from the use of the long side brace but also from
the design of the semi-circular seat support – which can be
read as being derived from a Neo-Classical curule chair
(an early-nineteenth century version of the ancient Roman
x-frame chair) or from a rocking chair – and the manner
in which the seat is not supported by traditional legs; from
some angles it appears to be cantilevered out from the
frame. Nearly all the wood parts are turned, a method of
decoration which Hunzinger preferred 'as being ornamental, but not expensive'[5] (Hunzinger advertised his
business as 'Ornamental Furniture [and] Fancy Chairs').
The grooves in the turned surfaces were painted bright
red to contrast with the light maple and to match the seat
(which is ornamented with grey-green flecks); together,
paint and textile give the chair a polychromatic effect.

The chair looks as if it might fold or disassemble into
parts for packing; it does neither, yet the articulation of
turned elements, especially where horizontal and vertical
elements meet, gives it a distinctly mechanical appearance
that further contributes to the unusual appearance and
particular identity of Hunzinger's designs.

Hunzinger was born in Tuttlingen, Württemberg,
Germany, into a family of cabinet-makers with whom he
served his apprenticeship.[6] He worked as a journeyman in
Geneva, Switzerland, for a time and came to New York in
the 1850s during the peak period of German emigration to
America. The New York furniture-making trade was
especially dominated by Germans who, by the 1870s,
comprised more than sixty per cent of all cabinet-makers
and upholsterers.[7] Hunzinger built a large and successful
business which prospered until the 1920s.   c.w.

1. R. Roth, 'Nineteenth-
Century American Patent
Furniture', in D.A. Hanks,
Innovative Furniture in America
(New York: Horizon, 1981),
p.38.

2. United States Patent
88,297, 30 March 1869.

3. The social significance of
tilting is discussed by K.L.
Ames in *Death in the Dining
Room and Other Tales of Victorian Culture* (Philadelphia:
Temple University Press,
1992), pp.195–215.

4. United States Patent
176,314, 18 April 1876.

5. US Patent 88,297, op. cit.

6. R.W. Flint, 'Prosperity
Through Patents: the
Furniture of George
Hunzinger & Son', in
K. Ames (ed.), 'Victorian
Furniture', special issue of
Nineteenth Century, vol.8,
nos 3–4 (1982), p.119.

7. S. Nadel, *Little Germany,
Ethnicity, Religion, and Class
in New York City, 1845–80*
(Urbana: University of
Illinois Press, 1990), p.63.

Chair

British (London): 1880–83

Designed by Christopher Dresser (1834–1900). Made by Chubb & Co. for the Art Furnishers' Alliance, London. Mahogany, ebonized and gilded

H: 81.3 cm; W: 40.6 cm; D: 45.8 cm
Museum No. W.35-1992
Purchased from Mr T. Powell, Wye, Kent

Christopher Dresser was one of the most successful and prolific commercial designers of the nineteenth century. He designed not only furniture but also metalwork, textiles, wallpapers, ceramics and glass.[1] A botanist by training, he contributed the plate depicting the geometric arrangement of flowers for Owen Jones's *Grammar of Ornament* (1856), and shared Jones's appreciation of Egyptian, Greek, Gothic, Middle Eastern and Japanese ornament. His expert knowledge of Japanese culture, art and design was fostered by examples displayed at the London Exhibitions of 1851 and 1862, and by his visit to Japan in 1876. Through his publications and notably in his book, *Japan, its Architecture, Art and Art-Manufactures* (London, 1882), he became a highly influential commentator on Japanese design and its relevance to contemporary British designers and manufacturers.

Dresser's knowledge of Japanese design may have influenced this chair, in particular its very unusual combination of vertical and diagonal uprights in the back. It illustrates his belief in the minimum of carving required for good decoration and his theories about honest construction, namely the use of straight sections for chair backs and legs (fig.1).[2] His criticism of curved legs and back supports was based on the inherent weakness of the cross-grained timber necessary in this construction. However, he approved of small brackets uniting the seat to the back, as in this chair, since these added strength to the frame.

Fig.1. Back view of the chair

Typical of Dresser's furniture are the incised decoration and the ebonized finish, which he used in other pieces designed for the Art Furnishers' Alliance. His choice of mahogany, although unusual considering it was to be ebonized, may have been prompted by its inherent strength and the exotic connotations of its origin. The chair, strikingly modern in its pared-down structure and lack of ornamentation, is the simplest and yet most complicated of designs, perfectly expressing Dresser's innovative and imaginative skill as a designer.

Dresser promoted his theories about good design through many articles, notably those in *The Technical Educator*, subsequently published in his book, *Principles of Decorative Design*. As Art Editor of *The Furniture Gazette*, 1880–81, he hoped to influence commercial furniture manufacturers by illustrating his own designs, including this chair, published on 21 February 1880 (fig.2). Highly critical of the current fashion for eighteenth-century styles, particularly the Queen Anne Revival, he recommended the use of forms and decorative motifs derived from Classical sources, particularly Ancient Greece and Egypt.

His commercial enterprises included the foundation of the Art Furnishers' Alliance in 1880, to provide a range of co-ordinated artistic house furnishings, sold through a shop at 157 New Bond Street.[3] The stock combined new designs by Dresser with pieces from current ranges produced by various manufacturers. The failure of the Alliance in 1883 was probably due to the lack of commercial success of the very advanced designs that it promoted in spite of complimentary comments in periodicals. After its liquidation the remaining stock was offered for sale by Chubb, who had manufactured the furniture. Their illustrated sale catalogue included this chair, described as suitable for a drawing room or lady's boudoir, price £1 13s.[4] F.C.

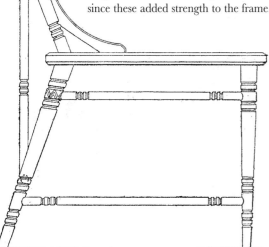

Fig.2. Design for the chair (The Furniture Gazette)

1. There is a surprisingly small number of firmly attributable surviving pieces of furniture. See W. Halén, *Christopher Dresser* (Oxford: Phaidon-Christie's, 1990).

2. In the chapter on furniture in *The Principles of Decorative Design* (London: Cassell, Petter & Galpin, 1873), Dresser discussed his theories about good design, constructional techniques, woods and decoration, with perceptive and critical comments on furniture by his contemporaries. He praised Burges's 'Yatman Cabinet' (see p.154) for its painted decoration but criticized its constructional dishonesty.

3. The opening of the shop in May 1881 received complimentary coverage in various contemporary journals, including *The Cabinet Maker*, vol.II (1 July 1881), pp.1–2, where a version of this chair is illustrated, with a slightly different arrangement of the back uprights.

4. Chubb Archive, Walton-on-Thames, Surrey. According to *The Cabinet Maker*, vol.III (1 August 1883), p.38, total sales at the Alliance amounted to £25,000 over two years. Arthur Lazenby Liberty, whose shop established in 1875 sold only oriental goods, was clearly influenced by Dresser's ideas for integral schemes of home furnishing.

Cabinet

British (London): 1878

Designed by B.J. Talbert (1838–81). Made by Jackson and Graham. Exhibited at the Exposition Universelle, Paris, 1878. Ebony inlaid with boxwood, myrtle, mother-of-pearl and ivory. Inlaid inscription 'DETUR.PUL/CHRIORI'

H: 234 cm; W: 206.5 cm; D: 54 cm
Museum No. W.18-1981
Purchased from the Fine Art Society Ltd, London

Fig.1. Detail of cabinet

The Judgement of Paris and its terrible consequence, the Trojan Wars, are commemorated in this cabinet, popularly known as the 'Juno Cabinet' when it was exhibited by Jackson and Graham in Paris in 1878. Cabinets offered plenty of scope to designers and makers for emblematic decoration, particularly when intended for display at exhibitions; other nineteenth-century examples include the 'Yatman Cabinet' (p.154) and the 'St George's Cabinet' (p.158). Both, like the 'Juno', rely on literary sources, Classical and medieval, rather than on religious iconography.

Juno is depicted in the centre of the upper tier (fig.1) below her emblem, the peacock, with Minerva on the left and Venus on the right. Peacock feathers separate the rival goddesses and panels depicting the Sea and the Earth. Venus' victory as the most beautiful of the three goddesses is commemorated below the right-hand mirrors, the centre panel is inlaid with a diadem and two rosebuds (her emblem), and the side panels have her prize, the golden apple, with the inscription meaning: Let it be given to the most beautiful.

The abduction of Helen by Paris followed by the despatch of the Greek army to Troy is probably the meaning of the ship shown below the left-hand mirror. Olives, emblematic of Minerva who supported the Greeks, are inlaid into the side panels. The rest of the inlaid decoration includes Talbert's familiar daisy-like flowers in the pediment, lilies on the doors of the cupboard and elegant geometric patterns.

Talbert's cabinet is not just a vehicle for this theme of Classical tragedy but perfectly illustrates his genius as a furniture designer in its superb proportions and balance of three-dimensional mouldings with flat pattern. His expert understanding of the possibilities of furniture design, and of luxurious materials such as ebony, ivory and mother-of-pearl, were matched by the cabinet-making skills of Jackson and Graham, renowned for their sophisticated furniture. The form of the cabinet, with its pediment, brackets, shelves and cupboards, is typical of Queen Anne Revival furniture, a fashionable style of the 1870s loosely based on early eighteenth-century architecture.

Jackson and Graham were awarded the Grand Prix d'Honneur for the British Section at the Exposition and this cabinet, probably the finest achievement of Talbert's career as a furniture designer, was bought by the Khedive of Egypt for £2,000, an enormous sum of money. As the *Cabinet Maker* pointed out in Talbert's obituary, 'This design was useful as showing the versatility of Talbert's genius, and his power to grasp Classicism with the same success as Gothic and Old English.'[1]

Talbert, a Scotsman, originally trained as a carver and then worked as an architectural draughtsman in Glasgow. He subsequently became a prolific commercial designer of metalwork, stained glass, wallpapers, textiles and carpets as well as furniture. His first publication, *Gothic Forms applied to Furniture Metalwork and Decoration for Domestic Purposes* (Birmingham: S. Birbeck/London: the author, 1867), was 'unquestionably the most successful attempt to utilize Gothic for domestic purposes which has yet been made.'[2]

As a professional furniture designer he was employed by several large businesses, notably Marsh, Jones and Cribb of Leeds, and Holland and Sons, and Gillows of London.[3] Gillows commissioned the 'Pet Sideboard' for the International Exhibition held in London in 1871 (fig.2).[4]   F.C.

Fig.2. The 'Pet Sideboard', oak with boxwood panels and metal hinges, English, 1871 (V&A Museum No. W.44-1953)

1. *The Cabinet Maker & Art Furnisher*, vol.II, no.13 (1 July 1881), p.5.

2. Ibid. His second publication, *Examples of Ancient & Modern Furniture* (London: B.T. Batsford, 1876) demonstrated changes in contemporary taste by illustrating Jacobean rather than Gothic designs.

3. Holland's exhibited various pieces of furniture designed by Talbert at the Paris Exposition of 1867.

4. Bought by the Commissioners for the 1851 Exhibition, this sideboard was lent to the South Kensington Museum from 1872 and subsequently given to the V&A.

Armchair

British (London): circa *1884*

Designed by Sir Lawrence Alma-Tadema (1836–1912). Made by Johnstone, Norman & Company, London. From a suite made for the Music Room in the house of Henry G. Marquand (1819–1902), New York. Mahogany, with cedar and ebony veneer, carving and inlay of ebony, sandalwood, ivory, boxwood and abalone. Casein label under front rail: 'JOHNSTONE, NORMAN & CO/ MANUFACTURERS/67 NEW BOND ST. LONDON'

H: 90 cm; W: 65 cm; D: 73 cm

Museum No. w.25-1980

Purchased from Haslam & Whiteway Ltd, London

Fig.1. Music Room in the Marquand residence (Metropolitan Museum of Art Archives, New York)

Sir Lawrence Alma-Tadema, who specialized in paintings of Classical subjects in appropriate Roman, Pompeian or Egyptian settings, also designed picture frames and furniture both for himself and for clients.[1] Three examples of his work are now in the V&A: this armchair, the studio seat from his house in St John's Wood (Museum No. w.3-1971) and the screen painted by Alma-Tadema and his future wife, Laura Epps, in 1870 (Museum No. w.20-1981).

The armchair was part of a suite commissioned by H.G. Marquand, a prominent collector and second President of the Metropolitan Museum of Art, New York, for the Music Room in his New York mansion (fig.1). The armchair incorporates his initials into the elaborate inlaid decoration on the back (fig.2). The suite included a grand piano, painted by Sir Edward Poynter, two piano stools, a music cabinet, small tables, settees, small chairs and a second armchair.[2] The theme of the Music Room, also designed by Alma-Tadema, was Grecian and the decoration included a ceiling painting by Sir Frederick Leighton and paintings by Whistler and Alma-Tadema.[3]

Favourable contemporary comment, both in Britain and in America, on the commission referred to the Greek style of the decoration and the exotic materials used for the furnishings.[4] This amount of publicity and the unusual display of some of the furniture in the New Bond Street shop of Johnstone, Norman & Co. in 1884 (inspected by the Prince and Princess of Wales), emphasized the importance of this commission from an American millionaire collector to an English artist and furniture manufacturer. The piano was subsequently shown in the same premises in 1887 before shipment to New York.[5]

The design of the various pieces of furniture clearly reveals Alma-Tadema's knowledge of the Classical world, based on his studies in the British Museum, on visits to Pompeii and Herculaneum, and on his extensive photographic collection of Classical antiquities and architecture. The armchair exemplifies his mastery of Graeco-Roman motifs with its elaborate carved and inlaid scrolling anthemia (flower heads) and acanthus, bell flowers, paterae (medallions) and Greek key patterns. The design of the back and legs can also be traced back to stone seats in Ancient Greece.

Alma-Tadema's personal taste for the Classical world combined with rich furnishings was well illustrated in the interiors and furnishings of his houses, Townshend House, Regent's Park, and 17 Grove End Road, St John's Wood. The studio couch, one of a pair designed for his own use, has one side decorated with Roman motifs taken from a bedstead excavated at Pompeii in 1868 whilst the other side is in the Egyptian style, enabling the artist to incorporate it successfully in several of his Classical paintings.   F.C.

Fig.2. Detail of the back of the chair

1. Alma-Tadema's importance as a popularizer of Classical civilization is discussed in the exhibition catalogue, *Sir Lawrence Alma-Tadema 1836–1912* (Sheffield: Mappin Art Gallery, 1976).

2. Despite sale at auction in 1903, some pieces, including the piano and armchairs, remained together at the Martin Beck Theatre in New York, until dispersal at Sotheby Parke-Bernet in 1980. One settee is now in the Metropolitan Museum of Art, New York; the other armchair is in the National Gallery of Victoria, Melbourne.

3. Marquand apparently chose Johnstone, Norman & Company on the recommendation of Alma-Tadema but it is not clear how he originally commissioned the artist. His new house, designed by Richard L. Hunt, also contained equally elaborate Japanese, Persian and Arabic rooms and his collections included paintings, furniture and porcelain, all sold after his death.

4. For example 'Classic Furniture for an American Mansion', *The Furniture Gazette*, vol.XXIII (1 August 1885), p.355. *The Building News* (24 July 1885), p.122, and *Cabinet Making and Upholstery* (New York: September 1885), p.104.

5. *The Building News* (27 May 1887), p.792.

Cabinet

British (London): circa 1893

Designed by George Washington Henry Jack
(1855–1932). Made by Morris & Co., London.
Mahogany with marquetry of sycamore and
other woods. Stamped: 'Morris & Co. 449
Oxford S. W. 1147'

H: 141 cm; W: 131 cm; D: 70 cm
Museum No. Circ. 40-1953
Purchased from the Trustees of the Middlemore
Estates, London

Fig.1. Detail of the interior showing the writing surface and pigeon holes

1. *The Cabinet Maker & Art Furnisher* (1 November 1889), p.114.

2. Ibid, p.115.

3. Surviving examples include one acquired for Ickworth, Suffolk, and two at Tapeley Park, Devon. Others were bought for Stanmore Hall, Middlesex, and Compton Hall, Wolverhampton. William Morris, 'The Lesser Arts of Life' (1878), published in *Architecture Industry & Wealth, Collected Papers by William Morris* (London: Longmans, Green and Co., 1902), pp.69–71.

4. The individual makers are identified in *Arts & Crafts Exhibition Society. Catalogue of the Second Exhibition* (London: Chiswick Press, 1889), no.412.

Although made by the firm owned and run by William
Morris, this cabinet is quite different from the furniture
commonly associated with him (p.158). It was first shown
at the Arts and Crafts Exhibition of 1889 where mixed
reviews included the comment that it looked like an
'exaggerated inlaid tea-caddy on a clumsy stand'.[1] Despite
this, it became quite a popular design for Morris & Co. It
was still available around 1912 in the firm's catalogue,
priced at 98 guineas for a version with decorative marquetry or at 60 guineas for plainer examples.

George Jack's design cleverly combines a modified
cabinet on stand with a fall-front and, although it is not
immediately apparent from the exterior, the cabinet is
quite functional. It is fitted with cupboards on each side
and the central panel falls down to form a writing surface
with compartments for papers above (fig.1). The shaped
top lifts up on brass quadrants to reveal a velvet lined tray,
possibly used for the display of medals or coins.

The naturalistic design of the marquetry, with its native
motifs of oak, thistle and ash on the front and stand,
contrasts with a restrained and subtle diaper pattern on
the sides and back. As was pointed out in 1889, 'If this
queer-looking thing does nothing else, it will render good
service by making apparent the possibilities of inlay and
the unrivalled beauty of Nature's own tinting in woods'.[2]

George Jack was born on Long Island, New York,
USA, of British parents and was brought to Glasgow at
the age of four. After his architectural apprenticeship in
the office of Horace K. Bromhead, he came to London in
1875 and joined Philip Webb (1831–1915) as his assistant
before 1880. Jack took over the architectural practice after
Webb's retirement in 1900.

Jack supplied furniture designs for Morris & Co. from
about 1880 and succeeded Webb as chief furniture designer from 1890. Although, like Webb, he favoured designs
derived from eighteenth-century furniture, his furniture was
less reminiscent of vernacular forms and more typical of
metropolitan designs. This, combined with his use of native
timbers and revival of marquetry, resulted in rather sophisticated and slightly fussy designs for Morris & Co. Such

pieces, like this cabinet, were clearly favoured by owners of
country houses as examples of the highest art of furniture
design, what Morris described as 'state furniture'.[3] Other
clients included Ralph Radcliffe Whitehead, founder of an
American Arts and Crafts community (fig.2).

By 1880 Jack had also begun carving in wood and subsequently taught this at the Central School of Arts and
Crafts and at the Royal College of Art. His book *Wood-
carving, Design and Workmanship* was published in 1903. Jack,
a regular exhibitor at the exhibitions of the Arts and
Crafts Exhibition Society, showed his carved chest there in
1894 (V&A Museum No. w.34-1972).

The original cabinet exhibited in 1889 was made by
George Turner, H. Green, W. Thatcher and A. Dicks.[4]
Morris & Co. took over the Pimlico furniture workshops
of Holland & Company, the large and well-established
firm of cabinet-makers, in about 1890 and the V&A's
cabinet illustrates the technical expertise and quality of
workmanship associated with experienced cabinet-makers.
The use of the firm's stamp and a serial or model number
on the edge of the fall-front is typical of large commercial
furniture making firms. The cabinet was purchased from
Melstetter House, Orkney. It was
probably acquired originally
by Thomas and Theodosia
Middlemore who commis-
sioned W.R. Lethaby (1857–
1931) to build the house in
1898–9. The Middlemores
were friends of May Morris,
daughter of William Morris,
who furnished the house
with Morris's textiles,
Georgian furniture and
several pieces designed
by Lethaby himself, in-
cluding a dresser for
the dining room (V&A
Museum No. Circ.41-
1953). F.C.

Fig.2. Cabinet secretaire designed by George Jack and made by Morris & Co., c.1889 (Philadelphia Museum of Art)

Desk

British: 1896

Designed by C.F.A. Voysey (1857–1941), for Mr and Mrs Ward-Higgs, London. Metalwork by W.B. Reynolds (1855–1935). Oak, copper hinges and fittings

H: 167.5 cm; W: 86 cm; D: 67 cm
Museum No. w.6-1953
Purchased from Mrs J. Bottard, London

Fig.1. Design for writing-desk, 1895 (V&A Museum No. E.274-1913)

The scene depicted on the pierced copper hinge plate on this desk shows a rural family group strolling through a bucolic English landscape, framed by an arrangement of heart motifs. This type of emblematic decoration demonstrates how central the ideals of home, family and England were to Voysey's architecture and domestic designs.

Voysey's furniture was often unornamented as he believed that 'Simplicity in decoration is one of the most essential qualities without which no true richness is possible. To know where to stop and what not to do is a long way on the road to being a great decorator.'[1] This restraint may go some way towards explaining why, from the 1930s, Voysey was seen as a forerunner of Modernism.[2] The asceticism of this desk should not be mistaken for plainness, however, as the construction and proportions are sophisticated. The improbably slender, chamfered legs run the full height of the desk, with the carcase suspended between them. The attenuated verticals produced by the legs are balanced by the broad horizontals of the desk-top and cornice. This severe, almost geometrical elegance is particularly apparent in Voysey's design for the desk (fig.1) in which it is stained green, with blood-red leather behind the copper panel. Neither of these coloured features was applied and the desk remained unvarnished, merely polished, as Voysey specified for much of his furniture. His concern for honesty extended beyond the surface to the construction of the furniture itself, which was not disguised by mouldings or veneers to conceal bad workmanship.

Voysey's houses were essentially enlarged and idealized cottages, principally for the well-to-do middle classes who were inspired by the Arts and Crafts Movement to seek a simple country life. This desk was, however, part of an urban commission to furnish an existing house, which Voysey undertook for William and Haydee Ward-Higgs in 1896 (fig.2). William Ward-Higgs was a successful City solicitor and the couple had advanced artistic taste. The desk was acquired by the V&A from the Ward-Higgs's daughter, and several other pieces from the house are in Cheltenham Art Gallery and Museum.[3]

Voysey was not a cabinet-maker himself, unlike his more purist Arts and Crafts contemporaries, and he employed a variety of commercial firms to produce his furniture. Although the maker of this desk has not been identified, an inscription on the design indicates that the metal fittings were undertaken by the architect and metalworker William Bainbridge Reynolds. Designs for other furniture for the Ward-Higgs's indicate they were intended to be made by the cabinet-makers F. Coote and F.C. Nielsen.

Voysey's designs were publicized by *Studio* magazine and his somewhat fey decorative style, described famously as 'only-little-me-ishness', influenced 'new art', or Art Nouveau, furniture made by firms such as Liberty around 1900.[4] In the 1930s his country houses became a model for the pseudo-vernacular architecture of inter-war suburban developments. In this at least, Voysey's belief in the importance of the Englishman's home was vindicated. G.W.

Fig.2. Haydee Ward-Higgs with furniture by C.F.A. Voysey at 23 Queensborough Terrace, Bayswater, 1908–10, photographed by W.H. Tingey (Cheltenham Art Gallery and Museums)

1. C.F.A. Voysey, 'The Aims and Conditions of the Modern Decorator', 1895 lecture quoted in E.B.S., 'Some Recent Designs by Mr C.F.A. Voysey', *Studio*, vol.VII, no.38 (May 1896), pp.209–19. The article includes an illustration of this cabinet.

2. N. Pevsner, *Pioneers of the Modern Movement: From William Morris to Walter Gropius* (London: Faber & Faber, 1936), p.146.

3. A. Carruthers and M. Greensted, *Good Citizen's Furniture; The Arts and Crafts Collections at Cheltenham* (Cheltenham and London: Art Gallery and Museums and Lund Humphries, 1994), pp.64–71. Voysey's dresser for the Ward-Higgs's is also in the V&A (Museum No. Circ.518-1963).

4. H.S. Goodhart-Rendel, 'The Victorian Home' in P. Ferriday (ed.), *Victorian Architecture* (Philadelphia and New York: J.B. Lippincott Co., 1964), p.83. Goodhart-Rendel describes Voysey's style in terms of '*mièvrerie*' which can perhaps be loosely rendered as "only-little-me-ishness". His houses were mostly very long, very low, with very small windows, very large chimneys – very artily artless altogether'.

Chair

British (Glasgow): 1898–9

Designed by Charles Rennie
Mackintosh (1868–1928), for
Miss Cranston's Argyle Street
Tea Rooms, Glasgow; this
example used in and probably
made for the Mackintosh flat,
Glasgow, 1900. Stained oak,
upholstery not original
H: 136.5 cm; W: 50.3 cm; D: 45.5 cm
Museum No. Circ.130-1958
Given by the Glasgow School of Art

This high-back chair is one of the best-
known examples of modern furniture, yet it
is also one of the most enigmatic. The details of its commission are well known but
an explanation of its appearance and design sources is not
simple.[1]

In 1896 Kate Cranston, the dynamic owner of Miss
Cranston's Tea Rooms in Mackintosh's native Glasgow,
commissioned the young designer to create murals for her
Buchanan Street Tea Room, within an interior designed
by a fellow-Glaswegian architect, George Walton.[2] Two
years later, Mackintosh was again asked to design for a
Walton interior, the new Luncheon Room for Miss Cranston's Argyle Street premises. Here, Mackintosh designed
the free-standing furniture, including chairs, benches,
settles (settees), tables and umbrella stands, as well as a
number of light fittings.

Many of Mackintosh's Argyle Street designs had their
roots in traditional furniture types – ladder-back chairs,
deep settles, wing chairs – as interpreted both by Arts and
Crafts designers and the commercial furniture trade. High-
back chairs enjoyed a vogue during the period around
1900, although it is difficult to cite any specific historical
precedent for this chair. Its attenuated and carefully con-
toured form, which clearly began as a drawing on paper
rather than on a joiner's bench, suggests the artistic and
abstract nature of much of Mackintosh's design.

To employ the word 'abstract' suggests furniture of an
exceptional nature and there can be no doubt that Mackintosh's furniture carried aesthetic and symbolic aspir-
ations and meanings more typical of painting or drawing
than furniture. As Mackintosh was not responsible for the
Argyle Street interior architecture it is possible that the
meanings were intended to be private while the ornamental qualities were shared.[3] For example, the cut-out
shape in the oval on the back (fig.1) appears to be a bird
in flight, possibly a dove, a bird with rich religious and
spiritual associations.[4] Similarly, when in use, the structure
of the chair back frames the sitter who appears to be

Fig.1. Detail of chair back

crowned by the halo-like oval. These hardly seem relevant
to a public tea room but Mackintosh's was an intensely
personal mode of design; the motifs and design of this
chair must have had particular meaning, conscious or
unconscious, to the designer. Indeed, Mackintosh used the
same chairs for his own flat, designed with his wife,
Margaret Macdonald, at 120 Mains Street in 1900; this
particular example may have come from the dining room
(fig.2).[5]

Careful shaping of the various elements of this chair is
difficult to appreciate in photographs. Although the long,
thin back splats are uniformly rectangular, nearly all the
structural elements are shaped to alter in plan and/or
section: most extraordinary are the back legs which are
rectangular in plan at the base and then curve and taper
upwards until they are circular in plan at the top. This
subtle shaping and joining of parts contributes to the
boldness, originality and beauty of this chair.[6]   C.W.

1. R. Billcliffe, *Charles Rennie
Mackintosh, the Complete
Furniture, Furniture Drawings
and Interior Designs*, 2nd
edition (London: J. Murray,
1986), pp.47–8, 260.

2. P. Kinchin, *Tea and Taste:
The Glasgow Tea Rooms,
1875–1975* (Oxford: White
Cockade, 1991), pp.91–5.

3. A. Crawford, *Charles
Rennie Mackintosh* (London:
Thames & Hudson, 1995),
p.44.

4. T. Neat, *Part Seen, Part
Imagined, Meaning and
Symbolism in the Work of
Charles Rennie Mackintosh
and Margaret Macdonald*
(Edinburgh: Cannongate,
1994), pp.156–7, in general,
a wildly speculative book.
Although recognized during
Mackintosh's lifetime (see
H. Muthesius, 'Die
Glasgower Kunstbewegung',
Dekorative Kunst, vol.9 [1902],
p.215), this aspect of
Mackintosh's work has only
recently been analysed.
See also D. Brett,
*C.R. Mackintosh: the poetics
of workmanship* (London:
Reaktion Books, 1992).

5. This chair came from the
'Set of 6 High Back Oak
Chairs' listed in the probate
inventory of Margaret
Macdonald Mackintosh
(13 February 1933). Copy
of document supplied by
Pamela Robertson,
Hunterian Art Gallery,
Glasgow.

6. A contemporary review
claimed that 'No artist owes
less to tradition than does
Mackintosh; as an originator
he is supreme'. J.E. Taylor,
'Modern Decorative Art at
Glasgow. Some Notes on
Miss Cranston's Argyle
Street Tea House', *Studio*,
vol.39 (1906), p.33.

*Fig.2. Dining room, 120
Mains Street, Glasgow
(T&R Annan & Sons)*

Table

German (Munich): 1898–9

Designed by Richard Riemerschmid (1868–1957).
Made by the Vereinigte Werkstätten für Kunst
im Handwerk GmbH, Munich.
Probably designed for the Music Room at the
Deutsche Kunstausstellung, Dresden, 1899.
Stained oak *(Wassereiche)*

H: 77 cm; W: 65 cm; D: 57 cm
Museum No. W.1-1990
Purchased from Verlag Dry, Munich

Fig.1. Music Room, German Art Exhibition, Dresden

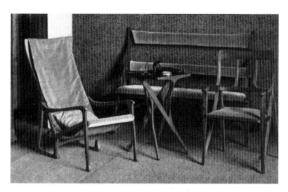

Fig.2. Detail showing slightly different version of the table

German furniture from about 1900 is neither as well
known nor as appreciated as contemporary French (p.186)
or Austrian (p.194) examples, yet German designers, especially Richard Riemerschmid, produced work as inventive and original as that in any Western country.[1]
'Jugendstil' (youth style) was the name given to the New
Art movement in Germany; it derived from the Munich
art magazine *Jugend* which, from 1896, published many
illustrations of work in that style. Munich was also Riemerschmid's native city and, like all German designers of the
period, his work was closely identified with the city in
which he worked.

This table was part of a Musiksalon (Music Room or,
more precisely, a room for 'a music loving collector' – figs
1–2), which also included Riemerschmid's best known
furniture design (fig.3).[2] The abstract form of the table,
and the sense of movement which it suggests, may have
been intended to give visual expression to some of the
qualities of music. Although the organic quality of the
design echoed more familiar, curvilinear Art Nouveau, the
use of plain oak, the simplified construction and appearance, and, especially, the thin, flat, undecorated surfaces
represented something novel; this is reflected in contemporary comments describing the 'plain, down-to-earth
effect' of the room, or the reaction that 'some people
consider the completely ornament-free furniture forms to
be ugly'.[3] Although the simplicity of Riemerschmid's work
was very much at odds with the prevailing decorative
tastes of 1898, the table was undoubtedly part of an
ensemble with a very particular ornamental intention.

In advanced German circles of the period, it was a
matter of consensus that interior furnishings were more
than decoration; an object such as this table deserved 'to
be acknowledged as a work of art, if it is marked by an
artistic individuality'.[4] This breaking down of the bound-
aries between design and art was one of the most
important and influential aspects of German design in the
period and was central to the special identity of the firm
that made and sold the table. It was typical of the period
that Riemerschmid's formal training was as a painter, and

that his first furniture designs dated only from 1895. It is
also worth noting that this table was displayed in an 'Art'
exhibition.

Riemerschmid's room was one of several designed for
group exhibitions of the Vereinigte Werkstätten für Kunst
im Handwerk (United Workshops for Art in Craft), whose
other leading members included Bruno Paul and Bern-
hard Pankok. Founded in 1897 and inspired by British
Arts and Crafts guilds and workshops (p.192), the German
company differed from its British forerunners in several important ways: it
accepted that the function of the
designer (or artist) was to give form
to objects, not to make them, and
thus craft practice was not central
to its ideology and machines were
freely accepted; it also lacked a
socialist political agenda, instead
promoting pan-German reform
of design and manufacture; and,
above all, it achieved striking
commercial success over many
decades, opening branches in
other German cities and selling
by catalogue.[5]   C.W.

1. W. Nerdinger (ed.),
Richard Riemerschmid
(Munich: Prestel Verlag,
1982), pp.142–5 on the 1898
exhibition.

2. F. Lattmann-Goslar, 'Die
Deutsche Kunst-Ausstellung
zu Dresden', *Deutsche Kunst
und Dekoration*, vol.IV (1899),
p.509.

3. P. Schultze-Naumberg,
'Die Dresdener Kunstaus-
stellung', *Dekorative Kunst*,
vol.II, no.9 (1899), p.91, and
Lattmann-Goslar, op. cit.,
p.511.

4. Ibid., p.493.

5. J. Heskett, *German Design
1870–1918* (New York:
Taplinger, 1986), pp.46–7,
93–101, and K. Hiesinger
(ed.), *Art Nouveau in Munich*
(Munich: Prestel Verlag,
1989), pp.12–15.

*Fig.3. Oak armchair desig.
for the same exhibition, the
version made by Liberty
Co., London, oak
(V&A Museum No.
Circ.859-1956)*

Cabinet
(Armoire étagère)

French (Nancy): 1900

Designed by Louis Majorelle (1859–1926)
and made by Majorelle, Nancy.
Kingwood veneer and carved kingwood,
purpleheart; marquetry panel in birch,
elm, oak, zebrano, rosewood, padouk
and other woods; carcase of oak and
mahogany (?); wrought iron mounts.
Inscribed and signed on top of shelf:
'L. Majorelle/nancy'

H: 180.3 cm; W: 68 cm; D: 23.5 cm
Museum No. 1999-1900
Given by Mr George Donaldson, London

Figs 1–2. Details of front of cabinet

In 1879 Louis Majorelle was forced by the death
of his father to abandon his studies at the École
des Beaux-Arts in Paris to return to Nancy to work in
the family business.[1] Within twenty years, he had transformed a local business devoted to retailing, decorating
and making furniture and ceramics into one of the most
important cabinet-making firms in France. The exhibition
of Majorelle furniture, including this cabinet, at the
Exposition Universelle in Paris in 1900, established Louis
Majorelle as the leading designer and maker of furniture
in the fashionable Art Nouveau style.[2]

Art Nouveau designers looked to nature rather than
historical styles as inspiration for their objects, or at least
their decoration. As this cabinet demonstrates
(figs 1–2), dynamic and stylized naturalistic forms, especially whiplash curves,
were employed not only to represent
nature but to suggest what Emile
Gallé (also from Nancy) had called,
'the life-lines … [the] muscles and
nerves' of flora and fauna.[3] Although
the vertical attenuation of this
object echoes French eighteenth-
century domestic forms
and Majorelle made
much furniture that
was recognizable as

*Fig.3. Chair by
Majorelle, 1900
(V&A Museum
No. 2001-1900)*

revivalist, this cabinet, which in its form has no direct
historic precedent, represents his attempt to develop new
furniture types.

Majorelle's design is based on contrast and tension
between the various elements of the cabinet, especially its
form and ornamentation. Its rectangular and distinctly
vertical form, emphasized by the tree motif which grows
from its base, is covered with dozens of unexpectedly
narrow bands of veneer laid horizontally. Superimposed
are the dynamic curvilinear iron fittings and the curiously
static, representational marquetry panel (a device for
which he was criticized at the time).[4] Finally, the carved
base, for all its skill, gives the impression that the slender
cabinet, with its thin carcase, crouches on the ground.

This cabinet was part of a large collection of decorative
art (fig.3) purchased at the Paris exhibition and given to the
V&A by George Donaldson. Its acquisition caused outrage
among part of the architecture and design community, a
number of whom wrote to *The Times* complaining that such
furniture was 'badly executed…a trick of design which,
developed from debased forms, has prejudicially affected
the design of furniture and buildings in neighbouring
countries…. The harm it may thus produce on our national
art cannot be easily gauged'.[5] It would be more than sixty
years before Art Nouveau came back into favour.

Despite the British reaction, the commercial rewards of
Majorelle's display at the Paris exhibition were large. In
1902 his workshop was described as 'organised…according
to the requirements of large industrial production' with
workshops devoted to 'mechanical woodworking, cabinet-
making, sculpture, marquetry, bronze work etc.'[6] The
business expanded, eventually publishing catalogues and
establishing branches in Lyon, Paris, Lille, Oran and
Algiers. C.W.

1. A. Duncan, *Louis
Majorelle, Master of Art Nouveau*
(London: Thames &
Hudson, 1991), provides
basic information on his life
and work.

2. The cabinet is improbably
called an *armoire étagère* in
Th. Lambert, *Meubles de Style
Moderne, Exposition Universelle
de 1900* (Paris: Charles
Schmid, 1900), pl.1, fig.3.
It is also illustrated as a
cabinet in 'The Victoria
and Albert Museum. Gift
of "New Art" Furniture for
Circulation', *Magazine of Art*,
vol.XXV (1901), p.468.

3. E. Gallé, 'Le Mobilier
contemporain orné d'après
la nature', *Revue des arts
décoratifs*, vol.20 (1900), p.377

4. O. Gerdell, 'Les Meubles
de Majorelle', *l'Art decoratif*,
vol.4, no.37 (October 1901),
pp.24–5.

5. *The Times* (15 July 1901),
p.12. The contoversy is
summarized in J.A.
Neiswander, 'Fantastic
Malady or Competitive
Edge', *Apollo* (November
1988), pp.310–13.

6. Gerdell, op. cit., p.24.

Dining Chair

American (Chicago): 1902

Stained oak; leather upholstery not
original. Designed by Frank Lloyd
Wright (1867–1959) for the Ward
Willits House, Highland Park, Illinois

H: 141.5 cm; W: 43.3 cm; D: 45.8 cm
Museum No. w.4-1992
Purchased from Mr Thomas S. Monaghan,
Ann Arbor, Michigan, USA, with the
assistance of the National Art Collections
Fund and the Rudolph Palumbo
Charitable Trust

Fig.2. Exterior, Ward Willits House (photo: H. Fuermann)

Guided by his philosophy of 'Organic Architecture', Frank Lloyd Wright believed in the underlying unity of all the elements of a building, its programme and site. This led him to conceive buildings in their totality and, accordingly, he designed interiors, furniture, metalwork, ceramics, stained glass, textiles, lighting and even sculpture and murals wherever possible. He fully subscribed to the notion that a building was a complete work of art requiring that each element contribute to the effect of the whole.

Furniture played a particularly important architectural role in his buildings, serving to define and organize interior space. When grouped around the dining table of the Willits House (fig.1) this chair and its five companion pieces offered not only an impressive phalanx of tall, screen-like backs but, by their arrangement, actually created a subsidiary space within the dining room. Dining was but one of many domestic rituals to which Wright sought to give unique architectural and symbolic expression, and it may well have been that he used his unusual furniture to suggest the sanctity of the ritual in the context of home and family.[1]

Although the form of this chair is severe and uncompromising it can be seen, like much of Wright's early work, as a clear expression of the Arts and Crafts Movement as transferred from Britain to America. Wright was well versed in the philosophy and aesthetics of the Arts and Crafts but he differed from some in his whole-hearted embrace of the machine which he called 'the normal tool of our civilization'.[2] While also indicating the profound influence of Japanese art and design, the simplicity and rectilinearity of this chair reflect Wright's view that wood furniture should be designed according to 'the clean cut, straight-line forms that the machine can render far better than would be possible by hand'.[3] Wright referred to the 'wonderful cutting, shaping, smoothing, and repetitive capacity' of the machine and it is precisely those characteristics which he emphasized in the Willits house chair.[4]

The extraordinarily high back and severe rectilinear form inevitably suggest contemporary European furniture, in particular the chairs designed around 1900 by Charles Rennie Mackintosh (p.182). Although the relationship, if any, between the two designers remains unclear, it is known that Wright designed his first high-backed chair in 1895 for his own house. Mackintosh's first such chair was designed in 1897.

Built in a suburb of Chicago, the Willits House (fig.2) was a large and accomplished example of what would become known as Wright's 'Prairie' house. The term referred to the emphatic horizontality of the design, inspired by the flat mid-Western landscape beyond the suburb in which the house was built. The clients became friends of Wright's and visited Japan with him in 1905. c.w.

1. N.K. Smith, *Frank Lloyd Wright, A Study in Architectural Content* (Watkins Glen, NY: American Life Foundation, 1979), pp.88.

2. F.L. Wright, 'In the Cause of Architecture', *Architectural Record* (March 1908), reprinted in B.B. Pfeiffer (ed.), *Frank Lloyd Wright Collected Writings*, vol.1 (New York: Rizzoli, 1992), p.88.

3. Ibid., p.97.

4. F.L. Wright, 'The Art and Craft of the Machine', 1901 speech reprinted in ibid., p.65.

Fig.1. Dining room, Ward Willits House (photo: H. Fuermann)

Wardrobe

British (Daneway, Gloucestershire): 1902

Designed by Ernest Barnsley (1863–1926).
Made at the Daneway House Workshops,
Gloucestershire, for the designer's home,
Upper Dorvel House, Sapperton. Oak

H: 177 cm; W: 114 cm; D: 66 cm
Museum No. W.39-1977
Purchased from Mr H.G. Fletcher, Cheltenham

Fig.1. Detail of wardrobe

The name of Ernest Barnsley forms part of the trium-virate of the most revered British Arts and Crafts furniture designer-craftsmen which also included Ernest Gimson (1864–1919) and Ernest Barnsley's younger brother, Sidney (1865–1926). The three met in about 1886 when Ernest Barnsley and Gimson were articled to the London-based ecclesiastical architect J.P. Sedding.[1] In 1887, his training completed, Ernest Barnsley left London to establish an independent architectural practice in Birmingham but in 1893 was persuaded to join his brother and Gimson and move to the Cotswolds, in Gloucestershire. There the three attempted to establish a rural community of crafts-men based on a revival of traditional crafts as advocated by William Morris, Philip Webb (p.158) and Sedding. At Ewen and later at Pinbury Park they established a work-shop where they designed and made their own furniture in addition to working on architectural projects.

While Sidney Barnsley devoted himself wholeheartedly to mastering the traditional cabinet-making skills neces-sary to make all his own furniture, Ernest Barnsley and Gimson decided to set up a workshop staffed by pro-fessional cabinet-makers, including a Dutch foreman, Peter van der Waals. This coincided with a move in 1902 to neighbouring Sapperton village where new workshops and a showroom were established at Daneway House, a typical Cotswold manor house. Nearby, Ernest Barnsley enlarged two cottages into a new home for his family, Upper Dorvel House, one of the most distinguished of Arts and Crafts houses. For the new house Ernest Barnsley built this wardrobe.

The wardrobe is an excellent example of Barnsley's simpler joined furniture. Its construction is clearly re-vealed, one might even say, celebrated: each door is com-posed of three planks, tongue-and-grooved together, and backed with narrow horizonal rails, the pegs fixing these clearly visible on the front surface of the door; the sides and back are of frame and panel construction, as are the three main horizontal elements – the flush top, a middle shelf and the base – which are joined to the wide uprights of the front with oversized, wedged, mortise-and-tenon joints (fig.1). (The topmost ones are treated as dove-tails

and are visible, as the wardrobe bears no cornice or cresting.) The material is quarter-sawn oak throughout. Solid wood only is used. Although oak was no longer the main material of every village carpenter – it had long become too expensive – it embodied the values of English-ness, simplicity and honesty which the Arts and Crafts held dear.[2] The decoration is of a type associated with everyday woodworking rather than more elaborate cabinet-making (fig.1): knife gouges create a simple, horizontal pattern enlivened by the various geometric forms of chip carving, created with a chisel.

The rustic simplicity shown in the materials and con-structional techniques of the wardrobe were but one strand of the work produced at Daneway House. Grander, highly finished furniture, made from expensive timbers and often related to historical, high-style rather than vernacular furniture, was also made, although such pieces are most associated with Gimson (fig.2) and Sidney Barnsley.

The rural idyll of Gimson and the Barns-leys lasted only until 1905 when the two Ernests famously fell-out and parted. Ernest Barnsley returned to the practice of archi-tecture and retained Upper Dorvel House, which passed to his widow upon his death. Upon her death in 1952 the contents of the house, including this wardrobe, were sold at public auction. The wardrobe was pur-chased by H.G. Fletcher, Librarian-Curator of the Public Library, Art Gallery and Museums of Cheltenham (1950–73), for his own use.[3] C.W.

1. M. Comino, *Gimson and the Barnsleys* (London: Evans Brothers, 1980), p.31.

2. M. Greensted, *Arts and Crafts Movement in the Cotswolds* (Stroud, Glos.: Alan Sutton, 1993), p.40.

3. Ovens and Sons, Ciren-cester, *Upper Dorvel House Sapperton, Catalogue of Antique Furniture and Furniture by E. Barnsley, E. Gimson and W.R. Lethaby*, 18 September 1952, lot 126. See A. Car-ruthers and M. Greensted, *Good Citizen's Furniture: The Arts and Crafts Collections at Cheltenham* (Cheltenham/ London: Art Gallery and Museums/Lund Humphries, 1994), pp.43ff. on Fletcher.

Fig.2. Walnut, ebony and gilt gesso cabinet, designed by Ernest Gimson, 1902 (V&A Museum No.W.27-1977)

Cabinet

British (Chipping Campden): circa 1905

Designed by C.R. Ashbee (1863–1942).
Made by W.W. Ride and J.W. Pyment (wood-work), and Annie (Statia) Powers (leatherwork), of the Guild of Handicraft, Chipping Campden, Gloucestershire. Walnut stand, sycamore carcase, cedar drawers; morocco leather, gold tooled; wrought iron fittings probably added after 1906.
Drawers numbered in pencil on back: 1–6

H: 139.2 cm; W: 107.2 cm; D: 63.2 cm
Museum No. Circ.234-1960
Purchased from Mrs P. Marshall-Purves, London

Fig.1. Cabinet closed

1. A. Crawford, *C.R. Ashbee* (London: Yale University Press), p.31.

2. Ibid., p.103.

3. Ashbee, *A Few Chapters in Workshop Re-Construction and Citizenship* (London: Guild and School of Handicraft, xx, 1894), p.78, cited by Crawford, op. cit., p.294.

4. Grafton Galleries, *Arts & Crafts Exhibition Society, Catalogue of the Eighth Exhibition 1906* (London: Grafton Galleries, 1906), p.75, cat. no.258.

5. Information from a handwritten card in Ashbee's hand found inside the cabinet. Crawford, op. cit., p.72, describes the house as 'part showroom' for the Guild.

Within the ranks of Arts and Crafts designers, C.R. Ashbee's life and work exemplified better than most the ideals and tribulations of that movement. Following the teachings of William Morris and others, Ashbee was a founder of the Guild and School of Handicraft established in East London in 1888. It was a technical and art school which also produced 'artistic' furniture, textiles, metalwork and ceramics based on an underlying premise of social reform.[1] In 1901, the Guild of fifty craftsmen and their families, led by the urban romantic Ashbee, moved to Chipping Campden in the Cotswolds in order to escape the 'squalor and ugliness' of city life.[2] It was in the furniture workshop of the relocated Guild that this cabinet was made.

Ashbee's cabinet (fig.1) demonstrates that the connection between historical and new objects was a vital one for Arts and Crafts designers. Although they are commonly associated with a return to traditional rural British furniture, high-style continental cabinets were an important source of inspiration and imitation. Among these, the Spanish *vargueño* (p.54) fascinated Ernest Gimson, Sidney Barnsley and Ashbee. Ashbee particularly admired the contrast between the plain exterior of such cabinets and their rich interiors. He wrote: 'There is, first of all, a stately structure with solid doors, delicately moulded and carved. In the centre is a golden key; you turn it, and open the doors, when within, you see the panels still more beautifully wrought…. The best work is within'.[3] He followed this convention in the design of a number of fall-front writing cabinets on stand, of which this example is the most traditional.

Like some Spanish *vargueños* and French seventeenth-century cabinets, Ashbee's cabinet is fitted with intricately tooled leather panels on the exterior, monochromatic and subtle. The same material covers the drawer and door fronts of the interior but here the leather is tooled with gold foil (fig.2). The connection between exterior and interior is thus established by the use of the same material,

but extravagance is reserved for the interior. The woodwork of the cabinet is restrained and simple although enlivened by contrasts of colour; frame and panel construction is employed and there is neither carving, except for the stand, nor inlay. In the relationship of cabinet to base, and the form of the base, Ashbee followed historicist designs of the nineteenth century. Although he often re-interpreted traditional forms, in this cabinet his concern was with the object type as it had evolved through the centuries.

The cabinet was shown in the Arts and Crafts Exhibition Society's exhibition of 1906, where it was available for sale at the very considerable price of £65.[4] Apparently unsold, the desk became part of the furnishings at 37 Cheyne Walk, known as the 'Magpie and Stump', the house belonging to Mrs H.S. Ashbee (the designer's mother); products of the Guild often ended up in Mrs Ashbee's house.[5] Sometime after her death in 1919, probably in 1923, it was taken by C.R. Ashbee who used it as his own desk in his library at Gooden Green, Sevenoaks, Kent. In 1942 it became the property of his daughter, Mrs P. Marshall-Purves, who sold it to the V&A. c.w.

Fig.2. Detail of interior showing tooled leather

Desk and Armchair

Austrian (Vienna): 1903

Designed by Koloman Moser (1868–1918).
Made by Caspar Hrazdil, Vienna (active
1890–*c*.1945). Designed for the Hölzl apartment,
Vienna. Veneered in thuya wood, inlaid with
satinwood and brass, engraved and inked;
mahogany interior, oak drawers, deal carcase;
gilt metal feet; upholstery not original. Printed
paper label of maker under right, lower drawer:
'Caspar Hrazdil/bürgerl. Bildhauer und
Kunsttischlerei/Wien/XVIII. Währing,
Czermakgasse No 21./Ubernimmt complette
Möbel-Einrichtungen/in allen Stylarten/
[handwritten in ink]1903'
Desk: H: 144 cm; W: 120 cm; D: 60 cm
Chair: H: 67 cm; W: 60 cm; D: 60 cm
Museum No. W.8&A-1982
Purchased from Haslam & Whiteway Ltd, London

The extraordinary flourishing of art, architecture and
design in turn-of-the-century Vienna resulted in the production of a very wide range of furniture designs, from
mass-produced bentwood chairs for cafés to exquisite,
one-of-a-kind cabinets for wealthy patrons. This cabinet,
one of the most lavish and beautiful produced in Vienna,
is clearly of the latter category. It formed part of a
commission to design two rooms for the apartment of a
prominent doctor, recently married.[1] Its designer, Koloman Moser, was one of the leading lights of Viennese
avant-garde design and, at the time, was Professor at the
Kunstgewerbeschule (Arts and Crafts School), a member
of the Secessionist group of artists and a co-founder of the
newly founded Wiener Werkstätte (Vienna Workshops), a
commercial enterprise dedicated to the manufacture and
sale of well-designed goods for the home.

The desk, designed for Mr Hölzl, was part of the
integrated scheme for the breakfast room of the Hölzl
apartment (fig.1) for which Moser designed at least seven
pieces of furniture all richly inlaid and decorated with
identical materials and motifs; all were similarly massive,
architectural in scale and rigidly rectilinear in form. They
were arranged in front of walls 'hung with mother-of-pearl
grey silk with white and gold stencilled ornament' and sat
on a grey, yellow and brown carpet with a border of
squares and lotus identical to that on the furniture.[2] Even
the metal fireplace had the lotus decoration punched into
its surface.

The flat surfaces of this cabinet well represent Moser's
talent as a decorative designer and his sure command of
ornamental forms. Rectilinear geometry and stylized ornament characterized his work; his interest in experimenting

Fig.1. Breakfast room, Hölzl apartment (Dekorative Kunst)

with flat pattern was characteristic of the period, as seen in
the magazine *Die Fläche* (literally, the surface), published
from 1902. Moser's stylized ornament drew not only on
the natural world but on historical form. Both the lotus
motif (or, in reverse, waterleaf) and the frieze of female
figures derive ultimately from Egyptian art, a rich source
for contemporary Viennese designers.[3]

Despite the boldness of its form, the desk (fig.2) was
also based on historic precedent. A desk with an integrated or hidden chair was part of the revival of the early
nineteenth-century Biedermeier style and was one used by
Moser numerous times.[4] Biedermeier furniture designers
had adapted such forms from French Empire models;
however, other precedents could be found in the elaborate
and carefully fitted constructions of the eighteenth-century
Russian cabinet-maker Heinrich Gambs (1765–1831).[5]
Although both German and French examples frequently
had the chair attached (and released) by mechanical
means, Moser simply inserted a large brass-line handle
into the back of the chair.   C.W.

1. S. Jervis, *Furniture of about 1900 from Austria & Hungary in the Victoria & Albert Museum* (London: Victoria & Albert Museum, 1986), pp.48–9.

2. B. Zuckerkandl, 'Koloman Moser', *Dekorative Kunst*, vol.XII (1904), p.336.

3. A. Alofsin, 'The Kunsthistorisches Museum: a Treasure House for the Secessionists', *Jahrbuch der Kunsthistorischen Sammlungen in Wien*, vol.88, new series vol.LII (1992), pp.189–203.

4. Desks of identical form but different decoration are in the collection of the Museum für angewandte Kunst, Vienna, and in the Palais Stoclet, Brussels.

5. A Chenevière, *Russian Furniture, The Golden Age 1780–1840* (London: Weidenfeld & Nicolson, 1988), p.102. Gambs sought to outshine the mechanical ingenuity of the German maker David Roentgen (p.128).

Fig.2. Desk with chair pulled out

Armchair

Dutch (Utrecht): 1918

Designed by Gerrit Rietveld (1888–1964).
Made by Rietveld with the assistance of G. van
der Groenekan, for Piet Elling, Utrecht.
Purpleheart wood, stained
H: 88.6 cm; W: 65.6 cm; D: 80.5 cm
Museum No. w.9-1989
Purchased from Barry Friedman Ltd, New York

Fig.1. Rietveld (sitting in a nearly identical chair) and assistants outside his shop, Utrecht, 1918 (Centraal Museum, Utrecht)

For those with even a passing knowledge of modern furniture, Rietveld's chair is a familiar design. However, as sometimes happens with designs which achieve iconic status, the history of this chair has become confused. This confusion arises because in about 1923 Rietveld began making versions of the chair painted in blue, red and yellow; it thus subsequently became known as 'the Red Blue chair' and, after 1951 especially, was treated almost exclusively as a piece of sculpture or a three-dimensional version of Dutch De Stijl painting, particularly that by Piet Mondrian.[1] The original design and all of the early versions were, however, simply stained, and it is in the present version that the designer's intentions can be seen most clearly.[2]

Far from being an abstract artist who dabbled in furniture, Rietveld left school at the age of twelve to work in his father's cabinet-making workshop. From the age of eighteen he attended evening classes in architecture and 'industrial arts' (including painting and drawing) and also worked as a draughtsman for a local jewellery firm. In 1917 he set up a cabinet-making business in his native Utrecht (fig.1). Among his earliest productions was this unusual chair.

Rietveld's design drew upon the simple geometry of furniture by an older generation of Dutch architects including H.P. Berlage (1856–1934) and Rietveld's former teacher P.J.C. Klarhaamer (1874–1954), as well as by the American Frank Lloyd Wright (fig.2), whose work was admired in Holland (p.188). In fact, Rietveld had apparently made reproductions of Wright pieces for a house designed by Robert van't Hoff.[3] In addition to the inspiration of specific furniture designs, Rietveld's chair was also a Utopian object, part of a search in European avant-garde circles for radically new forms of design

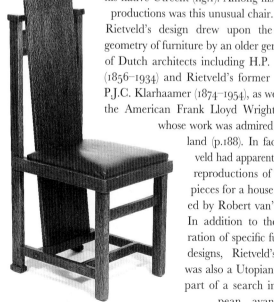

Fig.2. Frank Lloyd Wright, chair, oak, 1904 (Brooklyn Museum, New York)

and architecture arising, in part, as a result of the trauma of World War I. Although Rietveld was always interested in the comfort of his designs, and the chair is far more comfortable than it appears, he frequently quoted from a favourite poem which made clear his priorities:

> When I sit, I do not care
> just to sit, to suit my hindside,
> I prefer the way my mind-side
> would, to sit in, build a chair.[4]

Rietveld's armchair was a highly complex geometrical construction which, at the same time, aimed at simplicity and minimal bulk. It was originally made of machined, solid wood, the frame elements joined by dowels and the seat and back nailed to the frame. Although Rietveld wrote that the chair frame was to have been made from lengths of wood 2.5 x 2.6 cm in section, nearly all extant versions vary in fact in terms of size and materials. The articulation of the parts – especially the overlapping of each piece of wood – and the treatment of the joins emphasized the structural qualities of the design and the visual independence of each element. In a rare text on this chair Rietveld stressed his desire to maintain the intergrity of each element, 'without any deformations, so that no one part is too dominant or is subordinate to another; as a result, the design occupies the space clearly and freely as a single entity, the form being more important than the material.'[5]

The simple design and construction of the chair led Rietveld to offer, by 1932, both a serially produced version of the chair manufactured by another firm, as well as a more expensive, largely hand-made model from his own workshop. It was not until 1972, when the Italian company Cassina began producing highly finished examples (very different in character from the originals), that the chair can be said to have been mass-produced. c.w.

1. M. Küper and I. van Zijl, *Gerrit Th. Rietveld, the Complete Works 1888–1964* (Utrecht: Centraal Museum, 1992), pp.13–14, and P. Overy, *De Stijl* (London: Thames & Hudson, 1991), pp.15, 193–6.

2. M. Küper, 'Gerrit Rietveld', in C. Blotkamp *et al, De Stijl: the Formative Years* (Cambridge, Mass: MIT Press, 1982), pp.272–3 was the first to document the chair's early history. The present example, and the smaller version for Mrs Elling, were illustrated as the earliest extant examples of the design.

3. T. Brown, *The Work of G. Rietveld Architect* (Utrecht: Bruna & Zoon, 1958), pp.17, 23, and Küper, op. cit., pp.262–3.

4. From 'The Aesthete' by Christian Morgenstern, translated in Overy, op. cit., p.77. Rietveld printed this text in about 1930 (in the original German) on a paper label and attached it to many of his chairs.

5. Ibid.

Dressing Table

French (Paris): circa *1919–23*

Designed by Emile Jacques Ruhlmann (1879–1933). Made for Ruhlmann et Laurent, Paris. Oak carcase veneered with Andaman padouk (base and vase), purpleheart (amaranth) (top and mirror back, solid columns), inlaid with ivory and ebony; mahogany drawers; silvered bronze mirror frame and fittings.
Branded into underside of top:
'Ruhlmann' (script signature)
H: 119 cm; W: 76 cm; D: 52.5 cm
Museum No. W.14-1980
Purchased from Gallery 25, London

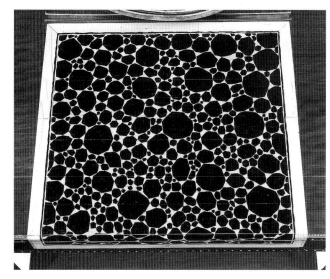

Fig.2. Detail of ivory-inlaid top

Ruhlmann's furniture represents one of the greatest achievements of what is now referred to as Art Deco. The term derives from the event which represented the acme of that wide-ranging style, 'L'Exposition Internationale des Arts Décoratifs et Industriels Modernes' held in Paris in 1925. As seen in this dressing table, Art Deco was characterized by the use of historically derived forms; rich and exotic materials, often from French colonies; stylized surface decoration; superb craftsmanship; and an emphasis on highly finished, mainly flat, surfaces.

The form of this table is loosely based on early nineteenth-century examples in which a pivoting mirror is attached to a table-top.[1] With characteristic bravado, Ruhlmann replaces the two rear legs with a flattened vase form which rises from an ogee-domed base. Although the lack of rear legs suggests a piece intended for placement against a wall, the entire back of the table (fig.1) is finished as if it were intended to be seen in the round or against a mirror: the tiny ivory dots and ivory and veneer dentil moulding along the sides of the top continue round the back; the back of the mirror is veneered; and the vase is treated three-dimensionally as in front and, indeed, is more prominent from the rear.

Ruhlmann's subtle, illusionistic use of ivory inlay was one of the most remarkable features of his work. The contrasting ivory and ebony inlay of the top (fig.2) suggests a fine textile draped over the table, an amusing reference to the centuries-old origins of the object type, called in French a *toilette*, the term derived from *toile* (linen) on which mirror, brush and other objects sat.[2]

Ruhlmann considered himself heir to the great traditions of French cabinet-making, specifically eighteenth-century *ébénisterie* (cabinet-making specializing in veneered, rather than carved, furniture) (p.58). The links between his work and French furniture of the eighteenth century were emphasized by the designer himself in writings and interviews and, by virtue of the form, materials, craftsmanship and extraordinary cost of his pieces, were apparent to contemporaries.[3] In the period after World War I especially, the patriotic, if not nationalistic, dimensions of his designs and craftsmanship were emphasized.

Although Ruhlmann designed some of the most luxurious and elegant furniture of the early twentieth century, he was not a trained cabinet-maker nor did he ever make furniture himself. He worked in his family's building and decorating business which he took over upon his father's death in 1907; in 1919 he set up independently.[4] Ruhlmann's partner, Pierre Laurent, ran the house-painting and building renovation side of the business and Ruhlmann devoted himself to building up the interior design practice he had begun in his family's firm. Until 1923 furniture making was contracted-out to firms in the Faubourg Saint-Antoine, the furniture-making district of Paris since before the Revolution, and it is likely that one of these made this dressing table.[5]

In response to increasing demand and, having received the commission to design an entire furnished pavilion (the 'town house of a collector') for the 1925 exhibition, Ruhlmann established his own cabinet-making workshop in 1923.   C.W.

1. N. de Reyniès, *Le Mobilier domestique*, vol.I (Paris: Imprimerie Nationale, 1987), p.347.

2. Ibid.

3. See J. Lacan, 'Notre Enquête sur le Mobilier moderne – E.J. Ruhlmann', *Art et décoration*, vol.XXXVII (January 1920), pp.4–5, and G. Janneau, 'D'André-Charles Boulle à Ruhlmann', *Revue de L'Art*, vol.LXVI, no.354 (December 1934), pp.185–91.

4. F. Camard, *Ruhlmann, Master of Art Deco* (London: Thames & Hudson, 1984), pp.196–9, which quotes unpublished sources without specific citations.

5. The precise date of this table is unclear. Camard, op. cit., who had access to original Ruhlmann papers, variously refers to it as the 'Lotus dressing table, 1919' (p.51) and the 'Vasque-tapis. *Circa* 1920. Ref. 1531 AR' (p.274). The latter is a reference to one set of Ruhlmann model numbers. Its illustration in a contemporary publication suggests a later date, see C.-H. Besnard, 'Quelques Nouveaux Meubles de Ruhlmann', *Art et Décoration*, vol.XLV (1924), p.69.

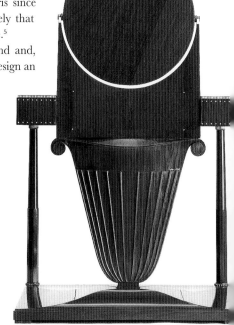

Fig.1. Detail of back

Screen

French (Paris): 1923

Designed and possibly made by
Eileen Gray (1879–1976), for her
shop, Jean Désert, Paris
Lacquered wood, brass rods

H: 189 cm; W: 136 cm; D: 2 cm
Museum No. W.21-1972
Given in memory of Charles and
Lavinia Handley-Read, by their
family

Fig.1. Gallery, Suzanne Talbot apartment, Paris, 1922 (V&A Archive of Art and Design, courtesy Miss Prunella Clough)

Although born in Ireland and educated, in part, at the Slade School in London, Eileen Gray spent her long adult life, from 1902, in Paris. She worked as designer, entrepreneur and architect, achieving considerable recognition during the 1920s; fortunately, she lived long enough to witness the revival of her reputation during a period of renewed interest both in French design of the 1920s and in women designers. Lacquer played an important role in her career, and this screen was one of her most accomplished and daring designs.

The screen was made from 28 panels, each of which pivots on brass rods. Within each panel is a raised square which gently enlivens the surface of the uniformly black panels. The screen is at once severe and luxurious, as abstract and complicated as such a form could be. Gray's use of separate panels to construct a screen was probably based on her design for a room in the apartment of Madame Mathieu Lévy (who worked as a designer under the name Suzanne Talbot).[1] Here (fig.1), a 'screen' made of 450 panels lined the walls and, in part, extended into the space of the room. In both the apartment and this free-standing screen, Gray's interest was in the screen as a flexible and dynamic architectural element, as well as in its sumptuous decorative effect. Throughout her career she had a fascination with, and designed, many pieces of adjustable or folding furniture (fig 2).

Gray first learned to make lacquer at a London shop during her student years but became accomplished at the arduous craft through the tutelage (begun about 1907) of a Japanese master in Paris, Sugawara, about whom little is known.[2] Considerable skill and commitment were required to learn how to build up more than 20 successive coats of natural resin on a base of resin mixed with fine earth, laid over cloth.

By 1913 Gray was exhibiting lacquer screens, one of which was purchased by the celebrated *couturier* and collector, Jacques Doucet. This preceded the wider fashion for lacquered screens following the end of World War I, and was to serve Gray well. The availability of expert Far Eastern lacquerists who had found work in France lacquering aeroplane propellers during World War I, provided Parisian workshops with skills that contributed to supplying, perhaps even creating, demand.[3] By the time Gray opened her own shop, named Jean Désert, in the Faubourg St Honoré in 1922, Sugawara was working for her and screens were a large part of her modest production.[4]

Gray's early work was very much in the luxurious, Parisian Art Deco style (p.198) but influenced by Modernist architects including Le Corbusier (p.204) and Robert Mallet-Stevens. She gradually developed her own synthesis of Modernist geometrical rigour and rich, sensual decoration. Although she never achieved great commercial success, some of her screens, described as 'big black lacquered' or 'plain black' were shipped to London for sale at Duncan Miller Ltd.[5]   C.W.

1. J.S. Johnson, *Eileen Gray: Designer 1879–1976* (London: Debrett, 1979), pp.18–23.

2. P. Adam, *Eileen Gray* (London: Thames & Hudson, 1987), pp.49–50.

3. P. Garner, 'The lacquer work of Eileen Gray and Jean Dunand', *Connoisseur* (May 1973), p.3 cites contemporary sources.

4. An inventory of the shop at the time of closing (1930) survives in the Gray Archives (V&A Archive of Art and Design, AAD 9-1980), published in Johnson, op. cit., pp.29–31.

5. Gray papers, AAD 9/11.

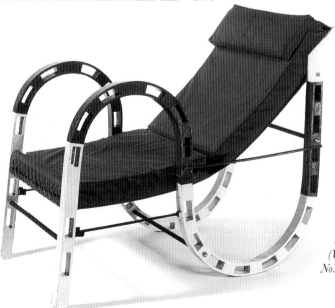

Fig.2. Folding chair, 1928 (V&A Museum No. Circ.579-1971)

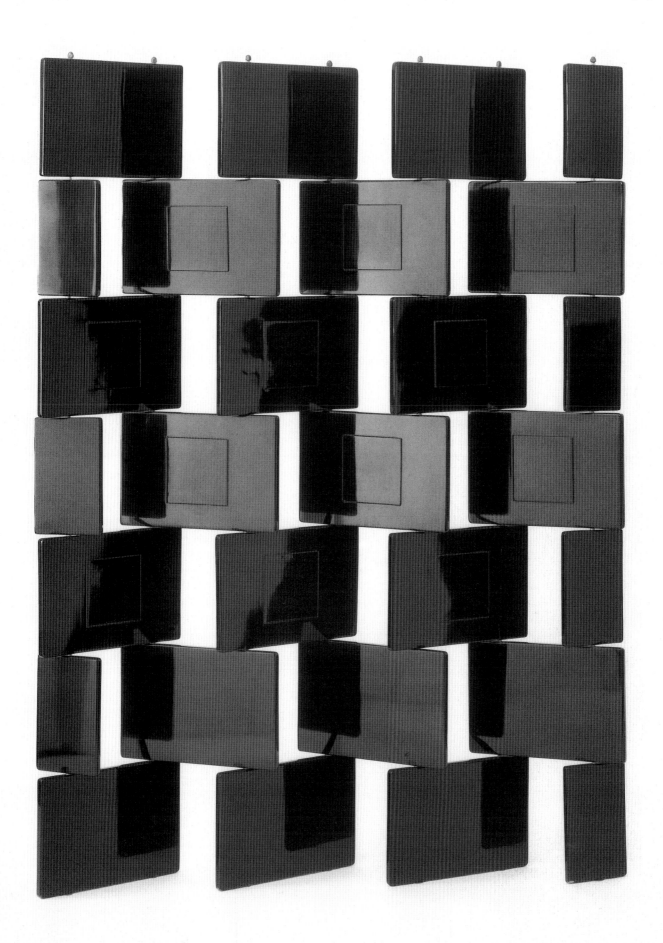

Desk

British (London): 1925

Designed by Sir Edward Maufe (1883–1974)
and made by W. Rowcliffe of Heal's for the
British Government Pavilion, Paris Exposition
Internationale des Arts Décoratifs et Industrielles
Modernes, 1925. Mahogany carcase, ebony
writing and top surfaces, gessoed and gilded with
white gold; haldu wood footrest and feet; ivory,
rock crystal and silk handles. Handwritten label
under centre drawer: 'This piece of furniture
was designed by/EDWARD MAUFE/and made by
/WILLIAM ROWCLIFFE/in 1925/It was first shown
in the British Government Pavilion/at the Paris
Exhibition of International Decorative Art'

H: 107 cm; W: 134.3m; D: 53 cm
Museum No. Circ. 898-1968
Given by Prudence, Lady Maufe

This desk was exhibited at the celebrated Paris exhibition
of 1925 and was clearly designed to demonstrate that
British furniture could compete with the latest fashions in
French furniture (p.198). More than anything else it is the
shimmering silver surfaces of this cabinet which associate
it with Art Deco. These are covered in the traditional
manner of gilded furniture, over a gessoed ground, not
with silver leaf but with a more costly substitute known as
white gold. The latter was chosen because the presence of
gold reduces the silver content, resulting in a surface which
tarnishes much less easily than silver leaf.

The boldness of the silver surface tends to divert attention from the form of the desk; indeed, if it had been
executed in stained, rather than gilded, mahogany we
would more readily see its rectilinear, stepped form and
fluted pilaster decoration as part of the 'stripped' or simplified Classicism common in British architecture and design
of the period. The traditional, albeit simplified, kneehole
desk form and the use of bun feet place the desk firmly
within a recognizable British furniture tradition. Thus,
although the designer emulated one aspect of the latest
Parisian style, he remained committed to the more solid
and traditional but less refined qualities of contemporary
British design. This comment might also be made of the
designer, the architect Edward Maufe, best known as
an eccesiastical architect – his work included Guildford
Cathedral (1932–66).

Both the design and construction of this cabinet exemp-
lify well the British tendency in the twentieth century to be
wary of the purer manifestations of modern continental
styles. The Department of Overseas Trade report on the
Paris exhibition specifically praised Maufe's desk for its
'"essentially right" wood construction' and contrasted
it favourably with the cabinetwork of Emile Jacques
Ruhlmann (p.198).[1] While acknowledging the 'technical
skill' of France's leading cabinet-maker, the report criticized his forms, which 'have no relation whatever to the
essential character and structure of [his] materials' and
which do 'violence to the nature of the material'. The
refined, curvilinear, feminine design of Ruhlmann's work
clearly did not appeal to the official British audience
whose preference was for traditional joinery as well as
traditional forms.

Although it is known that the desk was made for the
Paris exhibition, the precise circumstances of its commission – if, in fact, it was commissioned – remain unclear.[2] Maufe's wife, Prudence (1884–1976), chief buyer
and later a Director of Heal's, was responsible for the
'arrangement' of four rooms within the British Government Pavilion which was designed by London architects
Easton & Robertson (fig.1).[3] The desk was included in a
display variously described as a 'Town Parlour' or 'Pieces
of furniture suitable for a town house'. It was the only
design by Edward Maufe in the exhibition. The maker,
credited in the catalogue, was W. Rowcliffe, who is known
to have worked at Heal's.[4]

At the conclusion of the exhibition, many of the British
exhibits were available for purchase but it is not known
whether the desk was among these pieces. It was returned
to England and kept in the Maufe's Chelsea house until it
was given to the V&A in 1968. C.W.

*Fig.1. Easton & Roberton,
British Government Pavilion,
Paris Exhibition, 1925. The
Maufe desk is seen in the
room to the right, arranged
by Prudence Maufe*

1. *Report on the Present Position
and Tendencies of the Industrial
Arts as indicated at the International Exhibition of Modern
Decorative and Industrial Arts,
Paris 1925* (London: Department of Overseas Trade,
1925), p.63.

2. A drawing for the desk
is apparently in an
uncatalogued collection
of Maufe drawings in the
RIBA, London.

3. *British Section (Section
Britannique)* (catalogue)
(London: Department
of Overseas Trade, 1925),
pp.71–9.

4. According to Lady
Maufe, Rowcliffe was
'allowed to make [the desk]
from start to finish', letter
13/10/67, Prudence, Lady
Maufe to Peter Thornton,
Maufe Nominal file, V&A.

Chaise Longue

French: 1928–9

Designed by Le Corbusier (1887–1965), Pierre Jeanneret (1896–1967) and Charlotte Perriand (b.1903). Manufactured by Gebrüder Thonet, Frankenberg, Germany. Chrome-plated tubular steel, painted sheet steel, metal springs, rubber, horse-hide upholstery

H: 84 cm; W: 53.5 cm; D: 155 cm
Museum No. W.11-1989
Given by Barry Friedman Ltd, New York

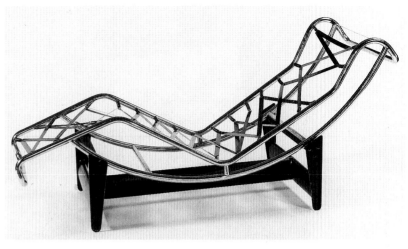

Fig.1. Frame of chair

The arrival of modern tubular steel furniture into the avant-garde architectural world during the period 1925–7 was a momentuous event.[1] This revolutionary, machine-age furniture, with its shiny nickel- or chrome-plated surface and futuristic appearance was welcomed as the uniquely appropriate furnishing for the New Architecture (as the new style of modern architecture was known at the time). Modern tubular steel furniture (from extruded steel) was first designed at the Bauhaus school in Germany by the head of the furniture workshop, Marcel Breuer (1902–81 – p.206). In the following years virtually every European architect with even vaguely Modernist tendencies tried his or her hand at designing the new furniture.

Le Corbusier, the Swiss born architect practising in Paris, was, in some circles, the best-known advocate and practitioner of the New Architecture. Although he had designed simple tubular steel tables and beds with his cousin Pierre Jeanneret, it appears that only after 1927, when he accepted a young graduate of the École des Arts Décoratifs, Charlotte Perriand, as 'a pupil for architecture and collaborator for furniture', did his office turn its attention to designing fashionable metal furniture.[2]

Le Corbusier had a life-long interest in furniture and in seating postures. He designed chairs, wooden and upholstered, and like contemporary German architects turned his attention during the 1920s to a narrow range of standard furniture types suited to the new interior. He described such furniture and fittings as *équipement*. In his buildings of the mid-1920s he generally used Thonet bentwood chairs, which he described as possessing 'nobility'.[3] However, like many contemporaries, he came to feel that wood was an inadequate expression of the new industrial age.[4] He famously described the house as 'a machine for living in', but also wrote of the chair as 'a machine for sitting in'.[5]

Le Corbusier was deeply concerned with the aesthetics of his furniture, perhaps more so than many contemporaries designing in tubular steel. The extraordinary elegance of this chaise longue – far removed from the functionalist utilitarianism of

équipement – arose from the designer's love of geometric form, expressed most noticeably in the carefully drawn line of the seat (fig.1). That seat adjusts simply by pulling the frame along the base; its weight and the rubber covering on the frame keep it in place. The construction of the chair is complex and expensive, using different types of metal and many more welds than bends. Le Corbusier did not share the social ideal of the inventors of modern tubular steel who were anxious to mass-produce furniture, and this chair was never manufactured in large quantity. As befitted a designer with a background as a painter, pure form and, perhaps less consciously, symbolic content, predominate.

Le Corbusier's love of Thonet bentwood furniture suggests that its sinuous rocking chaise (fig.2) may have been one of the sources of his designs, but he also drew and published illustrations of a variety of reclining chairs including Indonesian veranda chairs, commercial rattan chairs and French patent furniture.

The late twentieth-century view of this chair is based not upon the original version but on the reproductions made by the Swiss firm of Heidi Weber from 1959 and, since 1965, by the Italian company Cassina.[6] Like all reproductions these later versions, despite being 'authorized', fundamentally differ from the originals in terms of their construction and appearance. C.W.

1. C. Wilk, 'Furnishing the Future', in D. Ostergard (ed.), *Bent Wood and Metal Furniture: 1850–1946* (Seattle/New York: University of Washington Press/AFA, 1987), pp.121–43.

2. C. Benton, "'L'Aventure du Mobilier": Le Corbusier's Furniture Designs of the 1920s', *Decorative Arts Society Journal*, no.6 (1983), p.13, without source, but repeated in numerous interviews given by Perriand.

3. Le Corbusier, *Almanach d'architecture moderne* (Paris: Editions G. Crès, 1925), p.145.

4. Le Corbusier, *The Decorative Art of Today* (London: Architectural Press, 1987, transl. of 1925 original), pp.47–8.

5. Le Corbusier, *Towards a New Architecture* (London: Architectural Press, 1970, transl. of 1923 original), p.45.

6. R. De Fusco, *Le Corbusier, Designer: Furniture, 1929* (Woodbury, NY: Barron's, 1977, Italian edition 1976), funded by Cassina.

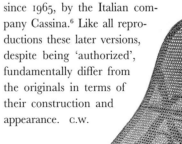

Fig.2. Thonet bentwood rocking chaise, c.1880 (Private collection)

'Short' Chair

British (London): 1936

Designed by Marcel Breuer (1902–81). Manufactured by the Isokon Furniture Company, London. Laminated birch frame with zebrano veneer, moulded plywood seat and back; lacks cushion

H: 79.2 cm; W: 62.2 cm; D: 98.5 cm
Museum No. Circ. 80-1975
Given by Mr and Mrs Dennis Young

Fig.2. Isokon 'Long' chair (V&A Museum No. Circ.83-1975)

Jack Pritchard was a zealous and life-long promoter of Modernist architecture and design.[1] He embraced fully the ideals and style of the Bauhaus, as well as the architecture of Le Corbusier (p.204), and believed that design had the moral power to transform society for the better. Towards this end Pritchard, who had a day job working for the Venesta plywood firm, founded a company called Isokon. A contraction of Isometric Unit Construction, it took shape during the course of discussions between Pritchard and the former Director of the Bauhaus, Walter Gropius (1883–1969), in 1935, following Gropius's emigration to England.[2] The Isokon Furniture Company grew out of the larger venture and was officially founded in January 1936.

Gropius played a major role in the new firm.[3] It was he who insisted that the former Bauhaus teacher, architect and furniture-designer Marcel Breuer should design for Isokon, and Gropius who also suggested that Breuer's first Isokon design should be a plywood version of a chair Breuer had designed in aluminium and steel examples in 1932–3 (fig.1). Breuer, as the designer of the first modern tubular steel chairs and one of the most influential furniture designers of the 1920s, was a natural choice. Pritchard's recent work experience made the use of plywood logical. It also served to temper British resistance to avant-garde Modernism, especially to metal furniture.[3]

Breuer's first Isokon chair, which came in 'Short' and 'Long' (fig.2) versions, was a direct translation into plywood of his metal reclining chair, albeit

more complex. The steel chair frame was made from two continuous lengths of metal which could support the weight of the sitter; the plywood version required a reinforced supporting frame each side of which was made from two separate pieces. The single-piece plywood seat was morticed into the top and bottom of the frame. The advantage of plywood was that it could be made under workshop conditions, whereas metal required a more elaborate factory setting.

Breuer's design was undeniably influenced by the plywood furniture of Alvar Aalto (fig.3). The curvilinear shape of Breuer's metal chair took on a sinewy, organic character similar to Aalto's furniture when translated into plywood, and it was Aalto with whom the use of a single-piece moulded plywood seat, suspended within a laminated frame, was most associated. This organic aesthetic signalled a move away from the rectilinear geometry that had dominated most Modernist furniture of the 1920s.

Although Pritchard hoped that Isokon would become a mass-market manufacturer, he accepted that his first task was to 'establish good-will for authentic modern furniture in the high-price market'.[4] By 1938 the firm was selling between three and six Long chairs per week but the coming of war in 1939 put an end to Isokon's manufacturing.[5] It is likely that only a few Short chairs were made. The Short chair was not manufactured again until about 1970 by Gavina (Italy) and then Knoll (USA), and is today produced under licence by Windmill Furniture in London. Breuer's Isokon reclining chairs are often illustrated without their original upholstered seats, thereby highlighting their plywood structure; however, they were never intended to be used without the cushion. C.W.

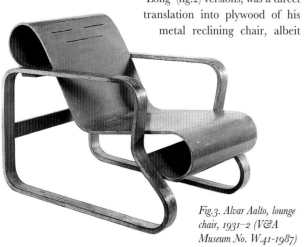

Fig.3. Alvar Aalto, lounge chair, 1931–2 (V&A Museum No. W.41-1987)

1. J. Pritchard, *View From a Long Chair* (London: Routledge & Kegan Paul, 1984).

2. C. Wilk, *Marcel Breuer: Furniture and Interiors* (New York: Museum of Modern Art, 1981), pp.127–9.

3. Wilk, op. cit., pp.68–9.

4. J. Pritchard, 'Draft History of the Isokon Furniture Company', note 3, undated mss., Pritchard Archive (file 18, section 2), formerly University of Newcastle-upon-Tyne, now University of East Anglia.

5. Letter from Pritchard to E. Reid, Venesta, 16 May 1938, Pritchard Archive (file 18, case 7).

Fig.1. Steel reclining chair made by Embru, Ruti, Switzerland, 1932–3 (V&A Museum No. W.12-1993)

Chair

British (London): circa *1930*

Designed by Denham Maclaren (1903–89).
Glass, metal fittings, zebra skin upholstery

H: 68 cm; W: 55 cm; D: 84.6 cm
Museum No. W.26-1979
Purchased from Mr Denham Maclaren, London

One of the hallmarks of the new Modernist design of the 1920s and 1930s (p.204) was an unbridled faith in the innovative use of manufactured materials. The period was seen as a new age in which the machine and its products could alleviate social ills and provide appropriate surroundings for modern living. Above all, such products were to embody and symbolize this new machine age.

Much as extruded tubular steel had been available since 1888 but not exploited for furniture until the 1920s, so large sheets of glass had been manufactured for a considerable time, although it was little used until advances in lamination had increased its strength. Despite this, glass still presented the risk of chipping, and its weight added to its impracticality as a furniture material. Beyond its obvious use for table tops, glass was used mainly for display or exhibition purposes. Display work undertaken by the designer Denham Maclaren for interior decorators Arundell Clarke may have led to Maclaren's experimentation with glass as a material for furniture.[1] Maclaren recalled that this chair was designed while he worked for Clarke in the late 1920s (although its form, particularly that of the sides, suggests it might well date from as late as the mid-1930s).

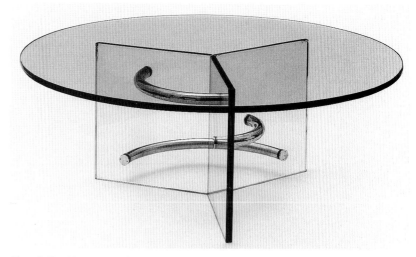

Fig.1. Coffee table, c.1929 (V&A Museum No. W.19-1979)

Not only are the sides of this chair made of thick, industrial glass but the metal fittings are of the type used commonly in shop fitting. Many of Maclaren's designs incorporated glass and, in addition to this chair, he designed at least one table made entirely of the material (fig.1). Although making innovative use of glass, this chair relates to a wooden model Maclaren used in his own flat (fig.2).[2] Its overall form is similar and its use of upholstered seat and back identical.

Maclaren's chair was fashionable and up-to-date not only in its use of glass but also in the choice of zebra skin upholstery (fig.3). Animal skins of all kinds were used by a wide variety of inter-war designers (p.204) and the use of zebra added a touch of exoticism, even Surrealism.[3]

That the details of Maclaren's career remain hazy may largely be due to the designer's independent income which made the necessity to work less urgent. By 1930 he was listed in the London directory as an 'interior decorator' in Mayfair, London, and his furniture had been published.[4] Although from 1936 he seems to have retailed his designs through Duncan Miller in London, he apparently moved into property development and continued his lifelong pursuit of drawing, painting and photography.[5] He gave up work as a designer by about 1937.   C.W.

1. Information supplied by Maclaren (Maclaren Nominal File, V&A), on whom nothing substantive has been published. Biographical details are included in an obituary by P. Greenhalgh, *Independent* (22 November 1989). An archive of some material on the designer exists in private hands. The designer's name was published during the 1930s both as Maclaren and MacLaren.

2. Sold as lot 117, Christie, Manson & Woods, London, 31 January 1990. The catalogue illustrated Maclaren's flat.

3. Maclaren was associated with English Surrealists, see P. Nash, 'Surrealism in Interior Decoration', *Decoration* (June 1936), cited by S. Calloway, *Twentieth-Century Decoration* (London: Weidenfeld & Nicolson, 1988), p.272.

4. P. Nash, 'Modern English Furnishing', *Architectural Review*, vol.LXVII, pp.43–8.

5. Tables sold at Miller's showroom were published in *Design for Today* (February 1936), p.71 and *Harper's Bazaar* (US ed. May 1936), pp.34–5.

Fig.3. Rear view of chair

Fig.2. Wood frame armchair, about 1930 (Christie, Manson & Woods)

Wardrobe

French (Paris): 1939

Painted by Eugène Berman (1899–1972).
Oil paint on canvas, varnished, on pine carcase.
Signed on canvas in keystone: 'EB/1939'

H: 251 cm; W: 147 cm; D: 50 cm
Museum No. W.27-1987
Purchased from Lewis M. Kaplan Associates Ltd,
London

Fig.1. Cabinet at Galerie Drouin, gown by Alix (Harper's Bazaar, September 1939, photo: Hoyningen-Huene)

Although painters often designed furniture in the Renaissance, the practice had become less common by the eighteenth and early nineteenth centuries. The conscious breakdown in the later nineteenth century of hierarchical conventions which separated the fine and decorative arts led numerous artists – for example, Dante Gabriel Rossetti (1828–82), James Whistler (1834–1903), Duncan Grant (1885–1978) and Salvador Dali (1904–88) – to design furniture.

Eugène Berman was a painter and print-maker who also achieved considerable distinction as a stage designer, especially for ballet and opera. Crucially, he was taught painting in his native Russia by an architect who worked in the Palladian tradition.[1] The architectural form and subject-matter of this cabinet relate directly to Berman's training as well as to his intense study of buildings through travel and drawing, and his collecting of architectural books and prints. The architectural fantasy, unusually dark and ruinous, was a frequent subject or motif in his work.

Unlike, for example, the artists of the London-based Omega group (1913–21), who often purchased ready-made furniture to paint on, Berman clearly designed this cabinet specially for its decoration. Its scale, and that of the painting, is monumental. Its design is simple. The complexity arises from the dramatic illusionism of the painting and the surreal and ominous nature of what is depicted. Berman's imagery suggests decay, destruction and the passing of time and may well have been related to when it was painted – on the eve of World War II.

Berman's art was not only decisively influenced by the mysterious and disturbing subject matter of European Surrealism, but also by the lesser known, classicizing, Neo-Renaissance art of 1920s and 1930s Italy.[2] From the 1920s he was closely identified with a group of Parisian artists, mainly former fellow students, dubbed the 'Neo-Romantic' painters, which included his brother Leonid (1896–1976), Christian Bérard (1902–49) and also Pavel Tchelitchew (1898–1957).[3]

This cabinet was shown at, and probably made specially for, an exhibition at the new Galerie Drouin, Paris, in 1939 (fig.1), which included, as one reviewer wrote, artists 'touched by the Surrealist attitude'.[4] Berman's furniture was not much published and was clearly not a major part of his work although he designed and painted furniture both for gallery exhibitions and as part of mural schemes for private clients in the United States. Furniture was a way to extend the illusionism of his painting into three dimensions in a direct and compelling manner rather than an attempt to engage with the complexities of furniture design itself.   C.W.

Fig.2. Detail of signature

1. J. Levy (ed.), *Eugène Berman* (New York/London: American Studio Books [1947]), p.v.

2. E. Cowling and J. Mundy, *On Classic Ground* (London: Tate Gallery, 1990).

3. M. Battersby, *The Decorative Thirties* (London: Studio Vista, 1969), pp.136–49, which illustrated the Berman cabinet. Also, S. Calloway, *Baroque Baroque* (London: Phaidon, 1994), pp.111–16.

4. M. Zahar, 'Paris', *The Studio*, vol.118 (October 1939), p.179, which also refers to 'painted cupboards' in the exhibition. The only proof that it was the present cabinet is its publication as backdrop to two fashion photographs in *Harper's Bazaar* (US ed., September 1939), pp.66 and 69. It is most likely the 'fake cabinet made last year for a Paris gallery' mentioned in R. Frost, 'Berman the Baroque Boy', *Art News*, vol.40 (1 March 1941), p.39. The later provenance of the Berman cabinet is unknown.

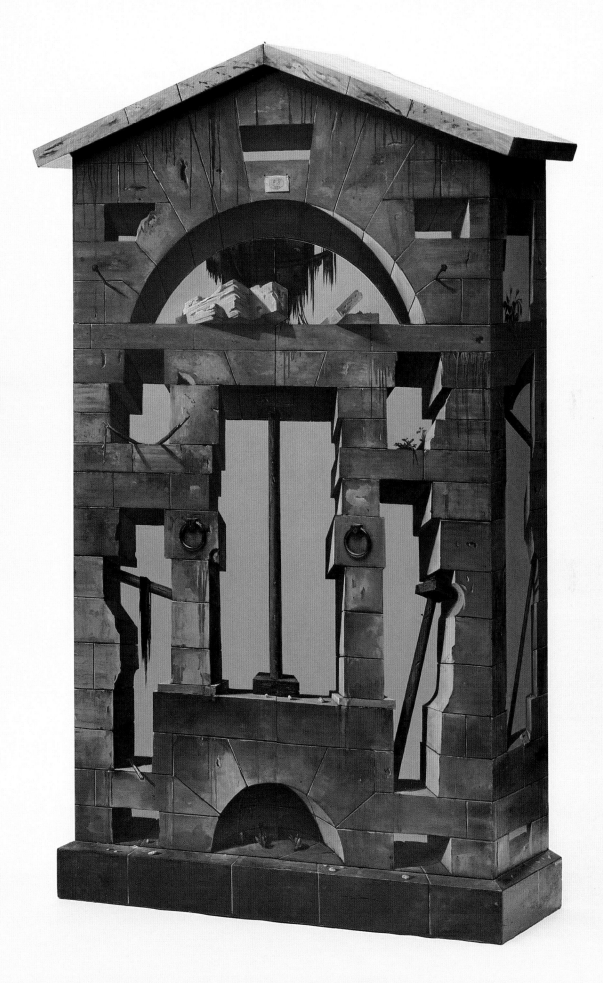

Writing Cabinet

Italian (Milan): 1951

Designed by Gio Ponti (1891–1979) and decorated by Piero Fornasetti (1913–88). Made by I Fratelli Radici, Milan, printing by Fornasetti. Exhibited at the 9th Triennale, Milan, 1951. Screen-printed wood-fibre board (masonite) on laminated and solid wood, varnished

H: 2,230 cm; W: 797 cm; D: 400 cm
Museum No. W.21-1983
Purchased from Dan Klein Ltd, London

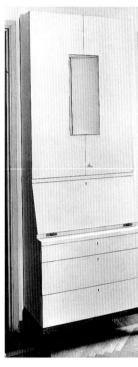

Fig.1. Interior of the cabinet

Fig.2. Later version of cabinet without decoration

Although the unornamented surfaces of Modernism have dominated much architect-designed furniture of the twentieth century (pp.196, 204), there have always been designers who believed that forms based on historical precedent as well as the use of applied decoration were an essential part of design.

Gio Ponti, architect of many celebrated Modernist buildings, including Milan's most notable skyscraper (the Pirelli tower), was a remarkably versatile designer who began his career as artistic director for the Richard Ginori ceramic factory, designing ceramics in the Neo-Classical taste. During more than fifty years of work he designed – as well as buildings – industrial products and virtually every type of decorative object.[1] He also founded and edited the influential magazine *Domus* which, in 1940, published a series of printed scarves designed by the talented young artist Piero Fornasetti.

Ponti had a keen eye for decoration and admired Fornasetti's exceptional skill as a draughtsman and his highly personal decorative style. Both men were profoundly influenced by the Neo-Classical 'return to order' which infused Italian art and design in the years between the wars and which was associated with the Fascist government. Although neither was politically active, Ponti and Fornasetti linked their work to the great traditions of Italian art and architecture. The architectural form and subject matter of this cabinet arose out of this tradition.

Although this tall cabinet with fall-front writing surface contained no mirrors (or decoration) within (fig.1), in Italy it was called a *trumó* or *trumeau*, a term elsewhere given to a pier glass.[2] Ponti's design was a handsome, modern version of an eighteenth-century form, but it was Fornasetti's remarkable decoration which transformed it into an extraordinary piece of furniture (fig.2). The technique used was unusual and precise details were always guarded closely by Fornasetti. It is known, however, that he created lithographs for each section which were printed onto transfer sheets and then applied to fibreboard panels which were fitted to the cabinet and varnished.[3]

The cabinet was produced at the height of the Ponti-Fornasetti collaboration which had begun in 1949. In a series of commercial, domestic and exhibition interiors, Fornasetti covered the surfaces of walls, display cases, bookshelves, furniture and textiles with illusionistic images, generally non-abstract, of his favourite themes including nature, playing cards, antiquities and architecture. Even though we are likely today to focus only on the incredible profusion of surface decoration, Ponti wrote that Fornasetti's applied printing was central to the forms that he (Ponti) had designed. The decoration gave, Ponti wrote, 'an effect of lightness and evocative magic. Everything becomes weightless.'[4]

Deceiving the eye was a lifelong passion for Fornasetti and his *trompe l'oeil* schemes drew upon, in particular, sixteenth-century Italian Mannerism as well as the Surrealism of the early twentieth century. His interpretation of architectural forms is based not upon observation but on an encyclopædic knowledge of printed books and engravings and although specific buildings are sometimes quoted, often the images represent Fornasetti's own architectural fantasies.[5]

This first example of the architectural cabinet was the one shown at the 9th Triennale exhibition in Milan.[6] Fornsetti continued to manufacture versions of the same cabinet with different decoration in the 1950s and 1960s and again in the 1980s, altering the form of both the base and top. It is still produced today by the Fornasetti family firm. c.w.

1. L.L. Ponti, *Gio Ponti, the Complete Work 1923–1978* (London: Thames & Hudson, 1990).

2. First described as such in, 'I mobili fantastici all Triennale', *Domus* 261 (September 1951), p.29.

3. G. Ponti, 'Printed Furniture', *Graphis*, vol.8 no.39 (1952), p.78.

4. G. Ponti, 'Una casa di fantasia', *Domus* 270 (1952), p.292.

5. Fornasetti himself identified the source of the lower section of the cabinet as 'Alessi's Palace at Genoa, now the University'. See P. Mauriès, *Fornasetti, Designer of Dreams* (London: Thames & Hudson, 1991), p.100. More likely, it is the Palazzo Tursi, Genoa, by D. and G. Ponzello, now the Town Hall.

6. It underwent some restoration around 1980, particularly replacement of lost feet (information from Barnaba Fornasetti, 10 May 1989 and 29 August 1995, and Dan Klein, 25 August 1995).

Storage Unit

American: 1949–50

Designed by Charles (1907–78) and Ray (1913–88) Eames. Manufactured by Herman Miller Furniture Co, Zeeland, Michigan, USA, as model ESU 421-C. Zinc-plated steel, birch-faced plywood, plastic-coated plywood and lacquered fibreboard (masonite). Printed label in top drawer: 'herman miller/furniture company/ zeeland, michigan [in script]/ DESIGNED BY/CHARLES EAMES'

H: 148.9 cm; W: 119.4 cm; D: 42.5 cm
Museum No. W.5-1991
Purchased from Fifty-50, New York

Fig.2. Eames House (detail), Pacific Palisades, California (Library of Congress, © Eames Demetrios, Eames Office)

Furniture designed by the husband-and-wife team of Charles and Ray Eames was the most influential and imitated furniture of the post-war period. Practising designers working today, regard it as among the most esteemed, even revered, of all modern furniture. Charles, trained as an architect, and Ray, trained as a painter, were remarkably versatile and prolific designers who achieved considerable success not only in furniture design but also as film-makers, photographers, architects, as well as interior, exhibition and graphic designers.[1] They were fortunate to have found a small group of clients (including Herman Miller) who allowed them to operate with enviable freedom; they only accepted jobs in which they were interested and, after their earliest working years, rarely found it necessary to solicit work. They were equally skilled at attracting able staff, with wide-ranging expertise, to collaborate with them.

Although best known for their chair designs (fig.1), the Eames' worked on modular storage systems throughout their career. The ESU (Eames Storage Unit) system was perhaps their most accomplished storage design although, unlike much of their mass-produced furniture, it did not achieve commercial success. This example was one of the larger cabinets from a collection intended for either commercial or domestic use, based on a system of interchangeable parts. Customers chose the size of the piece (this example is made from nine units), and the arrangement of panels (including both flat or 'dimpled'), drawers, materials, colours and finishes. The first versions of the storage unit, including the present example, were made with steel angle legs and were shipped knocked down to the customer. After 1952 the leg was modified and the units were shipped assembled. Production ceased in 1955.

The design represented a further development of modular storage systems developed for domestic use in Germany in the 1920s (made mainly to order), and of American metal office furniture of the early twentieth century. It was also, however, intimately related to the Eames's own house (fig.2), designed at precisely the same time.[2] A description of the house could be substituted for that of the storage unit: its framework was steel, the structure of which was emphasized by supporting struts and the manner in which different coloured panels were set into it. A desire to work with commonly available industrial materials was combined with a refined aesthetic sensibility, sensitive to the effects of colour and material. The elevation of this piece seems to have been unmistakably composed like a painting or sculpture. The overall impression is thin, delicate, structural and, owing to the screen-like effect of the panels, reminiscent of traditional Japanese architecture, this having been a powerful influence on American west coast design, even in the years after World War II.

Integrity and wit characterized all the work of the Eames. Not only does this storage unit have an air of sophisticated playfulness but included with each storage unit shipped fully assembled was an instruction sheet, designed by the Eames's, explaining how to turn the shipping box into a children's playhouse. C.W.

1. P. Kirkham, *Charles and Ray Eames* (Cambridge, Mass: MIT Press, 1995), passim.

2. J. and M. Neuhart, R. Eames, *Eames Design* (London: Thames & Hudson, 1989), pp.106–21. The relationship was widely recognized at the time.

Fig.1. Lounge chair, plywood, 1946
(V&A Museum No. W.17-1989)

'Universale' Chair

Italian (Milan): 1965–7 (model 4867)

Designed by Joe Colombo (1930–71).
Manufactured by Kartell, Milan.
Injection-moulded ABS plastic.
Impressed into underside of seat:
'Kartell BINASCO (Milano)/
860 e 861 5 [within circle] MADE IN
ITALY/DESIGN-Prof. Joe Colombo'

H: 72.5 cm; W: 43.5 cm; D: 43.5 cm
Museum No. Circ.887-1968
Purchased from Conran Contracts Ltd,
London

Fig.1. Stack of chairs

1. Inaccuracies in books and exhibition catalogues written in the 1970s have led to confusion about the dates of the earliest plastic chairs. This chair was first published in 'Una Sedia in Plastica Stampata ad iniezione', *Domus* (January 1967), p.51. See also I. Favata, *Joe Colombo and Italian Design of the Sixties* (London: Thames & Hudson, 1988), pp.30–31.

2. A. Morello and A.C. Ferrieri, *Plastiche e Design* (Milan: Arcadia Edizioni, 1984), a history of Kartell (pp.138–41 on the present chair).

3. N. Whitely, *Pop Design: Modernism to Mod* (London: Design Council, 1987), passim.

4. Ibid., pp.134, 138.

Plastic furniture is today both so taken for granted and so little used in the domestic interior that we are apt to underestimate its novelty and impact when first introduced, as well as its subsequent ubiquity. Designed in 1965 and mass-produced from 1967 or 1968, Joe Colombo's chair was the first injection-moulded all plastic chair to be manufactured and among the earliest plastic chairs to be sold in the marketplace.[1] It was manufactured by an innovative firm whose chief products were plastic laboratory and industrial wares, as well as lighting; housewares, and then furniture, represented the high-profile, design-orientated but much smaller part of the business.[2] Kartell exemplified the mixture of design and technical innovation and experimentation that turned Italy, and specifically Milan, into the post-war design powerhouse of Europe, a status which it retains even to the present day.

While Britain provided Pop culture with its identity, clothing and music,[3] it was Italian designers who added sophisticated, high-style design principles and aesthetics. Pop design was characterized by bold pattern, bright colour and new forms aimed at a young market. Plastic, a material formerly associated with cheapness and substitution, became fashionable, above all, for its novelty; plastic furniture was dramatically of the moment while suggesting the future that technolgy was making possible. Such furniture explicitly avoided all reference to past forms and materials. It was marketed as bold, multi-functional, stackable (fig.1) and portable, suitable for both indoor or outdoor use.

While the chief goal of many designers of plastic furniture was to manufacture chairs or other furniture types from a single piece of moulded material, not requiring assembly, Colombo consciously made his chair with detachable feet. This allowed for different height chairs (low for waiting areas, high for bars, as well as standard) and the largest possible number of forms from the smallest number of parts. Although this chair was manufactured in a range of bright colours, the designer in general chose to restrict his palette to a limited range of white, gray and yellow. The structure of Colombo's chair derived from a previous Kartell model, a child's chair designed by Marco Zanuso and Richard Sapper.[4]

The demise of plastic furniture for domestic use was due to the dramatic rise in oil prices in 1972 and the subsequent change in fashion; the bright, slick, plastic surfaces of Pop fell into disfavour and plastic furniture was subsequently restricted mainly to commercial or institutional use for which it has steadily been manufactured in large quantity. The novelty of the hard plastic surface gave way to a realization of its limitations for comfort, although the revival of 1960s design has led to reproductions of plastic furniture during the 1990s.   C.W.

Column of Drawers

British: 1977–8

Designed by John Makepeace (b.1939), made
by John Makepeace Ltd, Dorset.
Birch plywood, acrylic, stainless steel

H: 130 cm; W: 50 cm; D: 50 cm
Museum No. W.56-1978
Purchased from John Makepeace Ltd, Dorset

Fig.2. Column under
construction, 1977
(© Times Newspapers Ltd,
photo: Harry Kerr)

Exquisitely made cabinets have been a part of the western
furniture tradition since the sixteenth century. Although
nineteenth and early twentieth-century manufacturing
techniques made cabinets available to a wider range of
purchasers, the cabinet as display object has also survived
as a luxury item. Although relatively few such cabinets
were made during the middle years of the twentieth
century, the conscious revival during the 1960s and 1970s
of the tradition and ideology of the hand-made object led
to a new emphasis on making which has continued to the
present day, and which served as a stimulus to the
production of such luxurious furniture.

The word 'craft' is used in a variety of ways to describe
recent hand-made work, including furniture. Celebration
of the ideals and values of the handmade are central to
craft objects. Often, but not always (and not in Makepeace's case), the values are thought to be anti-industrial
and hark back to the Arts and Crafts Movement of turn-
of-the-century Britain (pp.180,
190, 192). Craft furniture is not
generally perceived as luxurious,
rather as simple, honest and
solidly made. However, much
as luxury Arts and Craft furniture existed a century ago (p.178),
there has more recently been
much luxury furniture produced
within the craft tradition.

Although the materials used in
this cabinet are neither rare nor
valuable, each was carefully
chosen and painstakingly worked
over many hours into a novel
form. Instead of a chest of
drawers housed within a supporting structure, Makepeace
designed a free-standing stack
of drawers which pivot from a
central steel spine (visible only

Fig.1. Side view of column

on the top) and rest on a thick wooden base (figs 1–2). Each
drawer is made from thin and narrow veneers bent and
stacked on a plastic drawer bottom which contrasts with
the colour of the wood and gives consistent dashes of colour.

Although generally identified as a furniture-maker,
John Makepeace gave up working at the bench relatively
early in his career. He decided to do this because he found
the demands of making left little time for serious attention
to design.[1] In the 1960s he produced simple, modern
furniture in the spirit of the recently opened Habitat shop
in London but, owing to its lack of success, decided to
embrace 'a more expressive and less rectilinear aesthetic'.[2]
(Indeed, the first version of this cabinet [fig.3] shared that
rectilinear aesthetic.[3]) From that time he devoted himself
to producing expensive, hand-made furniture to commission although, until the end of the 1960s, he also
undertook more modestly priced items made in
small series for retailers. The present cabinet
was purchased at a time when Makepeace – who had positioned himself to
address a market of collectors – sold
a relatively large number of pieces to
British museums and was (as he remains
today) celebrated as the leading British
designer of craft furniture.[4]   C.W.

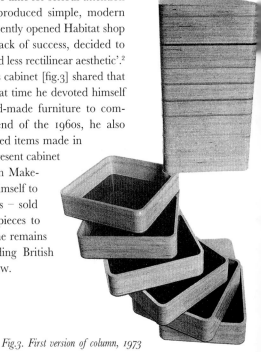

Fig.3. First version of column, 1973

1. J. Meyerson, *Makepeace,
A Spirit of Adventure in Craft
& Design* (London: Conran
Octopus, 1995), p.27.

2. Ibid.

3. Illustrated in *Craftsmen
of Quality* (London: Craft
Advisory Committee, 1976),
p.185.

4. It cost £3,500, equivalent
then to the price of a small
(economy) car.

'Casablanca' Sideboard

Italian (Milan): 1981

Designed by Ettore Sottsass Jr (b.1917).
Manufactured by Memphis, Milan.
Plastic laminate over fibreboard.
Printed and embossed label: 'Memphis/
Milano/E. Sottsass/1981/Made in Italy'
H: 230 cm; W: 161.5 cm; D: 39 cm
Museum No. W.14-1990
Purchased from Memphis with the assistance
of the manufacturer

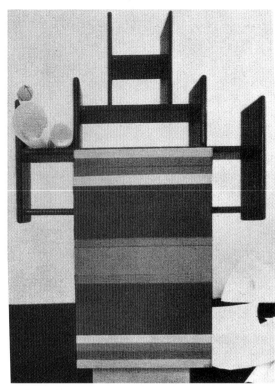

*Fig.1. The 'Architect's Harikari', 1966
(Domus, April 1967, Sottsass photo)*

1. M. Eidelberg (ed.), *Design 1935–1965: What Modern Was* (Montreal/New York: Le Musée des Arts Décoratifs de Montréal/Harry N. Abrams, Inc., 1991), p.326, and V. Gregotti, *Ettore Sottsass: Furniture and a few Interiors* (Milan: Arnoldo Montadori Editori SpA/Edizioni Philippe Daverio, 1985), p.36.

2. B. Radice, *Ettore Sottsass, a Critical Biography* (London: Thames & Hudson, 1993), p.148.

3. Ibid., pp.120–27, and Gregotti, op. cit., pp.52–7.

4. T. Hine, *Populuxe* (New York: Alfred A. Knopf, 1986), pp.7, 66.

With its garish colours and patterns, and outstretched cantilevered shelves, this monumental sideboard was designed as a challenge to preconceptions of good taste; it does not look like a conventional sideboard, its decoration is unsubtle and the materials are synthetic. Yet, for all its flouting of traditional values, it has great presence. This sideboard was part of the first Memphis collection for which Sottsass and his colleagues designed bold and often asymmetrical furniture, using unpredictable geometry which went against the Modernist doctrine of form following function. The brash decoration ran counter to the soberness and purity of much black and white minimalism, the unornamented style of the 1970s, which was rooted in the austerity of 1920s and 1930s Modernism. Memphis introduced a new spirit of fun and fantasy into contemporary design, perceived by Sottsass as having become restrictive, stale and bland.

Whereas Modernism asserted function as the principal basis of design, Sottsass recognized its emotional and symbolic properties. As early as 1960 he had designed *mobile a torre* (tower furniture), the purpose of which was to combine storage and display while also serving to divide rooms and provide specific areas for particular functions (fig.1).[1] By the 1980s his furniture had become more sculptural, and the form of this sideboard evokes the shape of a totem-pole, itself an object devoted to spiritual, rather than temporal purposes. By monumentalizing his furniture Sottsass imbued it with an emotional force and presence.[2]

Since the 1960s Sottsass had used brightly coloured plastic laminates inspired by contemporary Pop Art (fig.2).[3] For the decoration of this sideboard he looked back to the everyday products of 1950s popular culture, seen by many as a period of low taste. The laminates used on the Casablanca sideboard draw on Americana: the decor of the diner and the wipe-clean furniture of the kitchenette.[4] By drawing on low taste rather than high style, Sottsass was deliberately confronting traditional decoration, while

the improbable winged-form of his sideboard (the arms are angled to hold wine bottles) subverts the Modernist doctrine of functionality. These challenges to the seriousness of traditional Modernism identify the sideboard as Post-modern, the leading avant-garde design aesthetic of the 1980s.

Although the patterns and even the materials of Memphis furniture were drawn from popular taste, the furniture was not cheap or available to the average consumer. However, Memphis had a profound influence in many areas of design in the 1980s, particularly product design. The increased use of wit and colour and the disguising, rather than the expression, of function gave many products an emotional appeal to consumers and asserted individualism in the styling of mass-produced artifacts. These qualities became characteristic of a decade obsessed by design and were widely disseminated by Memphis. G.W

Fig.2. Desk/cabinet/bookcase, Tchou apartment, Milan, 1960 (Domus, September 1963)

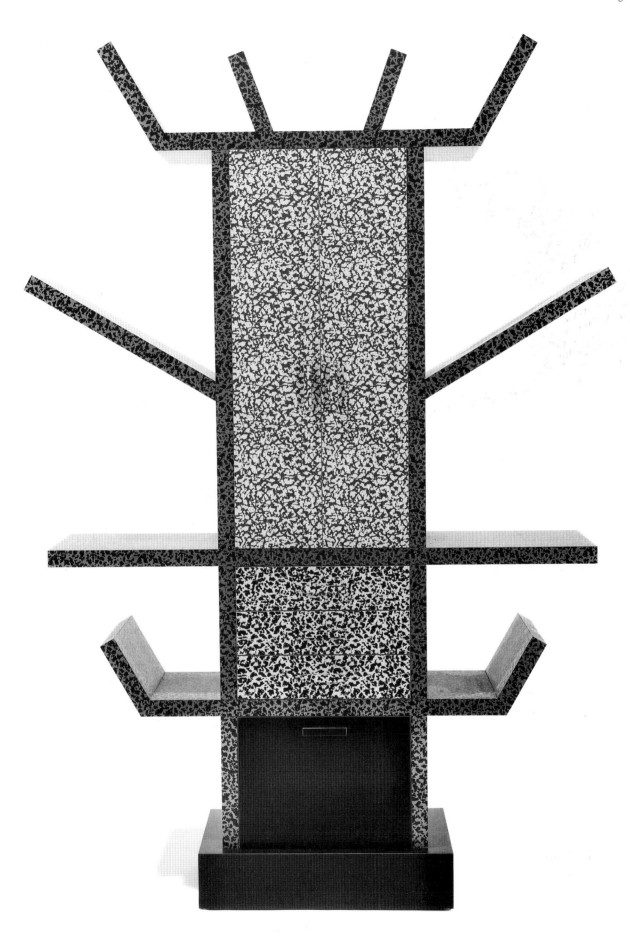

Sofa

British (London): 1988

Designed by Jasper Morrison (b.1959)
Manufactured by SCP Limited, London
Cotton and linen upholstery over foam, steel
springs, hessian and elasticized webbing on beech
frame; feather cushions and aluminium feet

H: 83 cm; W: 215 cm; D: 70 cm
Museum No. W.16-1990
Given by SCP Ltd, London

*Fig.1. Plywood chair,
manufactured by Vitra, 1988
(V&A Museum No. W.1-
1995)*

By the early 1990s, British furniture was admired and imitated throughout the European design world for the first time since the turn of the century.[1] Within Britain itself, the image most associated with contemporary furniture is that of 'craft' furniture, i.e., hand-made furniture (p.218) or furniture that espouses craft values made in small batches. Within the international context of the *avant-garde* furniture trade, in Italy, Germany and Scandinavia especially, it is British furniture designed for manufacture that has gained attention. The best-known designer of such furniture is Jasper Morrison; the most important manufacturer is SCP.

Following his graduation from London's Royal College of Art, Morrison was fortunate enough to have several student designs manufactured by SCP from 1986. However, he did not embark upon a career in the furniture industry, the frequent route for British design or furniture college graduates who receive a more specialized education than their continental counterparts. Instead, Morrison set about designing furniture and installations mainly for exhibitions at art or furniture trade fairs, and design displays or workshops.[2] The predecessor to this sofa was a *chaise longue* which Morrison manufactured in a series of ten and displayed at such exhibitions.[3]

The shape of the sofa, the fact that it is raised above the ground (without a 'skirt') and that it stands on aluminium feet, are unconventional elements in comparison to mainstream British upholstered furniture. However, its frame is made of beech and the upholstery consists of a conventional coiled spring structure, supported by hessian webbing and covered with foam (the latter essential to maintain its shape). This traditional construction would be unusual in a similar design manufactured on the Continent where elasticized webbing or even injected foam are employed in place of springs. The British market-place (which is said to buy more upholstered furniture per capita than any in the world) demands traditional methods in upholstered furniture. Even if a manufacturer could afford to risk selling upholstered furniture made by non-traditional methods, it would be impossible to find the skills in existing factories. Accordingly, it is not surprising that a small, recently

founded British firm would aim to market such a sofa, and that it would be made in a traditional way.

Although matters related to marketing played an important part in the decision to manufacture this sofa, its form and style are the explanation for Morrison's influence within the larger design community. Much 1980s design (pp.220, 224) represented a cathartic, self-conscious rejection of the simplified geometry, monochromatic palette and austerity of Modernism (p.204), especially in its often second-rate, post-war manifestations; Morrison, on the other hand, attempted to reinvent it. His sofa, and other contemporary pieces (figs 1–2), are characterized by great attention to detail, simplicity and restraint that result in low-key elegance and always avoid the grand gesture. They are also infused with a gentle wit. Because of its integrity and clarity, Morrison's furniture has led fellow designers away from the extravagant design of the 1980s into softer, more humane, but still intellectually charged work.   C.W.

1. For example, ten per cent of the designers listed in a guide to the leading designers and manufacturers showing at the prestigious Milan Furniture Fair of 1995 were British, a percentage inconceivable at any previous time during the post-war era (*Abitare*, supplement to April 1995 issue).

2. *Jasper Morrison, Designs, projects and drawings 1981–1989* (London: ADT Press, 1990), passim.

3. P. Teichgräber (ed.), *Jasper Morrison* (Vienna: Prodomo, 1988), p.23.

Fig.2. Thinking man's chair, manufactured by Cappellini, 1986 (V&A Museum No. W.15-1989)

'Little Heavy' Chair

British: 1989–91

Designed by Ron Arad (b.1951), 1989.
Made by One Off Ltd, London, 1991,
as number 9 of an edition of 20.
Stainless steel, beaten and welded

H: 75 cm; W: 59 cm; D: 72 cm
Museum No. W.17-1993
Purchased from Ron Arad Associates Ltd, London

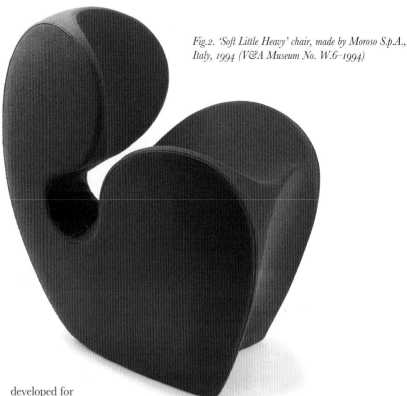

Fig.2. 'Soft Little Heavy' chair, made by Moroso S.p.A., Italy, 1994 (V&A Museum No. W.6–1994)

While unique examples of wood furniture have long been made by designers (p.218), and limited, even numbered 'editions' of such pieces appeared during the 1970s, a new phenomenon of 1980s British design was the designer-maker who worked with metal. The makers of wood furniture tended to extol their connection with nature as well as with traditional forms and materials; they located their workshops in the country and emphasized handwork through highly finished surfaces. New metal furniture designers, including Ron Arad, are urban and international in outlook, very much a part of forward-looking, contemporary culture and, although the surface of their furniture is often highly polished, it can also be rough and imperfect. Unlike modern design in the 1920s and 1930s, which often employed the imagery of efficient new industries and sleek, machine-made materials, the work of Arad and others lies within an aesthetic that suggests the collapse of the modern machine age.

Trained at London's Architectural Association, Israeli-born Arad is best known for his furniture and interior design, and from the early 1980s he produced welded metal furniture and lighting, often working with salvaged materials. There is nothing decorative or nostalgic in Arad's work. Designs such as the 'Little Heavy' chair reveal the nature of the material and the sometimes haphazard effects of the process of making, for example hammer and weld marks.[1] In general, Arad has not designed for a mass market; his pieces are produced in limited editions, employing sculptural forms. They are named and priced like works of art and were nurtured by the related 1980s phenomena of the growth of general interest in design and the huge boom in collecting of all kinds.

The 'Little Heavy' chair is one of an edition of twenty, ten of which were in highly reflective stainless steel and ten in dark, matt-finish, mild steel. This example was the last to be made in Arad's London workshop, and remaining examples in the edition are produced in Italy under his supervision. The seat and back of the chair are beaten from sheet steel using a rubber hammer. The bulbous, metallic form derives from a group of Arad's furniture from the late 1980s and early 1990s. He employs various types of metal not normally used in furniture, including tempered steel strips (fig.1) and woven metal originally developed for industrial conveyor belts.

A remarkable transformation occurred when Arad translated the 'Little heavy' and a group of related designs from metal to upholstered foam (fig.2) for a prominent, design-conscious Italian furniture manufacturer. The close connection between the original design and material disappeared at once. Although the volume and shape of the original were retained, the change of material from metal to foam fundamentally altered the character of the chair. From being harsh, unwelcoming and angular it became soft, comforting and enveloping. Furthermore, the precious, sculptural quality of the original gained a new sensuousness. The chair is now for daily use, not mainly for display or contemplation. This transformation of a radical, one-off design into a manufactured commodity suitable for mass consumption is symptomatic of the appetite of the design market for new work.

Arad's furniture is frequently exhibited and published because of its sheer novelty and bravura, but he is undoubtedly one of the most original designers of the period and a remarkably consistent one. He has worked doggedly at developing and refining his use of metal. Despite the unconventional nature of his work, he has attracted many imitators, both designer-makers and manufacturers. G.W.

1. D. Sudjic, *Ron Arad, Restless Furniture* (London: Fourth Estate/Wordsearch, 1989), pp.18–20.

Fig.1. 'Mortal Coil' bookcase, 1993 (V&A Museum No. W.18–1993)

Index

Note: numerals in **bold** refer to main colour and black-and-white plates; those in *italics* refer to figures in the text.

Footnotes which have been indexed are indicated by page number and n for footnote reference, eg 178n3.

Index of museum numbers

Museum numbers are unique to each piece and include the date of acquisition as the second element of the number.

Before 1910 a single sequence was used for all Museum acquisitions; since that time items in the Furniture & Woodwork Department have been prefixed by the letter w, the prefix Circ. being used for items acquired by the Circulation department.